1/13

Powering Achievement:
School Library Media Programs
Make a Difference:
The Evidence Mounts

3rd Edition

Keith Curry Lance
David V. Loertscher

Salt Lake City, Utah
Hi Willow Research & Publishing
2005

ISBN: 1-933170-14-X

Publisher: Hi Willow Research & Publishing
                    312 South 1000 East
                    Salt Lake City, UT 84102

Distributed by: LMC Source
and orders to: PO Box 131266
                    Spring TX 77393
                    sales@lmcsource.com (email)
                    http://lmcsource.com (url)
                    800-873-3043 toll free telephone

---

url for balance of content for this publication:
http://www.lmcsource.com
(under Freebies, see Powering Achievement 3rd Edition)

Contents

Preface to the 3rd Edition

The 3rd edition of this work summarizes the complete output of the Keith Curry Lance studies from 1999 through 2005. Keith vows that the Illinois study will be the last of this type of research (David Loertscher advises the reader to take this statement with a grain of salt). Keith is also found of asking: "How many times to we have to demonstrate that school libraries contribute to achievement before someone believes us?" In any event, the evidence continues to mount, not only from the work of Dr. Lance, but from other researchers. For the third edition, we have tried to list all the major studies linking school libraries with achievement and their availability. This list is updated on two sites where studies are added as they appear. The first is http://lrs.org (The Colorado State Library site) and http://www.davidvl.org (David Loertscher's personal website). For this edition, every presentation has been updated to add a combination of data from all the Lance studies. In addition, a major handout, entitled "Powering Achievement" invites school librarians to participate and report local action research done linking their programs to achievement. Also, a number of new handouts from the various research studies have been added to the Appendices, making this section of reprintable handouts almost as large as the rest of the volume. The authors are always interested in hearing from their readers about new research efforts in the area of school libraries as they are usually involved in the AASL Research Committee and the Treasure Mountain Research Retreat where such things are always on the agenda.

Introduction

Since the 1960s, school library media programs in the United States have been developing and changing from a classroom collection or tiny library filled with books to a modern library media center containing print and digital information. The multimedia information-rich environment is now extending far beyond the confines of four LMC walls into classrooms and homes. The LMC is fast becoming a vital 24 hour, 7 days-a-week information partner for teachers and learners.

But library media centers are expensive. They require huge investments to create the information technology networks, fund large quality collections, and particularly to staff with professional, paraprofessional, and technical personnel. Library media specialists fight the battle of the budget regularly. When teacher salaries rise above 90% of the total dollars available for a school district, the competition for scarce resources places tremendous pressures on administrators to find places in the budget to cut. The arts and libraries are often the first to be cut.

At first, library media specialists may seem self-serving when they try to present data showing how much they contribute to education. An audience may feel that jobs are at stake and that it is natural for any person or group to try to preserve the status quo.

However, there is a larger issue. Many local, state and federal government leaders target education as a top priority. These leaders realize that the nation's future depends on the next generation's ability to compete in a new world that places information, critical thinking, and problem solving at a premium.

The larger issue is this: The research is mounting that young people and teachers are at risk if they lack the types of information technology a strong library media program can deliver. Teachers suffer as their content knowledge ages and their teaching strategies become antiquated. Young people are in danger of piling ignorance, misinformation, and technological backwardness deeper and deeper. There is growing evidence that to cut LMC funding and effectiveness is to strike a blow at progress currently measured by academic achievement! To ignore the growth and development of solid library media programs contributes to the gap between the knowledgeable and connected vs. the ignorant and unskilled.

Simply stated, a teacher with a textbook is not enough. The world of information is simply too ubiquitous and too massive to ignore. Every young person and teacher must learn to survive information overload and data smog. And every learner needs an equal opportunity to succeed. In classes where 60% of the learners cannot read and understand the textbook, the challenge is obvious. Yet many communities expect teachers to magically compensate. It is a problem many love to ignore.

Then there are the quick-fix folks who want to hand the library a one-time budget pot, expecting that a feel-good contribution will salve the wound. These are the folks that somehow ignore the fact that libraries require the same care and feeding as paying the electrical bills, keeping school busses running, or paying teacher salaries. When the money stops, there are consequences. Somehow, though, the "stop" in the library is invisible. Today, we did not purchase the latest data for the library collection, but service went right on. No matter that the learner copied outdated or incorrect information into their reports. No matter if they still think that Bill Clinton is the President of the United States, or that they read "boys can become doctors and girls can become nurses" in an out-of-date book. The world is full of misinformation. What harm is a little more?

Luckily, the amount of evidence that strong library media programs and academic achievement are linked is rising. It is all too uncommon common sense.

The Lance studies and other research in this presentation booklet show that, as a whole, library media specialists and the programs they create do make a difference. This means that there are enough strong programs in a particular state being researched that their impact begins to show up in a "quality education" analysis. Sadly, there are also enough weak programs that they dilute the effect. And the weak cloud the potential for everyone.

The purpose of this short volume is to assist the busy library media specialist who desires to make presentations about the effectiveness of library media programs to various audiences and to begin discussions from the research about the direction local programs should take. Considering that there are differing amounts of time to present the research, the authors have created both brief and longer recommended presentations complete with the visuals and handouts to accompany them.

Part one contains six presentations:
> In a nutshell quotable quotes – when you have only time for a sentence or two.
> A one-minute presentation of the Lance and other studies

> ➤ A one-minute presentation about the Krashen/McQuillan research about school libraries and reading
> ➤ A one-minute presentation asking the question, "Do unsupervised clerks in the LMC make a difference in academic achievement?"
> ➤ A five-minute presentation of the Lance studies and other research
> ➤ A fifteen-minute presentation of the Lance studies and other research

Each of these presentations has a set of PowerPoint slides appended and also available for downloading on the web at www.lmcsource.com under "Freebies." In addition, right after the first presentation, there is a tri-fold brochure that can be reproduced freely to give to the audiences of any of the presentations. For the readers of the brochure who may have additional questions about the research, the authors have created a supplement to each of the important statements of the brochure on the web at www.lmcsource.com under "Freebies."

Part two contains eight discussion starters based on various aspects of the research. The idea is to focus groups of library media specialists, teachers, parent groups, or administrators on issues connected to school libraries. Each of the discussions is based on the Lance studies and other research that has brought some significant findings for focusing on academic achievement and library media programs. The authors recommend that these discussion starters be modified for your local groups and the particular concerns they have. PowerPoint slides accompany each of the discussion starters and the brochure from part one can be duplicated freely as a supplement to these discussions with its references to many studies and the supplementary information on the website.

Part three contains the authors' recommendations for planning to implement the research findings and measuring the impact of local programs on academic achievement. Most people want to know if national research would apply or has already applied to local programs. Do we already make a difference with our library media program, or could we plan an initiative to improve the local program and monitor the results on achievement?

Finally, in the appendix, various previously-published brochures and handouts have been reprinted here for the convenience of the user. All of these brochures and handouts may be freely reproduced.

For the users of this publication, reading the studies from which these presentations were created will help fill in many details. And the reader should know that future developments and other studies now being completed will be announced on the Colorado State Library's research page: www.lrs.org. That source should be accessed before any presentation just to see if any new information has been added.

Acquiring the background studies. Here is a list of the studies that were used to create these presentations and where to obtain them. They should be read carefully to build in-depth knowledge of the research studies. Throughout the publication, shorthand citations have been used for the studies. Consult the list below for the full citations.

All Studies   Links to all studies at:
http://lrs.org (Colorado State Library)
also at:
http://www.lmcsource.com under Freebies

Gaver
1963

Gaver, Mary V. *Effectiveness of Centralized Library Service in Elementary Schools*. 2nd ed. New Brunswick, NJ: Rutgers University Press, 1963 (out of print, find in many academic libraries or school district professional libraries).

Colorado I
1993

Lance, Keith C, Linda Welborn, and Christine Hamilton-Pennell. *The Impact of School Library Media Centers on Academic Achievement*. Castle Rock, CO: Hi Willow Research and Publishing, 1993 (available from LMC Source, PO Box 720400, San Jose CA 95172, and online at http://www.lmcsource.com).

Colorado II
2000

Lance, Keith C., Marcia J. Rodney and Christine Hamilton-Pennell. *How School Librarians Help Kids Achieve Standards: The Second Colorado Study*. San Jose, CA: Hi Willow Research and Publishing, 2000 (available from LMC Source, PO Box 720400, San Jose CA 95172, and online at http://www.lmcsource.com).

Alaska
2000

Lance, Keith C., Christine Hamilton-Pennell, Marcia J. Rodney, with Lois Peterson and Clara Sitter. *Information Empowered: The School Librarian as an Agent of Academic Achievement in Alaska Schools*. Revised ed. Juneau, AK: Alaska State Library, 2000 (available for $10 from The Alaska State Library, PO Box 110571, Juneau, AK 98811). Executive summary and order information at: http://www.library.state.ak.us/dev/infoemp.html

Pennsylvania
2000

Lance, Keith C., Marcia J. Rodney and Christine Hamilton-Pennell. *Measuring up to Standards: The Impact of School Library Programs & Information Literacy in Pennsylvania Schools*. Greensburg, PA: Pennsylvania Citizens for Better Libraries, 2000 (available online at http://lrs.org/html/school_studies.html). Also at: http://www.statelibrary.state.pa.us/libraries/lib/libraries/measuringup.pdf

Massachusetts
2000

Baughman, James C. *School Libraries and MCAS Scores*. Preliminary Edition. Boston, MA: Graduate School of Library and Information Science, 2000. See the study at: http://web.simmons.edu/~baughman/mcas-school-libraries/Baughman%20Paper.pdf

Texas
2001

Smith, Ester. *Texas School Libraries: Standards, Resources, Services, and Students' Performance*. Austin, TX: EGS Research & Consulting, 2001. Available at: http://www.tsl.state.tx.us/ld/pubs/schlibsurvey/index.html

Oregon
2001

Lance, Keith Curry, Marcia J. Rodney and Christine Hamilton-Pennell. *Good Schools Have School Librarians: Oregon School Librarians Collaborate to Improve Academic Achievement*. Salem, OR: Oregon Educational Media Association, 2001. Available in print from: LMC Source (http://www.lmcsource.com) and online at:

http://www.oema.net/Oregon_Study/OR_Study.htm

Scotland
2001

Williams, Dorothy and Caroline Wavell. *The Impact of the School Library Resource Centre on Learning*. Library and Information Commission Research Report 112: Report on Research Conducted for Resource: The Council for Museums, Archives and Libraries. Aberdeen, Scotland: The Robert Gordon University for The Council for Museums, Archives and Libraries, 2001. Available at: http://www.rgu.ac.uk/files/SLRCreport.pdf

Iowa
2002

Rodney, Marcia J., Keith Curry Lance and Christine Hamilton-Pennell. *Make the Connection: Quality school Library Media Programs Impact Academic achievement in Iowa*. A Research Project by Iowa Area Education Agencies, published by the Mississippi Bend Area Education Agency, 2002. Available at: http://www.aea9.k12.ia.us/download/04/aea_statewide_study.pdf

New Mexico
2002

Lance, Keith Curry, Marcia J. Rodney, and Christine Hamilton-Pennell. *How School Libraries Improve Outcomes for Children: The New Mexico Study*. Sante Fe: NM: New Mexico State Library, 2002. (Available from LMC Source online at http://www.lmcsource.com).

Michigan
2003

Rodney, Marcia J., Keith Curry Lance, and Christine Hamilton-Pennell. *The Impact of Michigan School Librarians on Academic Achievement: Kids Who Have Libraries Succeed*. Salt Lake City: Hi Willow Research and Publishing, 1993 (available from LMC Source online at http://www.lmcsource.com).

Illinois
2005

Lance, Keith Curry, Marcia J. Rodney, and Christine Hamilton-Pennell. *Powerful Libraries Make Powerful Learners: The Illinois Study*. Canton, IL: Illinois School Library Media Association (available via http:/www.islma.org).

Other Research Studies on School Libraries and Achievement

Florida
2003

Baumbach, Donna J. *Making the Grade: The Status of School Library Media Centers in the Sunshine State and How They Contribute to Student Achievement*. Salt Lake City: Hi Willow Research and Publishing, 2003. (available from LMC Source at PO Box 131266 Spring TX 77393 or online at http://www.lmcsource.com)

Ohio
2003

Todd, Ross J. *Student Learning Through Ohio School Libraries: A Summary of the Ohio Research Study*. OELMA. Study available at http://www.oelma.org/StudentLearning/documents/OELMAResearchStudy8page.pdf and other resources at http://www.oelma.org/studentlearning.htm

Minnesota
2003

Baxter, Susan J. and Ann Walker Smalley. *Check It Out!: The Results of the School Library Media Program Census*. Saint Paul: Metronet, 2003. Available at http://metronet.lib.mn.us/survey/index.cfm

Missouri 2003	Miller, Jamie, Jinchang Want, Lisa Whitacre, and Quantitative Resources. *Show Me Connection: How School Library Media Center Services Impact Student Achievement.* Available at http://dese.mo.gov/divimprove/curriculum/librarystudy/libraryresearch.pdf
North Carolina 2004	Burgin, Robert and Pauletta Brown Bracy. *An Essential Connection: How Quality School Library Media Programs Improve Student Achievement in North Carolina.* Salt Lake City, Hi Willow Research & Publishing, 2004. Available at http://www.rburgin.com/NCschools2003/NCSchoolStudy.pdf and an updated version from LMC Source at http://www.lmcsource.com
Indiana	Ongoing. Follow online at http://www.ilfonline.org/Units/Associations/aime/Data/index.htm
Delaware 2005	Todd, Ross. Should be released some time in 2005. A Google search plus notifications in library periodicals should provide access when published

Other Research Reviews of Interest

Krashen 1993	Krashen, Stephen. *The Power of Reading.* Englewood, CO: Libraries Unlimited, 1993 (available for sale online at http://www.lu.com).
McQuillan 1998	McQuillan, Jeff. *The Literacy Crisis.* Portsmith NH: Heinemann, 1998 (available for sale online at http://www.heinemann.com).

Also consider the recently published Research Review on reading sponsored by Scholastic and reprinted in Appendix T. It is also available online at http://www.scholasticlibrary.com/download/slw_04.pdf.

Tool Kit for Linking School Library Media Programs to Achievement:

Loertscher, David V. and Ross J. Todd. *We Boost Achievement!: Evidence-Based Practice For School Library Media Specialists.* Salt Lake City: Hi Willow Research & Publishing, 2003. Available at http://www.lmcsource.com.

Tips for presenting the findings of the Lance research:

For the shorter presentations and discussion starters, we recommend that they be adapted and then memorized. The PowerPoint slides should be clue enough to prompt you. Also, good presentation techniques such as pace of presentation, stressing of important ideas, and ability to speak clearly apply here. Do not hesitate to adapt the slides and the text for local use, but make certain that what you do add or modify is supported by the research.

Part One:

Presenting the Research Studies

Part one contains five presentations and some quickie quotes:

> ➢ In a Nutshell: Quotable Nuggets Concerning School Library Media Programs and Academic Achievement.
> ➢ A one-minute presentation of the Lance studies.
> ➢ A one-minute presentation about the Krashen/McQuillan research about school libraries and reading.
> ➢ A one-minute presentation answering the question: "Does an Unsupervised Clerk in the LMC Make a Difference in Academic Achievement?
> ➢ A five-minute presentation of the Lance studies and other research.
> ➢ A fifteen-minute presentation of the Lance studies and other research.

Each of these presentations has a set of PowerPoint slides appended and also available for downloading on the web at the url below. In addition, right after the first presentation, there is a tri-fold brochure that can be reproduced freely to give to the audiences of any of the presentations. For the readers of the brochure who may have additional questions about the research, the authors have created a supplement to each of the important statements of the brochure on the web at www.lmcsource.com under "Freebies."

In a Nutshell:
Quotable Nuggets Concerning
School Library Media Programs and Academic
Achievement

All Studies

- In research done in 14 states and over 8,700 schools since 2000, the positive impact of the school library media program is consistent. Strong school library media programs make a difference in academic achievement. That is, if you were setting out a balanced meal for a learner, the school library media program would be part of the main course, not the butter on the bread.

- Reading scores tend to rise with levels of:
    - Professional and support staff in LMCs,
    - The size of LMC collections,
    - Spending on LMC collections, and
    - The extent of school-wide networks that extend access to collection resources.
    - That is: More is Better

- Higher levels of librarian staffing are associated with:
    - Longer LMC hours,
    - Higher levels of LMC staff activity,
    - Higher student usage, and consequently
    - Higher test scores.

- The impact of LMC programs on academic achievement CANNOT be explained away by other school or community conditions.
    - School conditions include:
        - Teacher-pupil ratio,
        - Per pupil spending, and
        - Characteristics of teachers.
    - Community conditions include:
        - Poverty,
        - Low adult education, and
        - Race/ethnicity.

By State

According to the Alaska study:

- Test scores tend to be higher for schools where there is a librarian, a full-time librarian rather than a part-time one, and a part-time librarian rather than none.
- The more often students receive information literacy instruction in which LMC staff are involved, the higher their test scores.
- Where LMC programs have strong collection development policies that address the issue of reconsiderations, test scores are higher.
- Where LMC programs have relationships with public libraries, test scores tend to be higher.

According to the Colorado II study:

- Schools with stronger LMC programs average 10-18% higher reading scores.
- When library media specialists assert themselves as school leaders (meeting with the principal, attending faculty meetings, and serving on key committees), they are more likely to experience working conditions that encourage and support collaboration with teachers.
- When LMC staff collaborate with classroom teachers, reading scores increase 8-21%.
- When schools have computer networks that extend the LMC program's reach into classrooms and labs, reading scores rise 6 to 25%.
- Only individual student visits to LMCs were correlated with reading scores.
- When students have access to more up-to-date and accurate information from newer books and more current periodicals, their test scores are higher.

According to the Pennsylvania study:

- Reading scores increase with LMC staffing, information technology, and integration of information literacy with the curriculum.
- Activities that help to integrate information literacy with the curriculum include: teaching (cooperatively with teachers and alone), providing in-service training to teachers, serving on key committees, and managing information technology.

According to the Oregon, Iowa, and New Mexico studies:

- Both individual and group visits to LMCs were correlated with reading scores. Successful group visits depend on close collaboration between LMC specialist and teacher in planning and delivering instruction together in the LMC.

According to the Michigan study:

- As a school librarian's weekly hours increase, so does involvement in activities associated with teaching and learning.

According to the Illinois study:

- Test scores rise with the extent to which elementary students borrow circulating books and the extent to which middle and high school students visit libraries, both in groups and individually.

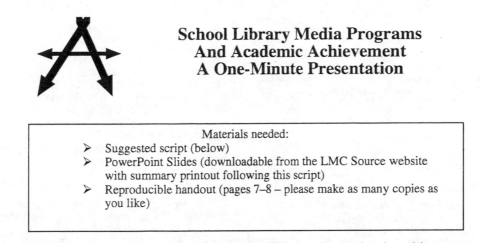

School Library Media Programs And Academic Achievement A One-Minute Presentation

> Materials needed:
> ➢ Suggested script (below)
> ➢ PowerPoint Slides (downloadable from the LMC Source website with summary printout following this script)
> ➢ Reproducible handout (pages 7–8 – please make as many copies as you like)

Strong school library media programs make a difference in academic achievement.

The evidence for this statement comes from numerous research studies dating back to a 1963 study in New Jersey. Since 2000, statewide studies in Alaska, Colorado, Florida, Illinois, Iowa, Massachusetts, Michigan, Minnesota, Missouri, New Mexico, North Carolina, Oregon, Pennsylvania, and Texas—studies involving over 8,700 schools—have added additional important evidence.

To build maximum impact, a school community should do two things to attain significant results:

First, create a quality information-rich and technology-rich environment easily accessible by students and teachers.

Second, employ professional and support personnel who provide leadership and tireless partnering.

Students and teachers who take advantage of this information-rich and technology-rich environment can expect:

> ➢ Capable and avid readers
> ➢ Learners who are information literate
> ➢ Teachers who are partnering with the library media professional to create high-quality learning experiences

When these things happen, scores can be expected to be 10-20% higher than in schools without this investment.

It's worth it.

(Give the handout to the listener, p. 7–8. It directs them to the Internet site for in-depth explanations.)

5

School Library Media Programs and Academic Achievement
PowerPoint Slides

Strong School Library Media Programs Make a Difference in Academic Achievement 1	**Since 2000:** **14 State-Level Studies** **Involving Over 8,700 Schools at** **Elementary, Middle & High School Levels** **Representing 2.6 Million Students** 2
Two Actions to Take for Maximum Impact: 3	**Step One** **Create a quality information-rich and technology-rich environment easily accessible by students and teachers.** 4

Step Two
Employ professional and support personnel who provide leadership and tireless partnering.
 	
5
	Results
	▪ Learners and teachers who take advantage of the strong library media center can expect:
	  o Capable and avid readers;
	  o Learners who are information literate.
	▪ Teachers who are partnering to create high-quality learning experiences.
	
	6

Impact **Scores tend to be 10-20% higher in schools with stronger libraries.** **It's worth the investment!** 7	

Invest in your...

School Library

To Build

Academic

Achievement

&

Equity

Fifty years of research studies, culminating in fourteen major studies done since 2000, involving over 8,700 schools at all levels, demonstrate that good school libraries make a difference!

| Alaska |
| Colorado |
| Florida |
| Illinois |
| Iowa |
| Massachusetts, |
| Michigan |
| Minnesota |
| Missouri |
| New Mexico |
| North Carolina |
| Oregon |
| Pennsylvania |
| Texas |

Here's the Evidence

Sources

Each phrase of this brochure is expanded and explained online at: http://www.lmcsource.com/ Click "Freebies" and look for "*Powering Achievement, 3rd Edition.*"

- Lance, Keith Curry and Loertscher, David V. *Powering Achievement 3rd Edition*, Hi Willow Research and Publishing, 2005. $30.00.

- Lance, Keith Curry, Marcia J. Rodney, and Christine Hamilton-Pennell. *How School Librarians Help Kids Achieve Standards: The Second Colorado Study.* Salt Lake City UT: Hi Willow Research & Publishing, 2000.

Studies on the Web:

- Research Studies from all states where they have been done are available on the web at http://www.lrs.org and http://www.davidvl.org

Additional Evidence:

- Krashen, Stephen. *The Power of Reading.* Englewood, CO: Libraries Unlimited, 1993.

- McQuillan, Jeff. *The Literacy Crisis.* Portsmith, NH: Heinemann, 1998.

Helpful Publications:

- Loertscher, David V. *Reinventing Your School's Library in the Age of Technology: A Guide for Principals and Superintendents*, Hi Willow Research and Publishing, 2002. $18.00.

- Loertscher, David V. and Achterman, Douglas. *Increasing Academic Achievement Through the Library Media Center: A Guide for Teachers.* $18.00.

- Loertscher, David V. and Ross J. Todd. *We Boost Achievement!: Evidence-Based Practice For School Library Media Specialists*, Hi Willow Research and Publishing, 2002. $30.00

(all publications published by Hi Willow are available from LMC Source, PO Box 131266, Spring, TX 77393 http://www.lmcsource.com)

"The nation's education system is not doing enough to prepare students to take advantage of the explosion in information technology."

- Alan Greenspan, Federal Reserve Chairman, July 11, 2000

What You Can Do

As a Young Person
- Be an avid and capable reader.
- Become a skilled user of technology tools.
- Become information literate:
  - An organized investigator
  - A critical thinker
  - A creative thinker
  - An effective communicator
  - A responsible information user

As a Parent
- Find out whether your school's library program contains the inputs and activities described in the brochure.
- If not, find out why and what can be done about it.
- Be aware of the changing world your child will compete in as an adult and work with parent organizations to improve education.

As a Teacher
- Seek out the school librarian and explore ways to enhance the learning experiences in your classroom.
- Support efforts to enhance the inputs and activities listed in this brochure.

As a School Librarian
- Be a leader in your school.
- Work on each of the activities listed in this brochure every day.

As an Administrator
- Understand the changing role of the 21st century high-tech school library.
- Hire a school librarian with a 21st century vision.
- Work with your librarian to build the inputs and implement the activities listed in this brochure.
- Monitor progress and help solve problems.

As a School Board Member
- Find out the status of the school libraries in your district compared to the issues listed in this brochure.
- Ask administrators to prepare plans to implement improvements for school library programs.
- Monitor improvements.

As a Taxpayer
- Remember that education is expensive, but cheaper than other social and corrective programs.
- Become informed about the quality of school and public libraries in your community.
- Communicate with school boards and legislators about the importance of building expertise in the generation who will be supporting an aging population and educating a new one.

$ Investments

Academic achievement increases as:

• The number of professional and support personnel in the school library increases.

• Quality information streams from the library into classrooms and homes.

• Sustaining budgets keep the information-rich environment current and of high quality.

• Easy access to the library is the norm.

Which young person has the best potential to succeed in the 21st century information economy?

A child with a teacher only.

A child with a teacher and a textbook.

A child with a teacher, textbook and a small library.

A child with a teacher, textbook, an information-rich and technology-rich environment.

A child with a teacher, textbook, an information-rich environment, and professional guidance.

The national average to educate a child is $6,563 (1997).
The national average to incarcerate a prisoner is $19,655 (1997).

↻ Activities

Academic achievement is enhanced when school librarians:

• Collaborate with teachers to create quality learning experiences using materials and technology.

• Are leaders in their schools.

• Teach information literacy.

• Promote reading.

🔔 Results

Achievement scores are likely to rise:

10-20%

Schools in the research with high-quality libraries scored higher than schools with poor libraries.

The relationship between high quality libraries and achievement cannot be explained away by at-risk factors such as parents' lack of education, poverty, or minority status.

Likewise, these results cannot be explained away by school differences such as teacher-pupil ratio or per-pupil expenditures.

Building Literacy:
Ideas from the Research
A One-Minute Presentation

> Materials needed:
> ➢ Suggested script (below)
> ➢ PowerPoint Slides (downloadable from the LMC Source web site with summary printout following this script)
> ➢ Copies of the handout p. 7-8.

Two major studies by Dr. Stephen Krashen[1] (1993) and Dr. Jeff McQuillan[2] (1998) collected the "startling" evidence from 100 years of research that children and teens surrounded by huge quantities of books they want to read, actually read more!

And equally startling: Those who read more score higher on any academic achievement test they take!

Actually, it is only common sense.

Translated into action, this means that any school can actually stimulate literacy by:

> ➢ purchasing a great many exciting books young people want to read,
> ➢ making them easily accessible from the library and every classroom,
> ➢ pushing these collections into the home.

In other words, think of large school library collections supplying:
> ➢ Large rotating classroom collections, and
> ➢ Large bedside collections for every teacher and student!

Think Flood!

It's actually cheaper than other reading program alternatives.

Added Bonus: Results are particularly spectacular in poorer neighborhoods where homes contain few or no reading materials.[3]

---

[1] Krashen, see chapter 1.
[2] McQuillan, see chapter 7.
[3] McQuillan, p. 80-83.

Building Literacy:
A One-Minute Presentation
PowerPoint Slides

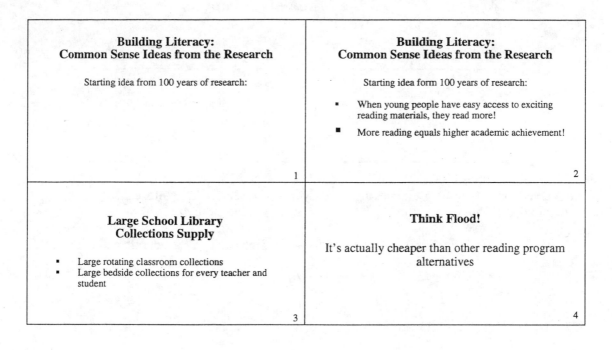

Building Literacy:
Common Sense Ideas from the Research

Starting idea from 100 years of research:

1

Building Literacy:
Common Sense Ideas from the Research

Starting idea form 100 years of research:

- When young people have easy access to exciting reading materials, they read more!
- More reading equals higher academic achievement!

2

Large School Library
Collections Supply

- Large rotating classroom collections
- Large bedside collections for every teacher and student

3

Think Flood!

It's actually cheaper than other reading program alternatives

4

Does an Unsupervised Clerk in the LMC Make a Difference in Academic Achievement?
A One-Minute Presentation

Materials needed:
➢ Suggested script (below)
➢ PowerPoint Slides (downloadable from the LMC Source web site with summary printout following this script)

In many school districts, the need to economize through budget shortfalls often creates the temptation to staff library media centers with clerical personnel rather than professionals. These unsupervised support staff keep the library open, allow students and teachers to use the collection and technology, and in the elementary schools, might provide a planning break for classroom teachers. But do unsupervised clerks make a difference in academic achievement?

The research from the Lance studies and other research document indicate clearly what actions by the LMC staff do make a difference:

➢ LMC staff planning & teaching cooperatively with teachers
➢ LMC staff providing professional development to teachers
➢ LMC staff meeting with principal, attending faculty meetings, & serving on standards & curriculum committees
➢ LMC staff managing computer network that provides remote access to LMC resources

When a clerk is unsupervised and is in charge of a library media center, why don't they perform these activities? Simply because NONE of these activities is properly in the job description of the clerk. Rather, their efforts center on the operation of the organization rather than reaching out into a leadership role in the school and its curriculum.

In the various Lance studies, this topic was not addressed in the final reports although present in the data collected. However, in the Alaska study, this comparison was addressed. Consider the difference between students scoring below average in schools having professional library media specialists vs. those where only a clerk is present.

LMC Staffing Level	Students Scoring BELOW Average	
	Elementary	Secondary
With a full time LMC specialist	17%	8%
With an unsupervised clerk – no LMS	41%	49%

The conclusion is that :

➢ Unsupervised LMC clerks do not engage in activities that make a difference. And,

➢ as a result, more students score poorly.

Because school libraries require a considerable investment in facilities, budgets for materials, salaries, utilities, computer networks, and the like, staffing the LMC with a clerk promotes a sense of false economy. Saving the cost of a professional negates the LMC's impact.

Does an Unsupervised Clerk in the LMC Make a Difference?
PowerPoint Slides

Do Unsupervised LMC Clerks Make a Difference in Academic Achievement?	Staff Activities That DO Make a Difference	Why Can't an Unsupervised Clerk Cover These Activities?
	▪ LMC staff planning & teaching cooperatively with teachers ▪ LMC staff providing in-service training to teachers ▪ LMC staff meeting with principal, attending faculty meetings, & serving on standards & curriculum committees ▪ LMC staff managing computer network that provides remote access to LMC resources	Because NONE of these activities is properly in the job description of a clerk
1	2	3
So What Difference Does It Make? Consider the Evidence from Alaska	**Thus, hiring only a clerk, produces a sense of false economy.**	**Conclusion** Unsupervised LMC clerks do not engage in activities that make a difference. As a result, students score poorly.

(Slide 4 contains the following table:)

LMC Staffing Level	Percent Students scoring below average	Percent Students scoring below average
	Elementary	Secondary
With full-time LMC specialist	17%	8%
With unsupervised LMC clerk – no LMS	41%	49%

| 4 | 5 | 6 |

School Library Media Programs and Academic Achievement: A Five-Minute Presentation

> Materials needed:
> ➤ Suggested script (below)
> ➤ PowerPoint Slides (downloadable from the LMC Source web site with summary printout following this script)
> ➤ Reproducible handout (pages 7-8)

Strong school library media programs make a difference in academic achievement.

The evidence for that statement began with a landmark study by Dr. Mary Gaver of Rutgers University in 1963.[4] She found that academic achievement was significantly higher when:

> ➤ There was a centralized library in the school building.
> ➤ The combined collection was large and easily accessible to every student and teacher.

Between 1963 and 1993, numerous other small studies supported the same findings.

However, in the early 1990s, during periods of financial retrenchment, questions about cost versus benefit arose again in the educational community.

In 1993, Dr. Keith Curry Lance and others published another major landmark study in Colorado[5] that probed whether school library media programs increase academic achievement. That study confirmed that academic achievement was affected in 220 Colorado schools when:

> ➤ There was a professional library media specialist on-site,
> ➤ The library media specialist collaborated with teachers to create exciting learning experiences using the library media resources, and
> ➤ The library media collection contained large amounts of quality materials including print and multimedia.

Since 2000, statewide studies have been completed by seven different research teams involving over 8,700 elementary middle, and high schools and an estimated 2.6 million students in 14 states.

---

[4] Gaver. See conclusions.
[5] Colorado I.

- ➢ Colorado (a second study) – 200 schools, grades 4, 7 (Lance, Rodney, & Hamilton-Pennell, 2000)
- ➢ Alaska – 211 schools, grades 4, 8, 11 (Lance, et. al., 2000)
- ➢ Pennsylvania – 435 schools, grades 5, 8, 11 (Lance, et. al., 2000)
- ➢ Massachusetts – 519 schools, grades 4, 8, 10 (Baughman, 2000)
- ➢ Oregon – 513 schools, grades 5, 8, 11 (Lance, et. al., 2001)
- ➢ Texas – 600 schools, grades 4, 8, 10 (Smith, 2001)
- ➢ Minnesota – 1,172 schools, grades 3, 5, 8 (Baxter & Smalley, 2001)
- ➢ Iowa – 506 schools, grades 4, 8, 11 (Rodney, Lance, & Hamilton-Pennell, 2002)
- ➢ New Mexico – 380 schools, grades 4, 8, 10 (Lance, et. al, 2002)
- ➢ Missouri – 782 schools, grades unknown (Miller, Want & Whitacre, 2003)
- ➢ Michigan – 729 schools, grades 4, 7, 11 (Rodney, et. al., 2003)
- ➢ North Carolina – 206 schools, grades 4, 8, 11 (Burgin & Bracy, 2003)
- ➢ Florida – 1,715 schools, grades 3, 8, 10 (Baumbach, 2003)
- ➢ Illinois – 759 schools, grades 5, 8, 11 (Lance, et. al., 2005)

Two other important studies connect school library collections and reading achievement, the first by Dr. Stephen Krashen[6] in 1993 and the second by Jeff McQuillan[7] in 1998. These two studies add a new dimension to the power a strong library media program provides to a quality education.

This presentation recommends steps to create a strong library media program that contributes to academic achievement. Each of the recommendations draws upon the research studies cited. A brochure and a web site provide access to many more details from the research.

To build maximum impact, a school community should do two things:

First, they create a quality information-rich and technology-rich environment easily accessible by students and teachers. That is, the school library now extends beyond its walls delivering quality information into the classrooms and into the homes of every learner 24 hours a day, 7 days a week. Learners flourish when quality information is close at hand.

Second, they employ a staff of both professional and support personnel in the library media center who provide leadership and tireless partnering with the teachers to deliver quality learning experiences. Achievement is affected by the two teaching partners using the best of information technology and learning strategies.

The results for learners and teachers who take advantage of this information-rich and technology-rich environment are:

- ➢ Capable and avid readers (learners who read a lot and enjoy it)

---

[6] Krashen.
[7] McQuillan.

➢ Learners who are information literate (these are learners who are taught how to locate information, evaluate it, use it well, and communicate that information effectively through an organized research process)
➢ High-quality learning experiences using information and technology far beyond what any textbook could offer.

Research indicates that schools with the most exemplary library media programs are those that are better staffed, stocked, and funded and thos characterized by stronger librarian-teacher collaboration and greater access to technology typically reap rewards ranging from 10 to 20 percent. And, these results[8] cannot be explained away by:

➢ Teacher/pupil ratio
➢ Teacher characteristics (education, experience, salaries)
➢ Student characteristics (poverty, race/ethnicity)
➢ Per-pupil expenditures
➢ Community demographics (educational attainment, poverty, ethnicity)

The results are well worth the investment!

School Library Media Programs and Academic Achievement
Five Minute Presentation
PowerPoint Slides

Strong School Library Media Programs Make a Difference in Academic Achievement 1	**Gaver Study, 1963:** Academic achievement is higher when: ▪ There is a centralized library in the school. ▪ The library collection is large and easily accessible. 2	**Lance Study Finding, 1993:** ▪ Academic Achievement was higher in Colorado schools when: ▪ There were more hours of professional library media specialist staffing ▪ The library media specialist spent more time collaborating with teachers to build exciting units of instruction ▪ The library collection was larger 3
Since 2000: **14 State-Level Studies Involving Over 8,700 Elementary, Middle & High Schools Representing 2.6 Million Students** 4	**Two Other Study Findings:** **Krashen (1993),McQuillan (1998)** ▪ Strong library media programs make a difference in academic achievement. ▪ Impact made by learners who read more from large library media center collections 5	**Step One:** Create a quality information-rich and technology-rich environment easily accessible by students and teachers. 6

---

[8] Colorado II, p. 79, Pennsylvania, p. 58, Alaska, p. 66.

Step Two:	**Results:**	**Impact:**
Employ professional and support personnel in the library media center who provide leadership and tireless partnering. 7	Learners and teachers who take advantage of the strong library media center can expect: - Capable and avid readers - Learners who are information literate - Teachers who are partnering to create high-quality learning experiences 8	Scores can be expected to be 10-20% higher than in schools without this emphasis. 9

Results are <u>not</u> explained by:
- Teacher/pupil ratio - Teacher characteristics (education, experience, salaries) - Student characteristics (poverty, race/ethnicity) - Community demographics (educational attainment, poverty, ethnicity) 10

School Library Media Programs
And Academic Achievement
A Fifteen-Minute Presentation

> Materials needed:
> ➢ Suggested script (below)
> ➢ PowerPoint Slides (downloadable from the LMC Source web site with summary printout following this script)
> ➢ Reproducible handout (pages 7-8)

Slide 1	**Background and Introduction**
	Strong school library media programs make a difference in academic achievement.
Slide 2	The evidence for that statement began with a landmark study by Dr. Mary Gaver[9] of Rutgers University in 1963. At this time, elementary schools were creating centralized school libraries by merging all the classroom collections and making those resources available to all the children of the school. Gaver found that academic achievement was significantly higher when: ➢ There was a centralized library in the school building. ➢ The combined collection was large and easily accessible to every student and teacher. That is, when teachers and students added a rich information environment in addition to a textbook environment, students read more, used more information sources, and therefore, learned more. Between 1963 and 1993, numerous other smaller studies supported the same findings. However, in the early 1990s, during periods of financial retrenchment, questions about cost versus benefit arose again in the educational community.

---

[9] Gaver. See conclusions.

Slide 3	In 1993, Dr. Keith Curry Lance[10] and others published another major landmark study in Colorado that probed whether school library media programs were holding their own in the push to increase academic achievement. That study confirmed that academic achievement was affected in 220 Colorado schools when: ➢ There was a professional library media specialist on site ➢ The library media specialist collaborated with teachers to create exciting learning experiences using the library media resources ➢ The library media collection contained large amounts of quality print and multimedia materials Some questioned whether those findings were valid only in Colorado, or if they might extend elsewhere.
Slide 4	Since 2000, 14 statewide studies have been completed by seven research teams involving over 8,700 schools and an estimated 2.6 million students. ➢ States include: Alaska, Colorado, Florida, Illinois, Iowa, Massachusetts, Michigan, Minnesota, Missouri, New Mexico, North Carolina, Oregon, Pennsylvania, & Texas
Slide 5	Two other major studies connect school library collections and reading achievement - the first by Dr. Stephen Krashen[11] in 1993 and the second by Jeff McQuillan[12] in 1998. These two studies add an additional dimension to the power a strong library media program has in a quality education. This presentation recommends steps to create a strong library media program that will contribute to academic achievement. Each of the recommendations draws upon the research studies cited. A brochure and a web site provide access to many more details from the research.
Slide 6	**The Vision** School libraries like all other libraries in the age of technology are building quality information-rich environments including books, multimedia resources, databases, electronic periodical collections, and access to quality Internet sites.
Slide 7	These resources are available in the library media center but also are extending into classrooms and beyond into the homes. The electronic part of this information-rich environment is often available 24 hours a day and 7 days a week. They are also available wherever the teacher or the learner might be. Thus, the school library is becoming an indispensable information portal for every student, teacher, and parent of school children.

[10] Colorado I.
[11] Krashen.
[12] McQuillan.

Slide 8	National guidelines[13] for school library media programs set clear expectations for every school. Strong school library media programs are expected to: ➤ Build capable and avid readers ➤ Teach all learners to become effective users of ideas and information ➤ Partner with teachers to create exciting learning experiences that take advantage of the richness of information technology In other words, the mission of the school library is to prepare learners to participate and compete in the information age, and to build life-long learning habits.
Slide 9	**Invest First in People** A strong library media program is led by ➤ A competent library media professional (The expert human interface) ➤ Paraprofessional staff (organization/service functions) ➤ Technical staff (technology support for the school) In addition, all the research studies[14] provide evidence that the larger the library media staff, the higher students score on academic achievement (as measured by reading scores). That is, as in every other program of education, people make the difference. The research suggests[15] that support personnel, including paraprofessional and technical staff, allow the professional more time to build quality learning experiences and make technology an effective learning tool. This translates directly into higher achievement.
Slide 10	Professional library media specialists[16] in any school can provide administrators, teachers, and parents with collaboration logs documenting their activities that research suggests are most effective: ➤ Collaboration with teachers in the building of quality learning experiences ➤ The teaching of information literacy (finding, using, and communicating information effectively) ➤ Promotion of reading
Slide 11	Consider a few sample findings from the research studies done in the five states of Colorado, Oregon, Texas, Iowa, and New Mexico. Comparing the top 25 scoring schools with 25 low scoring schools, note the difference professional staffing makes. Seven of the recent studies—those for Colorado, Illinois, Iowa, Michigan, New Mexico, Oregon, and Texas—compare levels of professional library media specialist staffing per 100 students for the 25 highest and lowest scoring schools in

---

[13] American Association of School Librarians and the Association for Educational Communications and Technology. *Information Power: Building Partnerships for Learning*. Chicago: American Library Association, 1998.
[14] Alaska, p. 65; Colorado I, p. 92; Colorado II, p. 57; Illinois, p. 103; Michigan, p. 65; Pennsylvania, p. 57.
[15] *Ibid.*
[16] *Ibid.*

each state. The following table summarizes those results across the five states:

LMC Specialist Staffing in 25 Highest & Lowest Scoring Schools (Multi-State Averages)[17]

School Level	Library media specialist hours per week per 100 students		% Difference (high/low)
	Highest Scoring	Lowest Scoring	
Elementary	9.4	5.1	84%
Middle	9.5	6.7	42%
High	11.5	8.2	40%

Slide 12   Conclusion across seven states: The level of professional library media specialist staffing contributes to academic achievement.

---

[17] Colorado II study, pp. 75-76; Illinois, pp. 126-37; Iowa, pp. 77-82; Michigan, pp. 92-96; New Mexico, pp. 54-59; Oregon, p. 86-88; Texas, pp. 177, 181.

| Slide 13 | Comparing the 25 highest and lowest scoring schools in Pennsylvania, note the levels of professional and support staffing that make a difference. |

LMC Staffing in 25 Top vs. 25 Low Scoring Schools

Pennsylvania[18] high/low	Top Scoring	Low Scoring	% Difference in
Professional staff hours/week			
5th Grade	34.31	29.36	17 %
8th Grade	38.40	37.63	2 %
11th Grade	45.06	43.25	4 %
Support staff hour/week			
5th Grade	25.92	12.48	108 %
8th Grade	30.30	15.80	92 %
11th Grade	49.57	19.28	157 %

| Slide 14 | Conclusion for Pennsylvania: Adding support staff is a key difference between strong and weak library media programs. Library media specialists understand these findings very well, since adding support staff allows them the opportunity to work more closely with teachers and students rather than tend to warehousing duties all day. |

| Slide 15 | From all these studies we draw the simple conclusion that the total LMC staff size contributes to academic achievement. It is not surprising that people make the difference. |

| Slide 16 | **Second, Invest in Materials, and Technology**

Learners provided with a rich information pool and access to technology[19] beyond the textbook outperform students in information-poor environments. |

---

[18] Pennsylvania study, pp. 54-56.

[19] Alaska, p. 66; Colorado II, p. 77; Colorado I, p. 92; Illinois, pp. 61, 87, 109; Iowa, pp. 48, 55, 60; Michigan, pp. 49, 65, 79; New Mexico, pp. 38, 40, 42; Pennsylvania, p. 57.

Slide 17	Krashen and McQuillan[20] collected the "startling" evidence from 100 years of research that when children and teens are surrounded by large quantities of books they want to read, they actually read more! And equally startling: Those who read more score higher on any academic achievement test they take! In other words, they found the obvious. Results are particularly spectacular in poorer neighborhoods where homes contain few or no reading materials. Translated into action, this means that any school can actually stimulate literacy by purchasing great quantities of exciting books young people want to read, and making them easily accessible from the library and through rotating classroom collections. Certainly, every learner will need quantities of books in the classroom and at home by their bedside.
Slide 18	Studies conducted by Dr. Keith Curry Lance and others[21] provide evidence that, beyond the collection to support reading, the extent to which every school library has a rich curriculum-centered information pool also affects how much children and teenagers learn. In addition, it appears that as technology[22] delivers that information via technology to the desktop of the student, achievement is further enhanced.
Slide 19	In today's school libraries, such collections consist of: ➢ Carefully selected Internet web sites relevant to the curriculum, ➢ Electronic periodical collections, ➢ Databases relevant to curricular topics, ➢ Attractive information books on all reading levels, ➢ Multimedia collections including video, audio, pictorial, graphic, and real objects, ➢ Special collections of print/electronic resources that meet all ranges of ability, cultural needs, and languages, and ➢ Collections that are authoritative, accurate, current, and curricular-related. Such collections allow learners to explore ideas and topics covered perhaps only in a paragraph of a textbook. This information can be found no matter the ability of the learner, the interest level, the cultural background, or the language of the learner.

---

[20] See Krashen and McQuillan.
[21] Alaska, p. 66; Colorado I, p. 92; Colorado II, p. 77; Illinois, pp. 58, 84, 106; Iowa, p. 73; Michigan, pp. 49, 65, 79; New Mexico, p. 59; Oregon, p. 83; Pennsylvania, p. 57;.
[22] *Ibid.*

Slide 20	Such collections add cost to the education budget since quality collections must be kept current. Again the research shows that schools spending more money for quality information beyond the textbook are actually boosting the bottom line – the amount learned.
Slide 21	**The Results** School communities who care enough to fund strong library media programs reap rewards. Those with stronger programs average 10-20% higher test scores than schools with weaker programs.[23]
Slide 22	These results,[24] as Dr. Lance points out cannot be explained away by: ➢ Teacher/pupil ratio ➢ Teacher characteristics (education, experience, salaries) ➢ Student characteristics (poverty, race/ethnicity) ➢ Per-pupil expenditures ➢ Community demographics (educational attainment, poverty, ethnicity) The message is increasingly clear that school communities who care enough to build strong library media programs also care about enough other vital elements in the education program, all of which combine to build academic excellence.

Fifteen Minute Presentation
PowerPoint Slides

Strong School Library Media Programs Make a Difference in Academic Achievement 1	**Gaver Study, 1963:** ▪ Academic achievement is higher when: ▪ There is a centralized library in the school. ▪ The library collection is large and easily accessible. 2	**Lance Study Finding, 1993:** Academic Achievement was higher in Colorado schools when: ▪ There was a professional library media specialist ▪ The library media specialist collaborated with teachers to build exciting units of instruction ▪ The library collection was very large 3
Since 2000: **14 State-Level Studies Involving Over 8,700 Elementary, Middle & High Schools Representing 2.6 Million Students** States Studied: Alaska, Colorado, Florida, Illinois, Iowa, Massachusetts, Michigan, Minnesota, Missouri, New Mexico, North Carolina, Oregon, Pennsylvania, Texas 4	**Two Other Study Findings:** **Krashen (1993),McQuillan (1998)** ▪ Strong library media programs make a difference in academic achievement. ▪ Impact made by learners who read more from large library media center collections 5	**The 21st Century Library Media Center** ▪ Consists of a quality information-rich environment: ▪ Books ▪ Multimedia resources ▪ Databases ▪ Electronic periodical collections ▪ Quality Internet sites 6

---

[23] Colorado II, p. 9.
[24] Colorado I, p. 92; Colorado II, p. 9.

The New Library Media Center: • Is available not only in the LMC, but • In the classroom, and • On beyond into the Home. *And is available 24 hours a day, 7 days a week.* 7	**Library Media Center Programs:** • Build capable and avid readers • Teach every learner to become effective users of ideas and information • Partner with teachers to create exciting learning experiences • Prepare learners to compete in the information age 8	**First, Invest in People** **Strong Library Media Programs have:** • A competent library media professional (The human interface) • Paraprofessional staff (Organization/service functions) • Technical staff (Technology support for the school) 9
Strong Library Media Specialists: • Collaborate with teachers to build quality learning experiences • Teach information literacy (finding, using, and communicating information effectively) • Promote reading 10	**Comparison of Top & Lowest 25 Scoring Schools in 7 States** Library media specialist hours per week per 100 students • Elementary: 9.4 vs. 5.1 -- 84% difference • Middle: 9.5 vs. 6.7 -- 42% difference • High: 11.5 vs. 8.2 -- 40% difference 7 states = CO, IA, IL, MI, NM, OR, TX 11	**Conclusion** • The level of professional library media specialist staffing is a key difference between strong and weak library media programs • … and between higher and lower scoring students on achievement tests. 12
Comparison of 25 Highest & Lowest Scoring PA Schools **Professional staff hours/week** • 5th grade 34.31 vs. 29.36 17% difference • 8th grade 38.40 vs. 37.63 2% difference • 11th grade 45.06 vs. 43.25 4% difference **Support staff hours/week** • 5th grade 25.92 vs. 12.48 108% difference • 8th grade 30.30 vs. 15.80 92% difference • 11th grade 49.57 vs. 19.28 157% difference 13	**Conclusion for Pennsylvania** • Support staff was the key difference between strong and weak library media programs in PA. • That is, professionals alone cannot make a major difference because of the load of clerical and technical work. 14	**Conclusion:** The total LMC staff size contributes to academic achievement. 15
Second, Invest in Materials and Technology • Create a quality information-rich and technology-rich environment easily accessible by students and teachers. 16	**Large School Library Collections Supply:** • Large rotating classroom collections • Large bedside collections for teachers and students 17	**Research Findings:** • Rich curriculum-centered collections boost learning. Information technology delivering information to the desktop of the learner enhances learning. 18
Today's LMC Collections are accessible through a library web page including: • Quality Internet sites • Electronic periodicals • Databases • Attractive information books • Multimedia collections • Materials meeting special needs • Materials of high quality 19	**Conclusion:** • Quality collections are expensive, but they earn their way by boosting achievement. 20	**Results of the total investment:** • Schools with stronger library programs average 10-20% higher test scores than those with weaker library programs. 21
Results are not explained by: • Teacher/pupil ratio • Teacher characteristics (education, experience, salaries) • Student characteristics (poverty, race/ethnicity) • Community demographics (educational attainment, poverty, ethnicity) 22		

Part Two:

Topical Presentations/Discussion Starters Based on the Research of School Library Media Programs

Part two contains nine discussion starters based on various aspects of the research. The idea is to focus groups of library media specialists, teachers, parent groups, or administrators on issues connected to school libraries. Each of the discussions is based the Lance studies and other research that has brought some significant findings for focusing on academic achievement and library media programs. The authors recommend that these discussion starters be modified for your local groups and the particular concerns they have. PowerPoint slides accompany each of the discussion starters and the brochure from part one can be duplicated freely as a supplement to these discussions with its references to many studies and the supplementary information on the web site.

Collaboration and Achievement:
A Two-Minute Discussion Starter
For School Library Media Specialists
And Teachers

Materials needed:
➤ Suggested script (below)
➤ PowerPoint Slides (downloadable from the LMC Source web site)
➤ Discussion questions

Library media specialists who collaborate regularly with faculty help build quality learning experiences that contribute to academic achievement.

This statement is supported by research done in schools in Colorado and elsewhere and published since 2000[25].

Collaboration for this study was measured by the number of hours a library media specialist worked with faculty:

➤ Planning units of instruction together
➤ Identifying materials for teachers
➤ Teaching information literacy to learners during the unit
➤ Providing in-service training to teachers
➤ Providing motivational reading activities
➤ Managing information technology in such a way as to push digital information beyond the LMC

In such collaborations, library media staff help raise scores by
➤ Enhancing learning experiences
➤ Building teacher effectiveness

Possible Directions the Discussion Might Take

➤ How can library media specialists and teacher maximize collaboration time?

➤ During what little time there is to collaborate, how do library media specialists and teachers use the time they do have effectively?

➤ How do library media specialists and teachers build a repertoire of effective learning experiences? (One by one? Planning several experiences in a professional development session?)

---

[25] Colorado II, p. 78; Illinois, p. xiii; Iowa, p. 42; .Michigan, p. xii; New Mexico, pp. 40-43; Oregon, pp. 49-50; Pennsylvania, pp. 6-7.

➢ What strategies of planning will maximize the number of students affected by collaborative planning? (Planning with grade level teams? Small teacher groups? Department level groups?)

➢ How can an entire faculty become a part of collaborative planning? (Large professional development sessions? Entire school initiatives? Large policy change programs?)

➢ How are collaborative efforts documented? (Collecting collaboration logs? Documenting collaboratively planned unit assessment results? Comparing achievement scores for teachers who collaborate regularly vs. those who do not?)

Collaboration and Achievement
PowerPoint Slides

Research Finding:	Collaboration Means:
Library media specialists collaborating with teachers to build quality learning experiences contribute to academic achievement. 1	▪ Planning units together ▪ Identifying materials for teachers ▪ Teaching information literacy to learners ▪ Providing in-service training for teachers ▪ Providing motivational reading activities ▪ Pushing digital information beyond the LMC 2
In Summary Scores rise when the LMC staff ▪ Enhance a learning experience ▪ Build teacher effectiveness 3	

No More Bird Units:
A Five-Minute Discussion Starter
For School Library Media Specialists
And Teachers

Materials needed:
- ➤ Suggested script (below)
- ➤ PowerPoint Slides (downloadable from the LMC Source web site)
- ➤ Discussion questions

If collaboration by the library media specialist with teachers in building learning experiences translates directly into academic achievement,[26] then it stands to reason that high-quality learning experiences ought to be the focus of the collaboration.

Sadly, library media center activities can be as ineffectual as poorly-designed classroom-based experiences.

Consider the bird unit.
- ➤ The teacher introduces the topic of "birds" to the class. (could be states, countries, scientists, etc.)
- ➤ Students then read a textbook chapter about birds and answer the questions – whatever required by the textbook.
- ➤ The teacher brings the class to the library so that each student can research a bird of choice.
- ➤ The teacher gives each student a worksheet containing fact questions.
- ➤ The librarian introduces the class to a few sources where facts about their birds can be found.
- ➤ The students find the answers to their fact questions and copy them on to their worksheets.
- ➤ They make a report back to the class about their bird.

Result: Nothing or very little! In fact, a well-designed classroom activity might be more productive.

A second result is that students have learned to cut and clip information from library resources, then regurgitate it back.

---

[26] Colorado II, p. 78.

Possible Discussion Questions

➢ Why are bird units (or any other fact-finding/copying exercise) generally a waste of everyone's time and effort?

➢ Why should bird units be banned from the library media program? Or, in the vernacular, how could we give the bird to bird units? (Cover higher-level questions, activities that require thinking to be successful, assessment that stresses thinking rather than fact regurgitation, etc.)

➢ What experiences in the library would cause students to <u>think</u> about the information they find rather than just cut, clip or copy, and report? (Have a group invent or modify bird units to guarantee higher-level learning) A few ideas might include:
  o Comparing and contrasting extracted data
  o Charting or graphing information
  o Drawing conclusions in groups about extracted data
  o Preparing position arguments using information
  o Re-formulating the original question(s) toward higher level thinking
  o Creating projects that require the integration of information to work
  o Redesigning questions to be more real or motivating to learners

➢ How could a faculty be weaned away from bird units?

No More Bird Units
PowerPoint Slides

Research Finding:	The "Bird" Unit
Library media specialists collaborating with teachers to build quality learning experiences contribut to academic achievement.<div align="right">1</div>	<ul><li>Teacher introduces topic.</li><li>Students do textbook work.</li><li>Class comes to the library.</li><li>Students pick a "bird."</li><li>Students are given a worksheet of fact questions.</li><li>Librarian introduces information sources</li><li>Students copy facts on to worksheets.</li><li>Students give reports on their "bird."</li><li>Result: Students learn to cut and clip information, then regurgitate it.</li></ul><div align="right">2</div>
Why Ban "Bird" Units? <div align="right">3</div>	**What learning activities in the LMC would be superior to "bird" units?** <div align="right">4</div>

Information Literacy and Achievement:
A Seven-Minute Discussion Starter
For School Library Media Specialists
And Teachers

Materials needed:
➢ Suggested script (below)
➢ PowerPoint Slides (downloadable from the LMC Source web site)
➢ Discussion questions

Learners who are exposed to integrated information literacy instruction as a part of their research projects in the library media centers score higher on academic achievement tests.

Support for this statement comes from major studies done by Dr. Keith Curry Lance, Marcia J. Rodney, and others in Colorado and several other states – all published since 2000.

Previously, school library media specialists, concentrating on library skills, would have helped students find and locate a few information sources, leaving the rest of the research process to the teacher.

Today, in an information-rich and technology-rich environment, library media specialists are finding that they need to teach many other concepts if students are to be successful investigators and better learners. Sample information literacy topics might include:

➢ Formulating a good research question
➢ Locating information
➢ Finding information in print and electronic environments including the Internet
➢ Judging the quality of information located
➢ Handling conflicting information sources
➢ Organizing the information found
➢ Reading and thinking about the information
➢ Synthesizing ideas across information sources
➢ Building creative presentations of findings
➢ Evaluating personal success as an organized investigator

Integrating Information Literacy: Teaching Cooperatively with Classroom Teachers
(Multi-State Averages)[27]

| School Level | Teaching Cooperatively with Classroom Teachers (Hours per Week) | | |
	Highest Scoring	Lowest Scoring	% Difference (high/low)
Elementary	3.5	2.5	40%
Middle	6.8	5.1	33%
High	10.4	8.8	18%

As teachers and library media specialists try to assist learners working in information-rich and technology-rich environments, they are beginning to recognize common problems. How could any of the following problems be solved?

Possible Discussion Questions

Small groups might be assigned different problems and then possible solutions across problems posed. The following list offers just a few possible topics.

➤ Learners wander and wander before settling on a researchable question or reasonable topic.

➤ Learners are unmotivated at the prospect of any library research.

➤ Learners either present copied information from print sources or they cut and clip from technological sources doing little thinking.

➤ Learners use the first few sources they find even though they have many other materials at their elbow.

➤ Learners want to use Internet sites exclusively.

➤ Learners rarely question the quality of the information they find.

➤ Learners spend almost all their research time finding information and cram the rest of the research process into a few minutes or hours.

➤ Learners' presentations are technologically attractive, but contain little substance.

➤ Learners' confidence levels during research are like roller coasters.

➤ Assessment shows little learning from the library activity, or students rate the experience low or counterproductive.

Information Literacy and Achievement
PowerPoint Slides

---

[27] States include Michigan, New Mexico, Illinois, Iowa, Oregon, and Pennsylvania.

Research Finding: Teaching integrated information literacy as a part of research projects affects academic achievement positively. 1	**Previous Practice:** ■ Concentrated on locating information ■ Left the balance of the research process to the discretion of the teacher 2	**Today's Research Process:** ■ Formulating questions ■ Locating information ■ Exploring online resources ■ Judging information quality ■ Handling conflicting information ■ Organizing information ■ Reading and thinking ■ Synthesizing ideas ■ Building creative presentations ■ Evaluating personal success 3

Pennsylvania's 25 Top Scoring Schools vs. 25 Low Scoring

■ 5th Grade 43% More time teaching
■ 8th grade: 1% More time teaching
■ 11th grade: 11% More time teaching

4

Differences in Time Teaching Information Literacy Cooperatively with Classroom Teachers
Highest & Lowest Scoring Schools
(Multi-State Averages)

5

Teaching Cooperatively with Classroom Teachers (Hours per Week)			
School Level	Highest Scoring	Lowest Scoring	% Difference (high/low)
Elementary	3.5	2.5	40%
Middle	6.8	5.1	33%
High	10.4	8.8	18%

Alaska's Schools

Significantly higher scores at the elementary level when information literacy was taught

6

How can the new problems learners face in an information-rich and technology-rich environment be solved?

7

Information Technology and Achievement:
A Five-Minute Discussion Starter
For School Library Media Specialists

> Materials needed:
> ➤ Suggested script (below)
> ➤ PowerPoint Slides (downloadable from the LMC Source web site)
> ➤ Discussion questions

Many school library media centers are acquiring the technology to push quality information beyond their walls into the classrooms and into the home. They are becoming 24/7 information providers. In schools with a rich information-technology environment, learners score higher on academic achievement tests.

Support for these statements comes from major studies done by Dr. Keith Curry Lance, Marcia J. Rodney, and others in Colorado and several other states – all published since 2000.

In high-scoring schools, there are a growing number of:

> ➤ Students who can link to the library media center remotely
> ➤ Databases/electronic resources available online from the LMC
> ➤ Computers linked to the Internet

When Colorado learners in the 25 most "connected" schools were compared with those in the 25 least "connected" schools achievement scores:

> ➤ At the 4th grade: 6% higher[28]
> ➤ At the 7th grade: 18% higher[29]

In the five states of Illinois, Iowa, New Mexico, Oregon, and Pennsylvania, the numbers of computers networked to the LMC in the highest vs. lowest scoring schools were:
- Elementary: 44 computers vs. 25 computers
- Middle: 64 computers vs. 38 computers
- High   87 computers vs. 65 computers

---

[28] Colorado II study, p. 72.
[29] Colorado II study, p. 73.

Thus higher scoring schools typically have 1/3 to 3/4 more computers in classrooms, labs, and offices that provide networked access to the LMC's information resources. Similar results in Alaska showed that students with higher tech library media centers scored higher on their achievement tests.[30]

Thus, in many schools, as quality information gets closer and closer to the elbow of the learner, academic achievement is affected. Such a finding makes sense since learners are interacting regularly with a pool of high quality information easily available. The concern, of course, is extending such an advantage to every learner.

Possible Discussion Questions

➢ What are school communities doing to insure that the percentage of "have nots" is decreasing each year in reference to connectivity to technology?

➢ What must happen in library media center programs as students become more and more connected to their resources online? That is, how is teaching and learning affected by connectivity?

➢ How can the effects of connectivity and its impact on teaching and learning be documented?

➢ What changes in "human interface" services need to happen as a higher and higher percentage of learners connect?

➢ What types of virtual/digital library media collections need to be built as connectivity increases?

➢ What features of library web pages are drawing learners to quality information sources?

➢ Are quality information sources delivered digitally actually showing up in learner research/products?

➢ Are carefully selected digital resources (provided by the LMC) preferred by learners or are learners wasting time surfing/fishing across the entire Internet?

---

[30] Alaska, pp. 56-57.

Information Technology and Achievement
PowerPoint Slides

Research Finding:	**In High Scoring Schools:**
Information pushed beyond the LMC into classrooms and into the home affects academic achievement. 1	▪ Students can link to the LMC remotely. ▪ Databases/electronic resources are available online. ▪ Computers are linked to the Internet. 2

In Colorado Connected Schools:

▪ 4th grade   6% higher for students in most "connected" schools.
▪ 7th grade   18% higher for students in most "connected" schools

3

School Computers Networked to LMC

Averages for Highest & Lowest Scoring Schools in 5 States

School Level	Highest	Lowest
Elementary	44	25
Middle	64	38
High	87	65

Higher scoring schools typically have 1/3 to 3/4 more computers in classrooms, labs, and offices that provide networked access to the LMC's information resources.

4

In Alaska Connected Schools:

Learners with higher tech library media centers scored higher on achievement tests.

5

Conclusion

▪ As quality information gets closer and closer to the elbow of the learner, academic achievement is affected.
▪ The concern is extending this advantage to every learner.

6

39

Making the Investment:
A Five-Minute Discussion Starter
For School Library Media Specialists,
Teachers, Administrators,
Boards, and Parents

Materials needed:
➢ Suggested script (below)
➢ PowerPoint Slides (downloadable from the LMC Source web site)
➢ Discussion questions

Research indicates that a certain level of investment in library media programs is needed to achieve improved academic achievement. The question is: "What level of investment is required to make a significant difference?"

For a discussion starter, let us examine the research done by Dr. Keith Curry Lance in Pennsylvania and Colorado covering 600+ schools. Specifically, let us compare the top 25 top scoring schools with the 25 lowest scoring schools in each state in terms of their commitment to library media staff, budgets for materials, and library media collection size.

LMC Staffing in 25 Highest vs. 25 Lowest Scoring Schools

Pennsylvania[31]	Highest Scoring	Lowest Scoring	% Difference (high/low)
Professional staff hours/week			
5th Grade	34.31	29.36	17 %
8th Grade	38.40	37.63	2 %
11th Grade	45.06	43.25	4 %
Support staff hours/week			
5th Grade	25.92	12.48	108 %
8th Grade	30.30	15.80	92 %
11th Grade	49.57	19.28	157 %

Conclusion for Pennsylvania: Adding support staff is a key difference between strong and weak library media programs. Library media specialists understand these findings very well, since adding support staff allows them the opportunity to work more closely with teachers and students rather than tend to warehousing duties all day.

---

[31] Pennsylvania study, pp. 54-56.

Colorado[32]	Highest Scoring	Lowest Scoring	% Difference (high/low)

Total library media staff hours/100 students

	Highest Scoring	Lowest Scoring	% Difference (high/low)
4th Grade	14.67	9.38	56 %
7th Grade	13.00	10.72	21 %

Conclusion for Colorado: The total staff size is contributing to academic achievement.

Budget in 25 Top vs. 25 Low Scoring Schools

Budgets were investigated comparing highest vs. lowest scoring schools in Pennsylvania, Colorado, Illinois, Iowa, Michigan, New Mexico, and Texas. Here are the results:

Expenditures for library materials

Pennsylvania[33]	Highest Scoring	Lowest Scoring	% Difference (high/low)
5th Grade	$ 7,240	$ 4,928	47%
8th Grade	$ 14,506	$ 8,386	73%
11th Grade	$ 23,730	$ 14,197	67%

Expenditures/students for library materials

Colorado[34]			
4th Grade	$ 21.60	$ 14.00	54%
7th Grade	$ 22.33	$ 13.44	66%

Illinois[35]			
Elementary	$20.71	$12.35	68%
Middle	$29.22	$12.92	79%
High	$25.13	$17.71	41%

Iowa[36]			
Elementary	$16.85	$14.67	15%
Middle	$25.55	$21.98	16%
High School	$23.38	$22.20	5%

---

[32] Colorado II study, pp. 75-76.
[33] Pennsylvania study, pp. 54-56.
[34] Colorado II study, pp. 75-76.
[35] Illinois study, pp. 126-37
[36] Iowa study pp. 76-78

Michigan[37]

Elementary	$14.14	$5.60	152%
Middle	$15.34	$7.82	96%
High	$20.56	$15.01	37%

New Mexico[38]

High School	$25.49	$22.08	15%

Texas[39]

Elementary	$36.02	$16.52	118%
Middle	$30.30	$20.60	47%

Conclusion: In all states studied, higher achieving schools spend more on materials for their library media programs.

Materials Available to Students in High vs. Low Scoring Schools

Measures were taken in eight states comparing the numbers of materials available to students in high vs. low scoring schools. These states included Pennsylvania, Colorado, Illinois, Iowa, Michigan, New Mexico, Oregon, and Texas. In Pennsylvania, the total number of volumes in the library collection was collected.

Pennsylvania

5th Grade	10.857 vs. 8,876	a 22% difference in materials
8th grade	13,507 vs. 10,744	a 26% difference in materials
11th grade	15,474 vs. 14,499	a 7% difference in materials

Looking across schools in the remaining states, volumes per student averaged as follows for the 25 highest vs. the 25 lowest scoring schools in each state:

Elementary schools	30 vs. 20	a 50% increase in materials
Middle schools	35 vs. 27	a 30% increase in materials
High schools	28 vs. 26	an 8% increase in materials

The conclusion was that stronger LMCs have richer print collections and this contributes to academic achievement. Higher scoring schools also have stronger periodical and electronic collections.

---

[37] Michigan study, pp. 92-96
[38] New Mexico study, p. 42
[39] Texas study, pp. 172-84.

Possible Discussion Questions

➢ Schools that invest more in staff, budgets, and the resulting larger information pools also see results in increasing academic achievement. Why does this happen? (If this is so obvious, why do libraries have to fight so hard for resources?)

➢ How do faculty and library media staff translate "things" into better learning experiences? (Obviously, since the figures are averages, not all schools that have high investments in the library media program automatically score higher.) The opposite is also true – some schools with poorer investments have high scores. How does this happen?

➢ If this school/district increased support of library programs, how could it document the impact of that decision?

Making the Investment
PowerPoint Slides

Research Finding:	Lance Findings in Two States	Comparison of 25 Top Scoring vs. 25 Lowest Scoring Schools
▪ A certain level of investment in the LMC program is necessary to expect improved achievement. ▪ What level of investment is required to make a significant difference?	▪ Pennsylvania (2000) 435 schools ▪ Colorado (2000) 200 schools	**Staffing in Pennsylvania** **Professional staff hours/week** ▪ 5th grade 34.31 vs. 29.36 17% difference ▪ 8th grade 38.40 vs. 37.63 2% difference ▪ 11th grade 45.06 vs. 43.25 4% difference **Support staff hours/week** ▪ 5th grade 25.92 vs. 12.48 108% difference ▪ 8th grade 30.30 vs. 15.80 92% difference ▪ 11th grade 49.57 vs. 19.28 157% difference
1	2	3

Conclusion in Pennsylvania	Finding in Colorado	Conclusion for Colorado:
▪ Support staff was the key difference between strong and weak library media programs. ▪ That is, professionals alone cannot make a major difference because of the load of clerical and technical work.	**Total library media staff hours/100 students** ▪ 4th grade 14.67 vs. 9.38 56% difference ▪ 7th grade 13.00 vs. 10.72 21% difference	▪ The total LMC staff size contributes to academic achievement.
4	5	6

Budget investment for five states	25 Highest Scoring vs. 25 Lowest Scoring Schools	
▪ Pennsylvania ▪ Colorado ▪ Texas ▪ Iowa ▪ New Mexico	**Pennsylvania budget for LMC materials** ▪ 5th grade $7,240 vs. $4,928 47% difference in scores ▪ 8th grade $14,506 vs. $8,386 73% difference in scores ▪ 11th grade $23,730 vs. 14,197 67% difference in scores	
7	8	

LMC Materials Expenditures per Student *Selected States & Grade Levels*

State/Level	Highest Scoring	Lowest Scoring	Percent Difference
CO Elem	$21.60	$14.00	54%
CO Middle	$22.33	$13.44	66%
IA Elem	$16.85	$14.67	15%
IA Middle	$25.55	$21.98	16%
IA High	$23.38	$22.20	5%
IL Elem	$20.71	$12.35	68%
IL Middle	$29.22	$12.92	79%
IL High	$25.13	$17.71	41%
MI Elem	$14.14	$5.60	152%
MI Middle	$15.34	$7.82	96%
MI High	$20.56	$15.01	37%
NM High	$25.49	$22.08	15%
TX Elem	$36.02	$16.52	118%
TX Middle	$30.30	$20.60	47%
TX High	$57.47	$23.92	140%

9

Conclusion

In all states studied, higher achieving schools spend more on materials for their library media programs.

10

Materials available in the LMC in seven states

- Colorado
- Iowa
- Illinois
- Michigan
- New Mexico
- Pennsylvania
- Texas

11

25 Highest Scoring vs. 25 Lowest Scoring Schools

Pennsylvania print volumes
- 5th grade 10,857 vs. 8,876 22% difference in scores
- 8th grade 13,507 vs. 10,744 26% difference in scores
- 11th grade 15,474 vs. 14,499 7% difference in scores

12

Volumes Per Capita

Highest & Lowest Scoring Schools in CO, IA, IL, MI, NM, OR, & TX

School Level	Highest Scoring	Lowest Scoring	Percent Diff.
Elementary	30	20	50%
Middle	35	27	30%
High	28	26	8%

13

Conclusion

- Stronger LMCs have richer print collections and this contributes to academic achievement.
- They also have stronger periodical and electronic collections

14

46

Leadership and Achievement:
A Ten-Minute Discussion Starter
For School Library Media Specialists
and Teachers

Materials needed:
➢ Suggested script (below)
➢ PowerPoint Slides (downloadable from the LMC Source web site)
➢ Discussion questions

Library media specialists who seek leadership roles and partnerships with administrators create strong library media programs translating into academic achievement. This is an indirect relationship. That is, leadership translates to higher collaboration with teachers in creating quality learning experiences that in turn, has a direct impact on academic achievement.

Support for this statement comes from a major study completed in Colorado[40] and published in 2000 that looked at a "leadership factor" and its relationship to academic achievement. Data were available for library media specialists who:

➢ Met regularly with administrators
➢ Served on standards committees
➢ Served on curriculum committees
➢ Attended school staff meetings, and
➢ Held library staff meetings (assuming more than a one-person staff)

Because this factor was so interesting, the analysis was repeated in Texas, Iowa, and New Mexico.

Notice the difference[41] between the top 25 highest scoring schools vs. the 25 lowest scoring schools on various measures of this leadership factor.

---

[40] Colorado II, p. 10-11.
[41] Colorado II, p. 25.

Measure/State	Highest Scoring	Lowest Scoring	% Difference in Scores

Meeting with administrators (hours per week)

Colorado
Elementary	.77	.37	108%
Middle School	.56	.49	14%

Illinois
Elementary	1.10	.60	83%
Middle School	1.10	,70	57%
High School	1.50	1.10	36%

Iowa
High School	.98	.78	26%

New Mexico
Middle School	.78	.62	26%
High School	1.16	.99	17%

Texas
Middle School	.80	.58	38%
High School	.99	.62	60%

Serving on committees (hours per week):

Colorado
Elementary	1.18	.74	59%
Middle School	1.63	1.12	45%

Iowa
Elementary	.61	.38	60%
Middle School	.75	.60	25%

New Mexico
Elementary	.54	.44	23%
Middle School	.53	.51	4%
High School	1.06	.76	39%

Pennsylvania
Elementary	1.52	.78	95%
Middle School	1.20	.40	200%
High School	1.16	.52	23%

Measure/State	Highest Scoring	Lowest Scoring	% Difference in Scores

Attending faculty meetings (hours per week):

49

Colorado
Middle School	0.83	0.60	38%

Iowa
Elementary school	0.71	0.48	48%
Middle school	0.88	0.82	7%
High school	0.92	0.78	18%

New Mexico
Middle school	0.83	0.81	2%
High school	0.80	0.59	36%

Attending library staff meetings (hours per week):

Colorado
Elementary	0.62	0.54	15%
Middle school	0.83	0.60	38%

Iowa
Middle school	0.80	0.76	5%
High school	1.58	0.76	108%

New Mexico
Middle school	0.78	0.62	26%
High School	1.28	1.08	19%

The correlation between test scores and time spent by library media specialists on leadership activities was positive and statistically significant. Thus, library media specialists are more likely to be leaders[42] in their schools if they:

➢ Have the ear and support of the principal and other administrators
➢ Serve with other teachers as members of the school's standards and curriculum committees
➢ Meet regularly with their own staff to plan and evaluate the effectiveness of LMC program activities in advancing student learning

Again, leadership is an indirect force. Library media specialists who are school leaders tend to collaborate more with classroom teachers, and that collaboration translates directly into academic achievement of students.

Possible Questions for Discussion:

➢ What other leadership factors of the library media specialist other than those studied in the research might contribute to academic achievement?

---

[42] Colorado II, p. 10-11.

➢ What leadership characteristics by both library media specialists and administrators will forge a powerful learning leadership team in a particular school?

➢ What communication patterns should Administrators and library media specialist team establish to move forward?

➢ What data flowing from the library media program to the administrator would trigger a focus on the contribution of the library media program on achievement?

➢ How can the leadership team in a school stimulate the organization of the school to put even more focus on student learning?

➢ How can the library media program focus on the whole school community's vision for academic success?

Leadership and Achievement
PowerPoint Slides

Leadership and Achievement

- Seeking leadership roles, and
- Creating partnerships with administrators
- Translate indirectly into:

ACADEMIC ACHIEVEMENT

1

Finding from Colorado:

Leadership translates into achievement when library media specialists:

- Meet regularly with administrators
- Serve on standards committees
- Serve on curriculum committees
- Attend school and staff meetings
- Hold library staff meetings (if appropriate)

2

Leadership in 25 High vs. Low Scoring Colorado LMC Programs

Meeting with Administrators
(hours per week)

Grade High Low   % Diff. in Scores

4th grade   0.77 0.37   108%
7th grade   0.56 0.49   14%

3

Weekly Hours Spent Meeting with the Principal

Averages for Highest & Lowest Scoring Schools for Selected States & Grade Levels

State/Level	Highest Scoring	Lowest Scoring	Percent Diff.
CO Elem	.77	.37	108%
CO Middle	.56	.49	14%
IA High	.98	.78	26%
IL Elem	1.10	.60	83%
IL Middle	1.10	.70	57%
IL High	1.50	1.10	36%
NM High	1.16	.99	17%
TX Middle	.80	.58	38%
TX High	.99	.62	60%

4

Weekly Hours Spent Serving on Committees

Averages for Highest & Lowest Scoring Schools for Selected States & Grade Levels

School Level	Highest Scoring	Lowest Scoring	Percent Diff.
CO Elem	1.18	.74	59%
CO Middle	1.63	1.12	45%
IA Elem	.61	.38	60%
IA Middle	.75	.60	25%
NM Elem	.54	.44	23%
NM Middle	.53	.51	4%
NM High	1.06	.76	39%
PA Elem	1.52	.78	95%
PA Middle	1.20	.40	200%
PA High	1.16	.52	23%

5

Weekly Hours Spent Attending Faculty Meetings

Averages for Highest & Lowest Scoring Schools for Selected States & Grade Levels

School Level	Highest Scoring	Lowest Scoring	Percent Diff.
CO Middle	.83	.60	38%
IA Elem	.71	.48	48%
IA Middle	.88	.82	7%
IA High	.92	.78	18%
NM Middle	.83	.81	2%
NM High	.80	.59	36%

6

Weekly Hours Spent in Library Staff Meetings

Averages for Highest & Lowest Scoring Schools for Selected States & Grade Levels

State/ Level	Highest Scoring	Lowest Scoring	Percent Diff.
CO Elem	.62	.54	15%
CO Middle	.83	.60	38%
IA Middle	.80	.76	5%
IA High	1.58	.76	108%
NM Elem	.57	.51	12%
NM Middle	.78	.62	26%
NM High	1.28	1.08	19%

7

Conclusions:

Library media specialists are more likely to be leaders in their schools if they:

- Have the ear and support of the administration.
- Serve with other teachers as members of important committees.
- Meet regularly with their own staff

8

However,

- Leadership is an indirect contributor to academic achievement, meaning that:
- Those who lead:
  - Collaborate with teachers more, and
  - Collaboration translates into increased achievement.

9

Five Key Things to Do Every Day:
A One-Minute Discussion Starter
For School Library Media Specialists

> Materials needed:
> ➤ Suggested script (below)
> ➤ PowerPoint Slides (downloadable from the LMC Source web site)
> ➤ Discussion activities

The Lance and Rodney studies (Alaska, Colorado II; Illinois, Iowa, Michigan, New Mexico, Oregon, Pennsylvania) plus studies by Stephen Krashen and Jeff McQuillan are providing more and more evidence that key program elements of a library media program are the factors accounting for increasing academic achievement. Thus, you could make your plans every day to make progress some way on each of the following five key factors:

➤ Collaborate with teachers to build solid learning experiences using the LMC resources.

➤ Teach information literacy as a part of collaborative experiences.

➤ Work to motivate students to read more.

➤ Manage the LMC in such a way to deliver quality information as close to the student as possible.

➤ Work on your leadership agenda.

The questions become:

➤ How can you plan a sensible strategy to do the five key elements every day and live to tell about it?

➤ How can you document easily these program components to explain to others when they discover you are still alive?

Possible Discussion Activities

After the one-minute presentation, ask groups of library media specialists to:

➢ Chart a sample day that might include all five activities.

➢ Chart a week's plan that would include all five activities.

➢ Predict what differences there would be in these plans depending on whether the library media specialist had some or a great deal of support personnel.

➢ Invent easy-to-keep measures (perhaps notes in their plan books) that could be tallied to track activities each week and then appear in a monthly report to administrators.

➢ How could the tracking of the five key elements:

- Be compared over time to growth in academic achievement by the students of teachers who actively participated in the Five Star LMC Program?

- Lead to documentation needed to make application for National Board for Professional Teaching Standards certification in the library media area (began in 2001)?[43]

Five Key Things to Do Every Day
PowerPoint Slides

Five Key Thinks to Do Every Day to Make A Difference!	Question
<ul><li>Collaborate with teachers to build solid learning experiences</li><li>Teach integrated information literacy</li><li>Motivate learners to read more</li><li>Push information beyond the LMC into the classroom and into the home</li><li>Work on the leadership agenda</li></ul>	How can the five key LMC program elements be documented?

---

[43] You may order a copy of the *Library media Standards* from the National Board for Professional Teaching Standards at http://www.nbpts.org

"To Which We Reply:" Discussing the Methodologies of the Lance Studies

Questions arise regularly about all educational research. Complaints abound about its inexact nature by those seeking definitive answers, cause and effect, and instant solutions to complex problems. In a day when test scores are published widely and when extreme pressure is made by various governments to "achieve," some criticisms of the Lance studies as with other educational research need to be aired. For a quality discussion to be held, knowledge of various research methods needs to be present in the group. However, various researchers like certain types of research – quantitative, qualitative, correlational, and other methodologies that gain fashion over time. As Keith Curry Lance presents to various audiences, common questions about methodology arise. Since he cannot be present in many arenas to conduct a question-answer period, the following answers to common questions have been written by him. Discussion leaders will want to take these into consideration as discussion questions are formulated, issues posed, panelists or experts invited and a host of other matters when methodology is the topic at hand.

Correlation vs. Cause and Effect

In statistical research, one of the easiest mistakes to make is equating correlation with cause-and-effect. Just because two variables—say, the level of LMC staffing and test scores—are correlated does not necessarily mean one causes the other. Indeed, there is no statistical test of cause-and-effect, only correlation. Further, it is a matter of logic and judgment which variable is the cause and which the effect. There is also no test to distinguish cause from effect.

Given these facts about the limits of statistical analysis, the best one can expect to do is to establish statistically that two variables are correlated, make reasonable assumptions based on theory and practice about which is the cause and which the effect, and rule out other variables that may explain away the correlation.

Regression

While the concept of correlation—two variables varying together from case to case—is fairly widely understood, regression is not. Regression is an elaboration of correlation analysis that makes it possible to assess the relative strength of multiple potential predictor variables on another variable all at once. In this research, such potential predictors include variables reflecting the LMC program's level of development and a variety of school and community conditions, such as the pupil-teacher ratio, per pupil spending, poverty, and adult educational attainment. Regression weighs the impact of each potential predictor while taking all of the other potential predictors into account. In a stepwise regression—the type employed in the Lance & Rodney studies—the strongest predictor is identified first, then the second strongest, etc.

Size of Correlation & Regression Coefficients

Generally, when correlation and regression analyses are conducted, the bottom-line question is "What percentage of the variation in one variable is explained by another?" In most fields of study, the expectation is that truly important predictors will explain large percentages of variation—say, upwards of 25 or 30 percent. Usually, variables that explain smaller percentages of variation—say, less than 10 percent—are discounted as not very important. For several reasons, such rigorous criteria have not been employed in this research.

From decades of educational research and statistics, it is widely recognized that socio-economic differences between schools and communities go far in explaining variations in the level of student performance from one school to another, indeed from one student to another. Because the impact of socio-economic factors is so powerful, because the number of potential predictors of academic achievement is so great, and because there are so many predictors for which data are not available (see below), there simply is not a lot of variation in student performance to be explained by anything in particular that a school can do—and for which data are available.

For these reasons, we believe it is noteworthy that data on school library media programs help to explain test score variations from school to school at all. Notably, in the Lance & Rodney regression analyses, some variables widely believed to be powerful predictors of academic achievement do not explain large percentages of variation at all. Such variables include the teacher-pupil ratio, per pupil spending by schools, and levels of adult educational attainment in the community. Indeed, more often than not, these variables are outweighed by library media variables.

Statistical Significance

One of the most misunderstood concepts in statistics is significance. Many believe that measures of statistical significance address the substantive importance of a finding. In fact, all an acceptable level of statistical significance means is that the sample in question—in the case of these studies, a few hundred schools representing all schools in a state—can be assumed to provide a reasonably accurate picture of the universe under study. The researchers have found that when the number of schools representing a particular grade level falls below 100 cases, it is difficult to achieve statistical significance. That does not mean that a correlation for a smaller number of cases is not valid or important; it simply means that, with relatively little data, it is impossible to know with reasonable certainty.

Quantitative vs. Qualitative Research

While quantitative research like the Lance and Rodney studies makes important contributions to understanding of the important role played by school library media programs, it has its limits. For instance, in these studies, data on instructional technology have been limited to numbers of computers in school libraries and elsewhere in schools and the number of typical weekly hours librarians spend helping to manage school computer networks. In order to truly understand the role played by technology in education, qualitative research is needed. Questions it could answer—that quantitative studies could not—include: How do teachers and librarians teach students using computers? How does the widespread availability of computers for instructional purposes alter the school's curriculum? How do computers affect the day-to-day interactions between teachers, librarians, and students?

Missing Data

In the Lance & Rodney studies, every effort has been made to include data on all major potential predictors of academic achievement. To be included in this research, however, data had to be available for an entire state on a school-by-school basis. Thus, data summarized only at the state level and data available only for selected students in a school were equally unusable in this context. Data on student participation in extra-curricular activities is an example of the latter. One of the most important contributions other researchers could make to this line of research is to generate or otherwise obtain appropriate datasets for other suspected predictors of student performance.

Discussion Questions

1. What is the difference between correlation and cause-and-effect?

2. How was regression analysis utilized to reduce the likelihood that correlations could be explained as something other than cause-and-effect?

3. How do findings about statistical significance as well as the replication of these studies in multiple states reduce the likelihood that correlations could be explained as something other than cause-and-effect?

Reinventing the Library as a Learning Laboratory: A Workshop Starter for School Library Media Specialists, Teachers, and Administrators

> Materials needed:
> ➢ Suggested script (below)
> ➢ Activity plans

Objective: To have teachers and administrators help the library media specialist do backwards planning to insure increased academic achievement.

Time: A minimum of one hour – two hours are better – three are best.

First activity: Present the one-minute presentation or the 15 minute presentation in this book about the potential of the library media program to enhance academic achievement.

Second activity: Put a library media specialist and one or two teachers and an administrator into small groups. Their task is to redesign a mundane instructional unit. Give them a sample unit on any topic containing the following usually boring elements:

➢ The teacher introduces the unit (one class period).
➢ Students read the chapter and answer chapter questions (one class period plus home work).
➢ Students select a topic of interest from the chapter and spend two class periods in the library constructing a two-page report (students are encouraged to come to the library before or after school if they need more information and are to write their report as homework).
➢ Students read their reports to the class (two class periods).
➢ Students take a test over the material covered (half a class period).

Rules for the redesign:

➢ The redesigned unit must not take any more time than the previous one.
➢ The library media specialist and the teacher must cooperatively plan, execute and evaluate the unit as a team.
➢ The new plan must guarantee to the administrator that the students will have learned more in the same amount of time or less.
➢ The experience in the library cannot be limited to students finding factual answers to a group of questions from library resources.
➢ The unit must draw upon the resources and facilities of the library media center.
➢ Student motivation/interest/involvement must be higher during the redesigned unit.

> ➤ There must be some form of information literacy integrated into the unit.
> ➤ There must be a drawing or chart/flowchart of the redesigned unit on a large piece of poster paper to post for the rest of the workshop participants to see. (The poster-size Post-a-Notes work very well)

Groups will need approximately 20-30 minutes to do the redesign.

Post all units and give a spokesperson no more than 30 seconds to explain their unit to the entire workshop (do not let more than 8-10 present).

Third activity: Present a new problem to the groups to solve: What were the common characteristics across the unit redesigns that would guarantee more learning in the same or less time? Give the groups 10 minutes to make a list as they view the posters.

Fourth activity: The workshop leader should then combine the best ideas into a set of principles with the entire group.

Fifth activity: Have the groups try to solve the following problem:
"Given the current resources (staff, materials, technology, and facilities), how many units a year could realistically be redesigned? And, if that number were to be doubled, what would have to happen to the organization of the school and the library to get the additional impact. Have groups prepare another poster for possible solutions to the problem.

Sixth activity: Have groups wrestle with the assessment of a learning activity to identify progress in learning. "How would you evaluate the effectiveness of these redesigned lessons? Would there be some way of determining which strategies worked best? How would you evaluate the impact of this kind of collaboration on student achievement?"

Seventh activity: Encourage the teams to make a realistic plan/commitment before they leave the workshop.

Important Resource: Obtain the book: *Ban Those Bird Units: Fifteen Models for Teaching and Learning in Information-Rich and Technology-Rich Environments* by David V. Loertscher, Carol Koechlin, and Sandi Zwaan published by Hi Willow Research & Publishing in 2005 (available at http://www.lmcsource.com). This book contains many ideas and transformations that can be used in workshops as models for creating high-level learning experiences.

Part Three

Implementing the Findings

Part three contains the authors' recommendations for planning to implement the research findings and measuring the impact of local programs on academic achievement. Most people want to know if national research would apply or has already applied to local programs. Do we already make a difference with our library media program, or could we plan an initiative to improve the local program and monitor the results on achievement?

The first essay makes major suggestions on how to create an initiative and an action research study in an individual school.

This essay is followed by the booklet: "Project Achievement" that is challenge to individual schools or districts to create and report action research. The bulk of this booklet contains major suggestions for measurements in four programmatic areas: Reading, collaboration, information literacy, and technology. It is a subset of many many measures available in a larger work:

Loertscher, David V. and Ross Todd. *We Boost Achievement!: Evidence-Based Practice for School Library Media Specialists.* Hi Willow Research & Publishing, 2004 (available at http://www.lmcsource.com).

Planning to Implement the Research Findings, and Measuring Local Impact

The inference of presenting the various research studies is that local programs make a difference in academic achievement as they do in Colorado, Pennsylvania, and Alaska and in other states as well. This is true, however, only in so far as a local program is like the strong library media programs in the research. Every library media specialist should be accountable by conducting various local studies that probe effectiveness.

Some statistics about library media programs are easy to collect but do not translate well into effectiveness. For example, a count of persons in the LMC each day will not account for uses of online resources 24/7 (24 hours a day, 7 days a week). Circulation figures have a little meaning, but do not measure amount read or information used. Currently, measures of the use of online information and information systems are just beginning to be developed. Watch for these or begin to develop them in your local area.

There are other tools that get closer to measuring impact. [44] Several are mentioned here that can be used.

Collaboration Logs. Collaboration logs are notebooks of "lesson plans" of jointly planned, executed, and evaluated learning experiences between library media specialists and teachers. If both the teacher and the library media specialist agree that a jointly-planned learning experience was "effective," then the record of that experience belongs in the collaboration log notebook. Unlike the football team, only <u>winning</u> games (effective units) would be counted. The first page of the notebook contains a summary chart of such experiences across the year and becomes a sort of "report card" for the LMC program. Collaboration logs are explained in several publications[45] and were used extensively in the major Library Power Project of the1990s.[46] The Lance research strongly suggests that there is a direct correlation between the amount of collaboration going on and academic achievement. Collaboration logs allow the library media specialist to demonstrate easily how much, with whom, and which parts of the curriculum are being affected the most by collaborative activities.

Another variation on collaboration logs can happen easily when the library media specialist uses the LMC web page to post units of instructions that are currently being done in the LMC. Students in the various classes would log onto the LMC home page

---

[44] See the evaluation chapter in: Loertscher, David V. *Taxonomies of the School Library Media Program.* 2nd edition. San Jose CA: Hi Willow Research and Publishing, 2000.

[45] Loertscher, David V. *Reinvent Your School's Library in the Age of Technology.* Hi Willow Research & Publishing, 1999, p. 14-15. Also by the same author: *Taxonomies of the School Library Media Program.* 2nd ed. Hi Willow Research & Publishing, 2000, p. 81-84.

[46] See Webb, Norman Lott. "Collaboration." In: Zweizig, Douglas L. and Dianne McAfee Hopkins. *Lessons from Library Power.* Englewood, CO: Libraries Unlimited, 1999. p. 53-78.

and in a section find their learning unit displayed. Clicking there would take them into their assignments, a webquest, or other directions. If the library media specialist adds the most current unit "at the top" of all the learning experiences listed, then older ones are pushed down the list. This list becomes the collaboration log of the units that were done in the library and can be printed out and analyzed by the library media specialist and administrators interested in tracking collaborative planning in the building.

Collection Maps. Collection maps are charts, diagrams, pictures, or maps of various segments of the library media collection that support the curriculum. This technique has appeared in the professional literature[47] for a number of years and was used extensively in the Library Power Project.[48] In the age of digital collections that are "invisible," collection mapping takes on an added dimension of reporting to stakeholders the quality of the collection and its strengths compared to the curricular demands placed on it. It is a tool for stakeholders to help push the direction collection development should take to support every teacher and learner. The Lance research indicates that there is a strong correlation between the availability of quality information at the student's elbow and academic achievement. Collection mapping is a technique to build the kind of information delivery system that will give every learner an equal opportunity to excel.

A Formal Locally-Based Research Project. Some schools and school districts need to carry out a longer-term assessment project of library media program effectiveness. Such research needs careful planning and should be long-term in nature rather than one-shot events. The description below is a brief outline of one possible study that could be tailored to local situations and available data.

Step One: Do a Baseline Study

First, analyze where your library media program is now on any or a combination of factors that the Lance studies probed. Then create a chart that can be shown to administrators, teachers, students, or parents.

Program Element	Brief Description	Graph of Changes over Last Five Years

Add a Graph of reading scores or other available assessment data from achievement tests for the past five years.

Report other baseline research from collaboration logs, collection maps or other program elements.

---

[47] See Loertscher, David V. *Taxonomies of the School Library Media Program*. 2nd ed. Hi Willow Research & Publishing, 2000, p. 207-15. Also by the same author *Collection Mapping in the School Library Media Center*. Hi Willow Research & Publishing, 1993.

[48] See Zweizig, Douglas L. and Dianne McAfee Hopkins. *Lessons from Library Power*. Englewood, CO: Libraries Unlimited, 1999. p. 19-52.

Step Two: Plan Improvement, New Programs, New Interventions

For each program element above, describe briefly how that element will be changed or improved. Include action plans, responsibility, budget, timelines, etc. Outline and obtain organizational support. The broader the support by faculty, administrators, and parents, the more likely the intervention will be successful. Some initiatives will take increased funding. Others will require a shift in attitude or practice. Some will require extensive reorganization of how the library media center operates in the school. Still others will involve extensive cooperation and support from the learners in the school. For example, learners should be involved in the planning to raise their own reading scores by maximizing the amount they read. Learners who are motivated to raise their own achievement using the tools provided are very likely to succeed. Rather than creating some sort of competition, the emphasis should be on a collaborative project designed to help every learner achieve.

For each element, select an evaluation measure or assessment to measure the impact of the change or improvement. These can be locally-created measures or standardized measures already being given in the school. Because there is so much time devoted to assessment in the schools, careful coordination and use of one measure for several purposes is advisable.

Changes in programs often take a long time to translate into increased scores. For example, an enhanced reading program will take at least six months to a school year to start showing results. Improving information literacy skills in a single class will require at least three "research experiences" complete with teacher and library media specialist instruction and guidance before students can be expected to adopt and implement an information literacy model. The impact of improved collections takes time to acquire, disseminate, and convince the appropriate teachers and learners to use before an impact on learning will result. You may set expectations for results high, but make sure that the improved program has the time needed to work.

Step Three: Chart Results for a Non-Librarian Audience

Prepare simple charts/graphs/pictorial records showing results in a simple enough way to be understood by an audience who may not be library media specialists.

Program Element	What We Did	Outcome at Mile Post 1	Outcome at Mile Post 2	Outcome at Mile Post 3

Or:

Program Element	What We Did	Reading Scores Mile Post 1	Reading Scores Mile Post 2	Reading Scores Mile Post 3

Or:

Program Element	What We Did	Other Assessments Mile Post 1	Other Assessments Mile Post 2	Other Assessments Mile Post 3

Baseline data might be used as the Mile Post 1 result. A trend chart over time is often an effective chart to show. For example, chart progress across time showing the creation of digital networks and the growth of quality information available in the LMC, classroom, and the home compared to achievement scores across the same time period.

A second technique that is effective is to chart the progress of at-risk learners. Learners who already read well and are information literate are not likely to show progress on any measure we use simply because they are already topping out on the assessments. They may benefit greatly by our improved programs, but the measurements may not show that improvement.

More dramatic results might be demonstrated by students who are likely to show large improvement on assessments. For example, track results of a reading initiative in classrooms where there are a high percentage of students who are learning English. Look for results with students who have consistently scored low on achievement tests but who have enthusiastically participated in your program initiatives. Show examples of improvement by individuals, small groups within a class, an entire classroom, or the school as a whole. Focus on every individual, not just the whole. Emphasize the number of teachers making more effective use of information, technology, and collaborative learning experiences.

A few comments on Accelerated Reader and other electronic motivational programs. Electronic motivational programs are immensely popular in schools throughout the nation and these systems provide evaluative techniques and statistical analysis built into their programs. There are, however, dangers to these types of programs as well as pluses.

Principle one: If a young person is not doing well in the program, design something else. Better to have a reader than a learner who can read but hates it.

Principle two: There are a number of abuses of these types of programs that will become apparent as they are implemented or that other schools have experienced. Cut the abuses to as close to zero as possible.

Principle three: Every book in the library should be a potential read in the electronic program. If tests have not been created for a particular book, then have learners help create those tests. They can have their "computer" points plus points for items not in the system.

Principle four: Readers may not score higher on reading tests if they read only fiction. Try increasing the amount of non-fiction read so that students experience more expository text. This means that large quantities of interesting non-fiction should be available.

Principle five: Learners are not likely to score higher on reading tests if they read only material at or below their level. While learners should be encouraged to read widely, they should also consciously select materials that will challenge them, knowing that these materials will help them build skill. Again, large collections of interesting non-fiction as a part of the program will naturally attract interest rather than forcing a reader into some mold.

Principle six: Competitions are rarely successful in reading simply because we want every learner, not just the already-motivated, to build a life-long reading habit. Create collaborative goals and personal goals that build the idea that everyone wins as a reader.

Principle seven: The readers needing the most attention in programs such as these are those learning English and readers in the bottom quartile of scores. These are the readers to track carefully since they will make the most dramatic gains. There will be a certain percentage of these readers who will thrive in electronic programs and another percentage who will not. Individualizing a program for the most at-risk is still the best approach.

Project Achievement

(A National Initiative to Collect and Present Evidence that Links
Library Media Programs to Student Achievement, 2003-05)

Brief Guide &
Handouts
(Sept.23, 2003 version)

by
David V. Loertscher

Salt Lake City UT
Hi Willow Research & Publishing
© 2003

This brief guide is a subset from the book: Loertscher, David V. with Ross J. Todd. *We Boost Achievement! Evidence-Based Practice for School Library Media Specialists*. Salt Lake City UT: Hi Willow Research & Publishing, 2003. Available at: http://www.lmcsource.com

Project Achievement
(A National Initiative to Collect and Present Evidence that Links Library Media Programs to Student Achievement, 2003-05)
by
David V. Loertscher

Library media specialists are invited to participate in Project Achievement sponsored by David V. Loertscher and supported by his web site at **http://www.davidvl.org**

Any credentialed library media specialist recognized as a professional and receiving a professional salary in a school or school district is invited to participate (sorry, no paraprofessionals or support personnel, please).

To participate, send an email message to: David Loertscher at **davidlmc@qwest.net** (Posal address: 312 South 1000 East, Salt Lake City UT 84102)

There is no charge to participate, but those who do are asked to commit to collect evidence of their program during the current school year and present that evidence to administrators, faculties groups, school boards, and try to get press coverage in the school, district, and community where the library media program is present. In addition, a brief report of your activities to David Loertscher would be appreciated for sharing beyond the local level. An online support group is also available as a link at **http://www.davidvl.org** under Project Achievement.

The measurements recommended in this handout cover four program areas: reading, collaboration, information literacy and technology. They are extracted from the following book where much more extensive instruction is available (however, you need not purchase the book to participate): Loertscher, David V. with Ross Todd. *We Boost Achievement! Evidence-Based Practice for School Library Media Specialists*. Salt Lake City UT: Hi Willow Research & publishing, 2003. Available from http://www. lmcsource.com for $30)

Evidence is divided into a number of perspectives, all covered in these handouts:

Program Emphasis Areas	Triangulation of Evidence:	Types of Evidence
o Reading o Collaboration o Information Literacy o Technology	o Learner Level o Teaching Unit Level o Organization Level	o Direct o Indirect

Note: The handouts in this packet are copyrighted by David Loertscher. They may be reproduced and modified for used by any person in Project Achievement without charge. Any other reproduction in any form requires the permission of the author.

The author is available as a consultant for states, districts or regions wishing to initiate more formal evidence collection initiatives. Both California and Massachusetts are already involved in state-wide initiatives.

The Library Media Center Reading Program
Ripple Effect Measures.[1]

Goals

LMC Agenda	Reading Agenda
• Capable and Avid Readers. • Learners who read a lot (amount counts). • Learners who like to read.	• Skilled readers. • Learners reading at grade level or above. • Taught using scientifically-based methods.

Pebbles to Measure

1. Access to a plentiful supply of materials learners want to read:
   a. In the Library Media Center
   b. In the Classroom
   c. At home
   d. Over digital networks
   e. As implemented in organizational policy

2. The Amount Read (Individuals, classes, the entire school).
   a. Free voluntary reading
   b. During topical unit studies

3. Whether a learner likes to read.

Justification:

The Krashen/McQuillan research review of 100 years strongly supports the notion that amount counts and that those who read a great deal score high in comprehension, grammar, spelling, writing style, and are just plain smart.

Demonstrate through research and practice that:
   ❑ Access is increasing and maxing out and that new materials are commonplace.
   ❑ The amount read is increasing and becoming a personal habit.
   ❑ The number of individuals who report they like to read is increasing.

Report:
   ❑ Steady improvement over time.
   ❑ Improvement related to an initiative.
   ❑ That success is already high and is remaining constant.
   ❑ Improvement related to organizational policy shifts.

---

[1] Ripple-effect measures refer to significant measures that are most likely to produce results in achievement and indicate maximum teacher collaboration and organizational effectiveness. Because you have these data, a ripple effect occurs, like throwing a pebble in a pool, triggering many other organizational practices and policies.

Value-Added Components of the LMC Reading Program: Candidates for Measurement

Learner Level

- Access to as much reading material as each learner can possibly handle in the LMC, the classroom, and in the home.
- Encouragement to read across the genres and for curricular pursuits.
- Encouragement to build a life-long reading habit.
- Involvement in conversation about reading.
- Personal readers advisory.
- Enjoyment of literature for literature's sake (no book reports, no tests, no critical analysis).
- Encouragement to participate in reading celebrations, events, initiatives, projects, and challenges (as opposed to prizes, rewards, contests, competitions).
- Individualized help for learners – particularly for those not doing well in classroom reading programs.

Teaching Unit Level

- Access to reading materials both for teaching units and recreational reading.
- Collaborative teaching of the language arts including appropriate information literacy skills and technology.
- Support of whatever skill-based reading program is in place; compensation for whatever weaknesses built into reading programs.
- Collaborative reading motivation both for free reading and for content reading.
- Reading aloud and storytelling both for fun and connected to teaching units.
- SSR (sustained silent reading program) for both fun and connected to teaching units.
- Endless booklists and booktalks for fun and connected to teaching units.

Organization Level

Access

- Easy access to reading materials kids and teens want to read:
  o   From the LMC.
  o   From the classroom (rotating from the LMC).
  o   In the home (as supplied by the LMC).
  o   In the preferred language.
  o   At desired reading level.
  o   Matching both curricular needs and personal interest.
  o   Constantly rotating to stimulate interest (as in bookstores).
  o   At the elbow for whatever device owned by patrons (cell phones, PDAs, wireless laptops).

- Pleasant places to read (inviting facilities, ambience, posters, banners, comfortable chairs, bathtubs, reading lofts).

Program

- Participate on or head the leadership team of motivational reading programs and events such as state young reader awards, and local initiatives, reading challenges, projects.
- Link to reading and literacy efforts in other libraries and from the community.
- Keep students and teachers apprised of what's new in publishing and in the collection.
- Connect with authors and illustrators.
- Create endless booklists and do booktalks.
- Sustain a SSR (sustained silent reading) program.

Materials

- A large and evolving collection of materials young people want to read.
- Materials to read in all formats: print, multimedia, and digital.

My Reading Log for _____ (topic of research/assignment/personal exploration)

Things I scanned (quick look/read)
- ❑ Books
- ❑ Magazines
- ❑ Web sites
- ❑ Online databases
- ❑ Video/multimedia sources

Time I spent:

What types of reading helped introduce me to the topic?

Easy reads that helped me understand more about the topic (could list fiction or nonfiction)

Rate each Item:

*   Not worth the time I spent

**   Somewhat helpful

*** Quite helpful

****Everyone should read this; it's that good

Items I really had to read slowly and carefully because they were so important or assigned.

Rate each Item:

*   Not worth the time I spent

**   Somewhat helpful

*** Quite helpful

****Everyone should read this; it's that good

Reading Evidence Plan Example #1

Goal: To increase exponentially every student's access to books they want to read in the LMC, the classroom, and the home.

	Learner Level	**Teaching Unit Level**	**Organization Level**
Direct Measures*	Through questionnaire or interview, the student should agree that access is at is maximum. Evidence that students actually take advantage of maximum access. The student's parents, teacher, and the library media specialist, along with the student, agrees that responsible behavior is equal to the maximum access I am allowed.	Student would agree that when they need to read for school work topics, there is almost always a wide choice of something to read. Assessment of an individual student's reading log required as part of a unit of instruction to see that access was maximized. The behavior of a teacher toward access issues pushed by the LMC program is apparent.	The behavior of almost all the faculty toward access issues pushed by the LMC program is apparent. There is documentary support by administrators for the access issues of the LMC reading program.
Indirect Measures**	Policies relating to access by individuals are in place to allow maximum access. Abuses in the use of electronic reading program (or any other initiative) are solved for the individual reader.	A classroom audit has resulted in changes in access for students in a particular classroom. A particular classroom has a rotating classroom collection and it is working.	There is an ample budget for the reading collection to support the needs of expanded access. Access policies for the entire school are in place and make provision for both groups and individuals Digital access to reading materials is ubiquitous. The physical environment of the LMC is conducive to access.

*Direct measures would be those so close to actual learning that confidence in an impact could be inferred. We have no thermometers to stick in a learner's mouth to gauge actual learning, but direct measures might challenge doubters to prove no impact.
** Indirect measures provide evidence that actions set the stage for, provide an environment for, give support to, enable, help, give encouragement to, mark progress toward, make change in direct measures over time the probable stimulus.

Reading Evidence Plan Example #2

Goal: To provide evidence that the new LMC reading initiative has actually increased the amount students read. The initiative could include access, a motivational program (see Read8), or an electronic reading program. Plan:

1. Take a measure before a major initiative is begun (to serve as the basis).
2. Implement the initiative, measuring during and after it is completed.
3. Judging the impact of the initiative.

	Learner Level	**Teaching Unit Level**	**Organization Level**
Direct Measures*	Build a questionnaire to ask students how much they read and whether they like to read (before during, and after the initiative). Measure the amount of reading on reading logs connected to a topical unit before, during, and after the initiative. On checktests, measure reading competence before, during, and after the initiative. Number of points earned on electronic reading programs (influenced by the LMC). Monitor standardized reading scores for an individual student over time (before and after the reading initiative). This is assuming that the initiative was planned as a long-term program.	Looking at any of the measures done for individuals at the classroom level before, during, and after the initiative. See Read10, 11, 12, 13, 14, 15, 16). Document amount read by a class for a specific initiative feature via logs, special counts, reader logs, circulation of physical items, hits on certain websites)	Looking at any of the measures done for individuals at the building level before, during, and after the initiative.
Indirect Measures**	Defend counting systems set up to measure the amount read during a special initiative for an individual	Defend counting systems set up to measure the amount read during a special initiative for a classroom.	Defend counting systems set up to measure the amount read during a special initiative for the school as a whole. Document efforts to spread the word about good books to read during whole school initiatives. The number and percent of learners participating successfully in the initiative.

*Direct measures would be those so close to actual learning that confidence in an impact could be inferred. We have no thermometers to stick in a learner's mouth to gauge actual learning, but direct measures might challenge doubters to prove no impact.
** Indirect measures provide evidence that actions set the stage for, provide an environment for, give support to, enable, help, give encouragement to, mark progress toward, make change in direct measures over time the probable stimulus.

The Library Media Center Collaboration Program
Ripple Effect Measures[2]

Goals

LMC Agenda	Curriculum Agenda
• Support state standards. • Build truly collaborative experiences. • Build high quality learning experiences.	• State standards met. • Achievement test scores high. • Learners at or above grade level.

Pebbles to Measure

1. The time professional library media specialists spend collaborating.
2. The move from "bird units" (low-level learning experiences) to quality learning experiences in the LMC.
3. The dispersion of collaborative experiences across the faculty and across the content areas.
4. Assessment of learning includes both classroom and LMC agendas including measurement of content learning, information literacy, amount read, and impact of technology.

Justification:

The pressure to achieve requires that precious time spent in the library media center produce the highest quality learning experience. The investment in information systems, technology, and facilities must pay its way in terms of achievement. The Lance studies all report the connection between collaboration and achievement.

Demonstrate through research and practice that:
  ❏ Collaboration is happening.
  ❏ The amount of collaboration and dispersion is improving over time.
  ❏ The quality of the collaboration is producing better and better learning experiences.

Report:
  ❏ Steady improvement over time.
  ❏ Improvement related to an initiative.
  ❏ That success is already high and is remaining constant.
  ❏ Improvement related to organizational policy shifts.

---

[2] Ripple-effect measures refer to significant measures that are most likely to produce results in achievement and indicate maximum teacher collaboration and organizational effectiveness. Because you have these data, a ripple effect occurs, like throwing a pebble in a pool, triggering many other organizational practices and policies.

Value-Added Components of the LMC Collaboration Program:
Candidates for Measurement

Learner Level

- ❑ A memorable learning experience is created.
- ❑ Collaborative learning experiences encourage more investigation even after the experience has ended.
- ❑ A successful collaborative learning experience includes content learning, information literacy, adds additional reading, and enhances learning through technology.
- ❑ Collaborative learning experiences seek to provide the learner with deep learning as opposed to surface learning.
- ❑ Successful collaborative LMC learning experiences motivate learners to be more engaged and interested not only in the topic at hand but in education and personal success.

Teaching Unit Level

Prelude:

- ❑ Collegial and trusting relationships characterize a collaborative experience rather than a servant/master stance (library media specialist being the servant and the teacher the master).
- ❑ Time for collaboration and planning is sufficient to build exciting learning experiences.
- ❑ LMC scheduling encourages individual teachers to collaborative learning experiences that can take advantage of the LMC facilities, collection, and networks.
- ❑ The entire LMC staff is available to teachers doing collaborative experiences: professional, clerical, and technical.
- ❑ Resources on beyond the LMC are tapped as needed (district, state, and national).
- ❑ Technology and facility support are available and reliable enough to use in planning the most exciting learning experience possible.
- ❑ The professional library media specialist has extensive knowledge of curriculum, teaching and learning, plus expertise technology, reading, and information literacy.

Planning and Execution Stage:

- ❑ Collaborative planning of a teaching unit begins with state standards from which goals and objectives for what learners are expected to know and do are created.
- ❑ Assessment strategies are designed so that both teaching partners will know what has been learned and how well. Rubrics or other assessment measures are jointly constructed so that learners understand that both teacher and library media specialist agendas must be satisfied to receive an "A."
- ❑ Collaborative units begin for students with clear goals and/or essential questions that need to be answered.
- ❑ Collaborative units draw upon the resources and technologies of the library media center and the information world beyond.
- ❑ Activities for a LMC-based learning experience are jointly taught by teacher and library media specialist thus reducing the pupil-teacher ratio and increasing the chances that learners will achieve.
- ❑ Activities in the LMC go far beyond the "cut and clip" mentality toward the "cut, clip, THINK" strategies ("bird units" are banned).[3]
- ❑ Culminating learning activities go beyond boring reports to pull together significant ideas of the research activities.

Postlude:

- ❑ All the partners of a collaborative LMC learning experience reflect on the learning produced and the collaborative experience itself to capture the best of what occurred and plan to overcome problems for future experiences.

Organization Level

- ❑ Administrators play a vital role in collaboration when they understand the role of the LMC as a curricular and achievement partner and do all in their power to encourage and make it happen.
- ❑ Administrators work with the LMC staff to provide the organizational structure necessary to make collaborative planning with the LMC staff work.
- ❑ The size of the LMC staff and its composition of professionals, support, and technical personnel is predictive of its impact on collaboration and the resultant impact on achievement.
- ❑ Professional development in the effective use of the LMC collaboration program to boost achievement is critical in any successful school culture.

---

[3] Loertscher describes "bird units" as the copying facts or downloading information to complete worksheets or fact-based assignments resulting in minimal learning.

Gauge the Dispersion of Collaboration
Across the Faculty

In this measure, the library media specialist documents the spread of collaboration through a faculty. Such a measure demonstrates an active rather than passive library media program. It makes the assumption that collaboration produces superior learning experiences (not always the case, but highly likely).

In the author's experience across the years, administrators who make a friendly compact or mutual goal with the library media specialist – a private challenge to see how far dispersion can be pushed – these are the schools in which the library media program makes the most difference.

The technique is known as the collaboration log described below and its critical summary page showing dispersion is given on the next page.

Collaboration logs are **direct measures** at the **teaching unit level**. The record of dispersion is a **direct measure** at the **organization level**.

Idea: Create a Collaboration Log.

Who: The library media and technology specialists and classroom teacher working as a team.

Activity: Each time there is a major collaborative learning experience jointly planned, executed, and evaluated by the library media specialist and classroom teachers, do the following.

➢ **File collaborative unit planning sheets** in a three-ring notebook in some sensible fashion. Only fully developed collaborative activities should be recorded — not every interaction between the library media and technology specialist and the teachers. An electronic record might be preferable.

➢ As the **first page** in the notebook, create **a collaboration log summary page** listing the collaborative activities as shown on the next page.

➢ **Principal's Activity:** Using the summary sheet, assess the collaboration log notebook as a whole looking for patterns.

- Who is being served?
- Which grade levels?
- Which departments?
- Which curricular subjects?
- Who is not being served?

Sample Collaboration Log Summary Page

During the school year, the teachers and the library media and technology specialists agree that the following units were successful collaborations, i.e., the learning was enhanced because the several partners exploited the resources and technology of the LMC and/or computer lab.

	LMS/TS Time	*#Students*
Social Studies		
Our Local Elections - grade 6 (Smith)	2.6 hours	24
Family Trees - grades 3 and 4 (Albright and Faire)	3.6 hours	45
Reading		
Newbery Novel Unit - grades 5 & 6 (Crane & Finch)	1.5 hours	47
Science		
Environment of the School Grounds - entire school (Principal, LMS and Dwight, leaders)	15 hours	465
Simple Machines - grade 3 (Truett)	1.4 hours	27
Nutrition - grades 5 and 6 (Handford and Zigler)	2.8 hours	48
Integrated Units		
Local Environmental Hazards – Social Studies and Science. gr. 4 (Todd and Lark)	4.5 hours	43
Labor Movements - SS and Art, grade 6 (Jones and Gregg)	3.7 hours	49
Totals	*35.1 hours*	*748*

Ideas:

➢ Create a summary chart similar to the one above that details collaborative units taught. Use a single sheet of paper for this summary page. This becomes the first page in the collaboration log.

➢ Create a graphic that summarizes the above list for use in the report.

➢ Enlarge the chart to poster size, use a transparency, or create a PowerPoint presentation when reporting collaborative efforts to the faculty, administration, and the community.

Note to the library media specialist: How many collaborative activities were there? What is the dispersal of collaboration among the faculty, grade levels, and subjects taught? How could I as the instructional leader encourage more and better collaboration? Which of the collaborative activities deserve recognition from the community? How would I assess the effectiveness of increased student learning?

Other Assessments of Collaborative Planning

Because the Lance studies[4] made a very strong link between collaboration in the LMC to academic achievement, the measures taken documenting this activity are vital. Collecting, reviewing, and reporting data at the organizational level, the teaching unit level and the learner level will help assess the impact collaboration is ready to make and is making in the school.

Level of Measure	Factor	Sources of Data
Collaboration at the Organization Level	The state of collaboration in the school and district.	❑ Evidence that district and school level administrators support collaborative planning by actions as well as word. ❑ Evidence that time for collaborative planning is built into the school day. ❑ Evidence that clerical and technical help are available to allow professionals to collaboratively plan.
Collaboration at the Learning Unit Level (class interaction and use)	The success that the class and the teacher experience during a unit of instruction both in the classroom and the LMC when collaborative planning is the norm.	❑ Evidence that collaborative logs are kept showing both planning and assessment of learning experiences. ❑ An analysis of collaboration logs showing spread of collaboration through the grade levels, the various disciplines, and through the faculty. ❑ An analysis of rubrics of classes as a whole for units of instruction done collaboratively. How they rate against instructional units done only in the classroom. ❑ "Teacher" to pupil ratio for this learning unit as compared with normal classroom-based instruction.
Collaboration at the Learner Level (as individuals)	Individual progress by each learner as collaborative planning enhances learning experiences.	❑ Rubric score that content knowledge, technology, and information literacy was enhanced through collaboration. ❑ Evidence that an individual learner was more engaged, interested, and motivated than "normal" as the collaboratively-taught unit progressed.

---

[4] Lance, Keith Curry and David Loertscher. *Powering Achievement*. 2nd ed. San Jose, CA: Hi Willow Research & Publishing, 2003.

The Library Media Center Information Literacy Program Ripple Effect Measures.[5]

Goals

LMC Agenda	Curriculum Agenda
• Integrated teaching of info. lit. • Each learner information literate. • Process learning a part of the school's curriculum.	• State standards met. • Achievement test scores high. • Learners at or above grade level. • All the above inclusive of process learning.

Pebbles to Measure

1. Information literacy is being integrated into joint classroom/LMC learning experiences.
2. Learners realize that information literacy is an integral part of LMC learning experiences.
3. Assessment of information literacy happens as it is taught.
4. Information literacy is a part of teacher assessment of student learning.
5. The school culture values both content and process learning.

Justification:

Content learning without process learning (information learning) gives learners only fish – not fishing poles. Learning how to learn is a life-long gift. The Lance studies all report the connection between collaboration and achievement.

Demonstrate through research and practice that:
- Information literacy is integrated into the curriculum.
- Learners are becoming more sophisticated over time in their information literacy skills.
- Information literacy skills are part of an entire assessment of learning package.

Report:
- Steady improvement over time.
- Improvement related to an initiative.
- That success is already high and is remaining constant.
- Improvement related to organizational policy shifts.

---

[5] Ripple-effect measures refer to significant measures that are most likely to produce results in achievement and indicate maximum teacher collaboration and organizational effectiveness. Because you have these data, a ripple effect occurs, like throwing a pebble in a pool, triggering many other organizational practices and policies.

Value-Added Components of the LMC Information Literacy Program:
Candidates for Measurement
(Items in Roman come from AASL InfoLit Standards; Items in Italics have been added;
The entire list is arranged in order of an information literacy model)

Learner Level
- ❑ Questioning
  - o Recognizes the need for information.
  - o Formulates questions based on information needs.
  - o *Understands that great questions have often been the basis for advancement in many fields.*
  - o *Understands the difference between a good and a poor question.*
  - o *Predicts possible answers to the question formulated.*
  - o *Revises questions as research proceeds.*
  - o *Understands that answers often lead to new questions.*

- ❑ Finding and Sorting
  - o Prelude
    - ▪ Recognizes that accurate and comprehensive information is the basis for intelligent decisionmaking.
  - o Finding and Searching
    - ▪ Identifies a variety of potential sources of information.
    - ▪ Develops and uses successful strategies for locating information.
    - ▪ Accesses information efficiently and effectively.
    - ▪ Seeks information from diverse sources, contexts, disciplines, and cultures.
  - o Sorting
    - ▪ Evaluates information critically and competently.
    - ▪ Determines accuracy, relevance, and comprehensiveness.
    - ▪ Selects information appropriate to the problem or question at hand.
    - ▪ Seeks information related to various dimensions of personal well-being, such as career interests, community involvement, health matters, and recreational pursuits.
    - ▪ Pursues information related to personal interests.
    - ▪ Identifies inaccurate and misleading information.

    - ❑ Consumes and Absorbs (reading, viewing, and listening)
  - o Appreciates literature and other creative expressions of information.
  - o Is a competent and self-motivated reader.
  - o *Understands skimming and scanning through text structure.*
  - o *Can pick out the main ideas from any form of media (text, video, lecture, digital) while reading, viewing, or listening.*
  - o *Can read and study carefully to understand challenging text and ideas.*
  - o *Can take notes of important ideas while reading, viewing, or listening.*

- ❑ Thinks and Creates (analysis)
  - o Distinguishes among fact, point of view, and opinion.
  - o Identifies inaccurate and misleading information.
  - o Applies information in critical thinking and problem solving.
  - o Organizes information for practical application (*charts, graphs, concept mapping, timelines*)
  - o *Can sort, compare, classify, and identify patterns and trends.*
  - o *Recognizes cause and effect or trends.*
  - o Derives meaning from information presented creatively in a variety of formats.
  - o Respects others' ideas and backgrounds and acknowledges their contribution.
  - o Thinks outside the box.

- ❑ Summarizes and Concludes (synthesis and decionmaking)
  - o Integrates new information into one's own knowledge.
  - o *Experiences the "Ah Ha!" of learning when pieces of the puzzle come together.*
  - o *Forms a point of view, opinion,conclusion, or supportable argument based on solid evidence.*
  - o *Makes decisions or takes action based on the best information available.*

❑ Communicates
  o Uses information accurately and creatively.
  o Designs, develops and evaluates information products and solutions related to personal interests.
  o Develops creative products in a variety of formats.
  o Produces and communicates information and ideas in appropriate formats.
  o Shares knowledge with others.
  o Acknowledges others' contributions.
  o Respects intellectual property rights.

❑ Reflects on Process and Product
  o Strives for excellence in information seeking and knowledge generation.
  o Assesses the quality of the process and products of personal information seeking.
  o Devises strategies for revising, improving, and updating self-generated knowledge.

❑ Throughout:
  o Group work
  o Participates effectively in groups to pursue and generate information.
  o Collaborates with others, both in person and through technologies, to identify information problems and to seek their solutions.
  o Collaborates with others, both in person and through technologies, to design, develop, and evaluate information products and solutions.
  o Attitudes and behaviors
  o Recognizes the importance of information to a democratic society.
  o Respects the principle of equitable access to information.
  o Practices ethical behavior in regard to information and information technology.
  o Respects the principles of intellectual freedom.
  o Uses information technology responsibly.
  o *Can follow the guidelines of an information literacy model to conduct a research project.*
  o *Can develop control over self-learning by creating a personal information literacy model.*

Teaching Unit Level
❑ Discovering information literacy skills within content objectives/state standards
❑ Adding to existing unit goals appropriate information literacy skills.
❑ Identification of or adopting an information literacy model as the scaffold of the teaching unit.
❑ Building rubrics for the unit that include and reward mastery of information literacy skills taught.
❑ Teaching a teacher to include process learning even when we are not collaborating.

Organization Level
❑ Teaching teachers through professional development the principles of information literacy and how to incorporate them into teaching.
❑ Adopting a school-wide or discipline-wide information literacy model.
❑ Integrating information literacy models/programs into state standards.
❑ Setting policies for the inclusion of information literacy in the curriculum and the methods by which it will be integrated.
❑ Organizing the LMC program in such a way that there is time to work with a wide cross section of teachers on information literacy.

Build a Joint Rubric (Teacher and LMS)
for a LMC-Based Unit

An amazing pebble to throw in the pool for a ripple effect is the joint teacher / library media specialist rubric constructed as a part of a library media center-based unit of instruction. Appendix A contains an account of this technique as used in a wide variety of library media centers across the United States.

The technique is rather simple, but may be a challenge to implement at the beginning. Here is how: During the planning stage of the unit, build with the teacher a rubric for students that will:

- Cover the content or skills required by the state standards governing the topic.
- Measure the information literacy skills the students need to demonstrate for this particular unit.
- Measure the amount read by the students and any technology skills that both the teacher and the library media specialist expect. (The more a learner reads about a topic on beyond the lecture and the textbook, the smarter they will be, and, the technology should assist learners in accomplishing their tasks).

What you are really asking the teacher to do is to consider all work done in the classroom and in the library media center to be contributing factors to the success of the learning experience. For some teachers, this may be a major shift in teaching strategy, but really a necessary one. If a student's total grade comes from what happens in the classroom and what happens in the LMC is, in fact, irrelevant, then the teacher would be better off staying in the classroom and saving the time and effort of the library media specialist.

Users of this technique throughout the country report amazing results. Once a teacher accepts the fact that LMC learning is co-equal to classroom learning and allows rubric items to measure both efforts, a major ripple effect happens:

- Both the teacher and the library media specialist agendas will be covered. (content and process learning)
- Learners will immediately understand that classroom and LMC learning are connected. (They will behave differently).
- The two professionals can help each other achieve each other's goals – thus building a true partnership in teaching.

The tough thing at first is to get the teacher to accept your items on a project's rubric. If this is not an acceptable practice in your school, a model or demonstration project is in order that could be tested first and then modeled to the faculty.

Let us say that a project is usually worth 100 points. If the library media specialist could capture just 10 of the 100 points or have 10 extra credit points that could be awarded, an amazing change would occur. The LMC rubric items would count for the difference between an A and a B or at least an A- and an A; a B and a B+. Students who did well on our process items could raise their grades! Ten points; it's all we want and need to effectively measure our impact and change teaching and learning.

The Joint Rubric Technique

During the unit planning process, the teacher/LMS team first identifies what state standards are to be achieved. Then together, they create a rubric that covers the teacher's concerns and adds the library media specialist's concerns for information literacy, reading and technology as illustrated below:

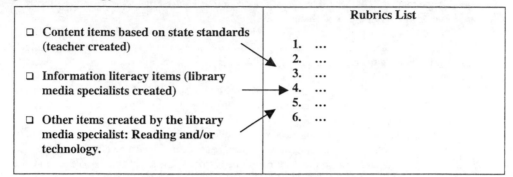

For students, the team may wish to create a self-assessment rubric to be completed by students or learning groups. This rubric can be the same as the above rubric or adapted for self-rating. As an example, suppose the library media specialist wanted to teach and assess **analysis** as part of a history timeline project. The following two rubric items might be on the joint list:

3	Historical events our group gathered were checked and rechecked for placement on our timeline.
2	We did some checking of the facts on our timeline, but ran out of time.
1	We did not have time to check any of our facts on our timeline.

3	During the checking of our historical facts, we found that one/several sites had bad information so we eliminated all information from that source on our timeline.
2	We noticed that some Internet sites had conflicting information from other sites. We did not have time to check which were right so just guessed at which facts to include on our timeline.
1	We used information for our timeline from any source we accessed on the Web.

For scoring, the library media specialist might score the information literacy items and the teacher the teacher-created items. This might happen several times until the teacher understood how to rate all the items at which time the library media specialist would pass off the assessment responsibility to work on another project with the same teacher.

This technique produces **direct evidence** of the impact of information literacy instruction upon student learning at the **learner level**. It is an effective and reportable piece of evidence. Furthermore, as you know how individuals perform based on your teaching, you will discover the most effective techniques of teaching and integrating information literacy into instruction. It is a vital component of evidence-based practice.

Research Logs: Writing and Learning about Research and About Me

In the Short Term:

How can we get good at anything in our lives without reflective practice? We can't. Sports skills, piano playing, and research skills are all in the category that requires reflective practice to see genuine improvement. With new emphasis on writing in the national curriculum, it strikes us that writing about what we are researching will not only help us reflect, but with guidance, will help us get better.

In case you have not noticed, students spin their wheels during the research process so much during the <u>time they think they have to devote to research</u>, that they often grasp at straws when deadlines are looming. The goal of reflective practice would be to build an individual's efficiency (one of the definitions of information literacy).

Research logs provide a way for both the learner, the teacher, and the library media specialist to peer into the world of research in a unique way so that coaching, guiding, and teaching all zero in on individual needs.

Have learners keep a log of their research with the rubric for the research project printed as a thumbnail on the log. Have the log accompany the final project and then score the log for the appropriate number of points to add to the student's total. For a teacher who has never experienced this type of logging, the library media specialist would need to score the log and have discussions with the teacher until the teacher could score the logs and the library media specialist move to other projects with that teacher.

In the Long Term:

Collect research logs after projects are complete and file them under a teacher's name. When students have completed two or three project logs, pass them out toward the end of the school year. Students should arrange them in chronological order from left to right on their desk in front of them. Have students write a reflection:

> Am I making progress as an organized investigator and researcher over time?

Have students attach their final reflection to the logs (still in order chronologically) and pass them in. Use these reflections to look not only to look at patterns of individual student success and failure but across classes and finally the school. This reflection could be done orally in an interview or as a reflection session with an individual or with a class. During a report to faculty, administrators, or boards, show what percentage of learners claim to be making progress as organized investigators vs. your own assessment of their progress. What type of individual seems to be making the most progress? The least?

This measure is **direct evidence** at the **learner level**, the **teaching unit level** and the **organization level** and is a powerful predictor of the impact of information literacy on learning.

Logging and Assessing the Investigative Experience:
A Sample Form
Learner Level

During a major research project, have learners track their progress and evaluate
themselves on the rubric created for the assignment. Create a form for your own learners.

My Research Log

My name: _____ Assignment title: _____
(Make a list/log of what you did first, next, next, etc. Include comments about problems you had.)

Self-Assessment Rubric	Comments	Teacher/LMS Rubric
(Am I an organized investigator? And, am I making improvement?) ■ ■ ■ ■ ■ ■ ■ _____My Score		Your work will be judged on the following rubric criteria: ■ ■ ■ ■ ■ _____ Your Score

The Library Media Center Technology Program
Ripple Effect Measures.[6]

Goals

LMC Agenda	Technology Plan
• Enhance teaching and learning through technology. • Build and information-rich environment available 24/7. • Build efficient learners.	• Connect every teacher and learner. • Integrate technology into teaching and learning. • Affect teaching and learning positively.

Pebbles to Measure

1. Information systems emanating from the LMC are available 24/7 and are reliable.
2. LMC information systems are available at the elbow (in the LMC, the classroom, in the home, and on any technological device owned by the learner).
3. Learners prefer LMC information systems over full Internet access.
4. LMC information systems and tools add to learner efficiency.
5. Enhancement of learning through technology is a part of teacher assessment of student learning.

Justification:

LMC information systems provide "smaller," safe, and very high quality information intranets to its clients in contrast to the wild world of the entire Internet. The Lance studies all report the connection between LMC technology and achievement.

Demonstrate through research and practice that:

☐ LMC information systems are at the elbow.
☐ Learner efficiency is being affected.
☐ LMC information systems are the first choice with students and teachers.
☐ LMC information systems are indeed "smaller," safe, and of very high quality.

Report:

☐ Steady improvement over time.
☐ Improvement related to an initiative.
☐ That success is already high and is remaining constant.
☐ Improvement related to organizational policy shifts.

---

[6] Ripple-effect measures refer to significant measures that are most likely to produce results in achievement and indicate maximum teacher collaboration and organizational effectiveness. Because you have these data, a ripple effect occurs, like throwing a pebble in a pool, triggering many other organizational practices and policies.

Assessment of Technology's Impact

Both learners and teachers are often quite willing to invest time and effort to integrate technology when it is accessible and it works. Collecting, reviewing, and reporting data at the organizational level, the teaching unit level and the learner level will help assess the impact technology is ready to make and is making in the school.

Level of Measure	Factor	Sources of Data
Technology at the Organization Level (District vision for effective technology use)	The state of the technology infrastructure in the district and at the building/ LMC/ classrooms	❑ Percent of learners who could find an Internet ready computer when needed. ❑ Number and percent of operational computer connections in the LMC. ❑ The annual budget to upgrade networks to meet technology plan needs. ❑ The size and competence of the technology staff for the school. ❑ Percent of staff who know the technology vision.
Technology at the Learning Unit Level (class interaction and use)	Technology's contribution to the teaching and learning.	❑ The percent of students who would rate the technology as helpful in completing their assignments during a unit of instruction. ❑ The number and percent of teachers who would report during a sample month that technology had "contributed to learning" during a collaborative activity in the LMC.
Technology at the Learner Level (as individuals)	Individual progress by each learner as technology becomes a trusted tool.	❑ Rubric score for use of technology in a project. ❑ Rubric score that content knowledge was enhanced through technology. ❑ Rubric score that information literacy standards were met.

Helpful publications for more measures to consider:

> ➤ *NCREL's enGauge: 21ˢᵗ Century Skills: Digital Literacies for a Digital Age*. Naperville, IL: NCREL, 2002.

> ➤ Jones, Beau Fly, et. al. *Plugging In: Choosing and Using Educational Technology*. Oakbrook, IL: NCREL, 1995.

> ➤ "Technology in Schools: Guidelines for Assessing Technology in Education." A publication of the National Center for Education Statistics, U.S. Dept. of Education, November, 2002. At: http://nces.ed.gov/

> ➤ Johnston, Jerome and Linda Toms Barker, eds. *Assessing the Impact of Technology in Teaching and Learning: A Sourcebook for Evaluators*. Ann Arbor, MI: University of Michigan, Institute for Social Research, 2002.

> ➤ *Planning for DET (Data-Driven Decisions About Technology)*. Naperville, IL: NCREL, 1999.

> ➤ *Technology Counts* - A yearly report focusing on how technology is changing education. At: http://www.edweek.org/sreports/tc02/

For more resources on assessment, see the web page for this book at http://www.indianalearns.org and http://ideanet.doe.state.in.us/technology

Evidence-Based Practice Plan

Detail in the appropriate box possible measures to be used in measuring a program element and its impact on achievement.

Goal:

	Learner Level	Teaching Unit Level	Organization Level
Direct Measures*			
Indirect Measures**			

*Direct measures would be those so close to actual learning that confidence in an impact could be inferred. We have no thermometers to stick in a learner's mouth to gauge actual learning, but direct measures might challenge doubters to prove no impact.
** Indirect measures provide evidence that actions set the stage for, provide an environment for, give support to, enable, help, give encouragement to, mark progress toward, make change in direct measures over time the probable stimulus.

Appendices

In the appendices, various previously-published brochures and handouts have been reprinted here for the convenience of the user. All of these brochures and handouts may be freely reproduced.

Appendix A

Five Other Studies of Interest

Five other recent studies are linked to the effectiveness of strong library media programs: one from Indiana, another from Massachusetts, one from Scotland, another from California, and the last from Ohio. The Massachusetts and Indiana studies are of particular interest because they include mathematics as one of the topics studied. Historically, the teaching of mathematics and the use of libraries were not thought be associated. Math teachers and librarians were not the closest of collaborative partners. However, looking at both the following excerpts from the research, it would appear that there is a way that mathematics in strong schools is taught and the strength of the library media program.

In the Indiana study, strong mathematics programs are far beyond the old "plug and chug" mathematics mentality (learning the rules of math without learning its meaning). Strong math programs emphasize mathematics as a way of thinking. Couple this with strong library media programs that integrate information literacy into units of instruction and encourage wide reading, and suddenly a new possibility becomes more obvious. Wide reading and "thinking about information" rather than just cut, clip, copy, and regurgitate fall in the same strong school environment supportive of higher achievement.

The Indiana Study

The following Executive Summary is reprinted here from: *A Study of the Differences Between Higher- Lower-Performing Indiana Schools in Reading and Mathematics.* Prepared for The Indiana Department of Education by NCREL (North Central Regional Educational Laboratory, February, 2000. 37 p. Available on the web at: http://www.doe.state.in.us/reed/newsr/00May/reports0504200/ncrel.pdf

The authors' comments in the margins emphasize certain of the findings.

Executive Summary

In July 1999, Superintendent of Public Instruction Dr. Suellen Reed invited the North Central Regional Education Laboratory (NCREL) to submit a proposal to study the differences between higher- and lower-performing Indiana schools in grades K-3 in reading and mathematics. Dr. Reed stressed that she was most interested in gaining insight about why two schools, serving similar groups of students in similar geographic regions, often reflect markedly different performance levels.

Our study included a total of 20 rural, urban, and suburban elementary schools from across the state. The schools were matched along demographic and geographic variables. One school in each pair was higher performing than the other. NCREL conducted the study using observation, survey data, and interviews with teachers, the curriculum coordinator, and the principal at each school.

Results

Three of the four original research questions focused on the differences between schools that performed higher than would be expected and those that did not in regard to three issues: state test scores, school-based characteristics, and instructional practices. These questions were answered in unison.

What emerged was a set of findings that links well with the research on effective reading and mathematics instruction. Namely, the research suggests that higher-performing schools tend to implement a coherent instructional framework and then continuously improve on it. Higher-performing schools, for example, may use a wide array of literature, including trade books, newspapers, and basal readers to support their reading/language arts program. They teach skills well, but do so in a context of higher purpose. All pieces work together to create a coherent plan for teaching reading and for moving all students to proficiency by the end of the third grade.

Authors' Comments

Notice how these schools follow the advice of Krashen and McQuillan saying that learners should have a mountain of materials for free voluntary reading.

Higher-performing schools also tend to hold high expectations for all students, engage in continuous student assessment, and use those assessments to guide daily instructional practice. Simply put, student program is consistently monitored and used to inform good teaching. When students show gaps in understanding, effective teachers use that information to quickly identify the problem and redirect to quickly identify the problem and redirect their instructional practice. Teaching practice is adjusted to ensure that all students move forward in their learning.

Finally, and most likely through exemplary and sustained professional development experiences, teachers at higher-achieving schools tend to act as coaches and guides for student discovery. Students are expected and encouraged to contribute to the learning process. Instead of one-way communication from the teacher to the student, knowledge at higher-performing schools tends to be shared and generated among the teacher and his or her students, and between the students themselves. Students become active coparticipants in their own learning. They discuss their thinking and strategies for solving problems. As a result, students in higher-performing schools tend to gain deeper conceptual understanding of reading and math content. This understanding often translates into higher performance on both basic skills and the problem-based tests.

Notice the identical goals of teaching information literacy in the library and those applauded here in the teaching of math.

Policy Implications

The fourth research question dealt with policy that might be formulated as a result of this inquiry. The implications of this study for policy must be interpreted carefully, however. The following points are examples of options policymakers might consider appropriate for action to the extent that they relate to improving student achievement in reading and mathematics in Indiana. It is important to note that these policy options are a result of the observed differences between higher- and lower-performing schools in Indiana, and while they closely mirror national research on the same issues, they may be more-or different ways-to improve student achievement in reading and mathematics.

1. Increase student access to instructional and print materials in lower-performing schools, including regular and flexible access to a working library.

    Sage advice.

2. Based on the findings in this study, lower-performing schools would appear to benefit from additional analyses of their instructional materials by a reading specialist to avoid over-reliance on the one approach to reading in the early grades.

3. Develop a state database of alternative student reading assessment and intervention materials that all schools could easily access to provide teachers with a useful benchmark on each student's progress through Grade 3.

4. De-emphasize the push to cover mathematics content over meaning especially in lower-performing schools.

    Notice the emphasis in teaching thinking and meaning

5. Provide sustained opportunities for teachers in lower-performing schools to team-teach mathematics with mentor teachers in higher-performing schools to improve classroom implementation of new mathematics curriculum.

6. As teachers are increasingly asked to teach in ways very different from the training they received, ongoing opportunities for professional development in both reading and math instruction continue to be of critical importance.

Conclusion

The compulsion to respond to a perceived crisis leads some policymakers – as well as school and district leadership – to suggest the adoption of what they believe to be teacher-proof" commercial materials for reading or math instruction. This response fails to give appropriate weight to the teacher, along with many other elements of the school context (e.g., high-quality instruction, strong links with parents, systematic evaluation of progress), in explaining the lack of achievement in mathematics and reading in lower-performing schools. No school, no classroom, no child is exactly like any other. Good teaching of reading and mathematics cannot simply be a matter of using the "right" method, because any method may be more or less effective depending on its fit with the school, the classroom, the teacher, and the needs of individual children.

The Massachusetts Study

The second study was conducted in Massachusetts with the purpose of looking specifically at school libraries and math scores.

The study citation is: Baughman, James C. *School Libraries and MCAS Scores: A Paper Presented at a Symposium Sponsored by the Graduate School of Library and Information Science, Simmons College, Boston, Massachusetts, October 26, 2000.* Preliminary Edition. Available on the web at: http://artemis.simmons.edu/~baughman/mcas-school-libraries/

Executive Summary
School Libraries and MCAS Scores

Authors' Comments

School libraries and student achievement are strongly related. The results of the Simmons Study of school libraries, based on a statewide survey, confirm the value of school libraries. The findings from the Simmons Study can be summarized as follows:

➢ At each grade level, school with library programs have higher MCAS (Massachusetts Comprehensive Assessment System) scores.

➢ At each grade level, students score higher on MCAS tests when there is a higher per pupil book count.

Replicates the Lance studies.

➢ At each grade level, schools with increased student use have higher MCAS scores.

➢ At each grade level, school libraries with more open hours score higher on the MCAS tests.

➢ At the elementary and middle/junior high school levels, students score higher on the MCAS tests when there is a library instruction program.

Again, the correlation between information literacy and good math thinking.

➢ At the elementary and middle/junior high school levels, average MCAS scores are higher in schools with larger per pupil expenditures for school library materials.

➢ At the elementary and high school levels, students who are served by a full-time school librarian have higher MCAS scores than those in schools without a full-time librarian.

Corroborates the Lance studies.

➢ At the elementary and high school levels, library staff assistance (nonprofessional help) makes a positive difference in average MCAS scores.

➢ At the elementary level, students score higher on the MCAS tests when the library is aligned with the state curriculum frameworks. (This fact is especially true in schools that have a high percentage of free school lunches.)

Good math thinking shows up both in Indiana and Massachusetts.

➢ At the high school level, schools with automated collections have higher average MCAS scores.

The Scotland Study

Researchers Dorothy Williams and Caroline Wavell, researchers at The Robert Gordon University in Aberdeen Scotland did a two-year study in Scotland probing the impact of school libraries and achievement which they reported late 2001. Their study was conducted in two phases.

Phase One: Perceptions of Impact

Librarians, students, teachers, and senior management staff were asked to rate the most important impacts that the library program **MIGHT** deliver. The collective e perceptions of impact were expressed as:
- The acquisition of information and wider general knowledge;
- Skills development in the areas of finding and using information, ICT skills and reading skills and their cross-curricular use and potential for equal opportunities;
- Higher achievement in school work;
- Developing a study and reading habit encourage independent working;
- Motivation to learn and enjoyment of learning;
- The ability to use these skills confidently and independently and the ability to transfer these skills across the curriculum and beyond school;
- The development of interpersonal and social skills, including working collaboratively.

Phase Two: Case Studies Analyzing Evidence of ACTUAL Impact

Specific learning activities in six schools were studied in depth to probe what the researchers termed "indicators of impact." The indicators included:
- Evidence of motivation (attitude, desire, and willingness of students to perform a task)
- Evidence of progression (success of students doing assigned tasks)
- Evidence of independence (students making progress as independent learners during a research project)
- Evidence of interaction (students working in a collaborative atmosphere)

To measure the above indicators, the researchers used the following data collection techniques:
- Observation of pupils at work in the library.
- Discussion and questioning of pupils during and after doing research.
- Examination of pupil's work in progress and written work.
- Discussion with members of the teaching staff.
- Examination of reading records.

Findings:

Evidence of motivation was seen across all the case units by pupil enjoyment and participation and absorption in the tasks set whether that was a project, looking for reading materials or in the commitment of the pupil librarians. The indicators were identified as:

- Verbal and written expression of enthusiasm by pupils;
- Pupil willingness to participate in the activity set;
- Pupil application and absorption in the task;
- Willingness of pupils to continue their work either by returning to the SLRC [library] or at home;
- A change in attitude towards work over a period of time.

Evidence of progression was most easily identified as awareness of or ability to use a specific skill associated with the finding of information and sometimes the use and presentation of information. It was also possible to identify examples of the application of skills in new contexts. The indicators were identified as:

- Awareness of or the ability to use specific skills associated with finding, using and presenting information;
- The use of new knowledge in work or discussion of new knowledge;
- Personal achievement or quality of work;
- The ability to apply skills or knowledge in a new situation.

Evidence of independence was identified in individual pupils who appeared to have mastered a skill and were seen to have the confidence and competence to proceed and progress unaided, either in the class session or in their own time. The pupil librarians were able to use their initiative by instigating their own activities and tasks. The indicators were identified as:

- The ability and confidence to continue and progress with a task unaided;
- Awareness of the need for help and the confidence to seek it;
- Awareness of the need for organization and time management in work;
- Use of initiative;
- Increased self-esteem.

Evidence of interaction was particularly relevant in the junior curriculum related activities and with the pupil librarians, where discussion and interaction were encouraged. Interaction was seen as a learning experience in itself, as a means of enhancing the learning in other themes and as a means of establishing the learning that individuals were engaged in. The indicators were identified as:

- Discussion with others about the task;
- Peer cooperation;
- Ability to mix with other groups;
- Use of appropriate behavior.

The Topsy Smalley Study

In the state of California, few elementary schools have professional librarians (library media teachers as they are named there). And, while professionals are more plentiful in secondary schools, districts often tend to replace professionals with less expensive clericals if the library is operational. Thus, the burden of doing library research falls upon the college librarians who get hundreds of novices appearing on their doorsteps each semester.

Topsy Smalley, an instructional librarian and advocate of information literacy at Cabrillo College (in Aptos, CA near Santa Cruz) noticed that there was quite a difference in the success rate of freshmen students and so formalized his investigation into a study published in the *Journal of Academic Librarianship* in 2004.

From Spring 2001 to Spring 2003, 506 students who had attended all 4 years of high school and had completed the freshman English and Library credit were examined. The librarians graded library research workbooks for all students and discovered that students who had attended high schools with full-time librarians scored higher than those students without high school librarians. Topsy concluded that "students whose high schools include librarians and library instruction programs bring more understanding about information research to their college experiences" (197, source below).

Source: Smalley, Topsy N. "College Success: High School Librarians Make the Difference." *The Journal of Academic Librarianship* 30 (3): 193–198.

The Ohio Study

The first of an anticipated many studies done by Ross Todd (a researcher from Australia, now on the faculty at Rutgers University) is quite different in research design than those done by Keith Curry Lance. Todd uses more qualitative methodology rather than quantitative designs. In the Ohio study conducted from October 2002 to December 2003, Todd looked at the qualities of the best school library programs and the impact these programs have on students. In other words, he is looking at the best-case scenario to see what one would expect to find when all the right components are in place for a student to flourish in a rich information environment. Such an investigation helps "set the bar" of what to expect if the investment in a library is made and when it is staffed by quality professionals.

Todd concluded: "Collectively, the data show that effective school libraries in Ohio are dynamic rather than passive agents of learning. The findings indicate that the effective school library helps the strongest as a resource agent and a technical agent, providing access to information resources necessary for students to complete their research assignments and projects successfully. However, the qualitative responses show that the school library's strength is not just as a passive information supply and exchange agency. Clearly helpful is the library's part in engaging students in an active process of building their own understanding and knowledge—the library as an agent for individualized learning, knowledge construction and academic achievement." (1, "Student Learning Through Ohio School Libraries: The Ohio Research Study Fact Sheet", OELMA, 2003). The OELMA fact sheet for this study has been reproduced in Appendix M.

Appendix B

School Libraries and Reading in Secondary Schools – Still a Good Idea to Raise Academic Achievement

By David V. Loertscher, Victoria B. Winkler, and Janet Lynne Tassell[1]

Introduction

For many reasons, teachers in the secondary schools of this country face the challenge of many students who are not reading at grade level. The impact, of course, is evident in every single department of the school, and it depresses the achievement scores of every student who does not read at grade level or above. In a recent visit to a conference in Indiana, Phyllis Land Usher, the Asst. Superintendent in the Indiana State Department of Education introduced me to Victoria Winkler, a school librarian. As Victoria and I talked, she began to explain the reading program in her high school that had made a major difference in achievement. Since such programs are in short supply and since librarians and teachers are often at a loss to combat the pernicious disease of illiteracy, I asked Victoria to write a one-page description of her program. Many school librarians have turned their attention, as they should, to the teaching of information literacy and away from the reading program. However, the challenge of the 21st century and its information technology still seems to require excellent readers to participate in an information-rich and a technology-rich environment. Where many librarians formerly spent the majority of their time promoting reading, they now find themselves providing less time. But that does not solve the reading crisis in many schools. Victoria's experience as a school librarian is an exemplar of taking a leadership role rather than trying to conduct the entire literacy campaign alone. Where a school librarian may have had an 80/20 split of time with 80% of time spent on reading, that balance shifts to 20/80 with the 80% spent in a leadership role.

The following is Victoria's brief letter to me describing what has happened in her high school. I have added footnote commentary at critical points to amplify certain aspects of the program. The reader is encouraged to do several readings of the letter to absorb its fascinating content and gain the full impact of its concepts.

[editor: If the following letter could be reprinted in a box with the footnotes on the side rather than at the bottom of the page, it would be wonderful. The layout is critical for full impact.]

---

[1] Victoria Winkler is library media specialist at Heritage Hills Jr.-Sr. High School and Janet Tassell is Director of Learning and Assessment in North Spencer School Corporation, Santa Claus, Indiana.

The Letter

Heritage Hills Jr.-Sr. High School in Lincoln City, Indiana has a student enrollment of approximately 1100 students, with 375 of those being seventh and eight graders. The school is located in a rural area in southwestern Indiana, principally serving people from farming and industrial backgrounds. In the early 1990s, we became aware of too low reading scores and too few students reading for pleasure. How do you get students to read for pleasure? How do you make students hungry for good reading? Independent reading for the school community became a top priority.

We read Krashen's *the Power of Reading* aloud to each other at a faculty meeting.

Absolutely amazing! How does a faculty take the time and have the sustained interest to do this in any school? Yet, what a wonderful beginning.

We visited other schools with exemplary reading initiatives.

Finding and visiting exemplary programs is a critical but time-consuming and expensive commitment. Obviously, this faculty and administration were committed.

We hired a reading consultant who taught us the value of reading aloud to the students.

Hiring consultants is another major expenditure. Hiring quality consultants is a challenge.

We began selling paperback novels in our bookstore.

They sell books because there is no local bookstore that every students can visit easily.

The focus of our annual summer institute for administrators, faculty and staff is reading and its impact on student learning.

Notice that this effort is just not a "single workshop and forget it" event, but interest and study is sustained over time.

Because of our new awareness of the value of sustained silent reading (SSR) for students, we initiated a fifteen-minute session at the beginning of the day once every two weeks. This has evolved to thirty minutes of SSR daily for middle school students and twenty minutes of SSR daily for high school students. Our sustained silent reading time called READ-IN is always held at the beginning of the school day.

Note that SSR began slowly but had a mid-course correction. SSR is only effective when it is a regular occurrence in the school and has the potential to establish a long-term reading habit.

When we started READ-IN, teachers complained of students not having access to pleasure reading materials in the classrooms. Today we have 400-500 books in every classroom in the school. These libraries consist of popular young adult paperback novels, nonfiction books on everything from cars to cooking to sports, magazines, and newspapers.

Classroom collections are a necessary feature of a good reading program, but the historic problem with these collections is that they are usually too small and they are only interesting to students for the first month of school and then ignored after that. I would recommend that these classroom collections rotate out of the library and that the students in the classroom care for these collections to make sure that they not only rotate but have fresh and exciting titles students want to read.

Teachers have been trained to be reading role models by our reading consultant. Also, we try to keep teachers abreast of the latest young adult literature that is going to hook the students. Teachers make semiannual trips to a large bookstore to select books for their classroom libraries.

When teachers are readers and talk to their students about it and students see them reading, the tone is set for the entire school.

All seventh graders also make a trip with their teachers to the bookstore to select a book for their homeroom library. For almost 80% of the seventh graders, this is the first time they have ever been to a bookstore.

Students need to have regular visits to both public libraries and bookstores. We have here a rural school that does not have a local bookstore, but even in many urban settings, students cannot visit public libraries or bookstores because these resources are located across gang territory lines. Notice that the school is paying the bill for the books students select.

We also have a teacher book club where each member has a month to read the same book. This group, called R.E.A.D. (Readers Eating and Discussing), meets for their book discussions. Talk in the teachers' lounge is now frequently about books and ideas instead of work conditions and job stress.

This is an amazing testimony that the reading program has made a difference in the culture of the faculty – a critical element in any school whose administration and faculty "get it together."

Some of the R.E.A.D. selections are purposely the same as Young Hoosier and Eliot Rosewater state award books that the students are reading. This leads to more discussions of book literature among faculty, staff, and students.

Note that the librarian links the school to state reading initiatives and no doubt a number of national initiatives that fit the school's agenda.

Teachers read aloud across the curriculum.

This is high school! So many secondary teachers feel that reading aloud is an elementary activity. Not so!

Both students and faculty engage in book swaps.

Another good idea, book swap, is a strategy in which students and teachers exchange books every few minutes to read where the other person left off. The benefit is that students are exposed to many different genre.

Students swarm the library before the school day begins looking for more of what they found in their classroom libraries. Students gather at the stacks recommending books to each other.

Remember that lots of research studies show that recommendations from a friend are the number one reason children and teens select their next book to read.

Author visits, read and feeds, book fairs, and love of reading advertising throughout the building further support our reading initiative show us that everyone of us is reading more because we enjoy it.

Notice that there are numerous ideas and activities going on throughout the school year – the faculty and librarian are not content with a one-shot reading motivational event.

Our reading climate is improving as shown in our research.

[end of letter]

Building a Reading Community

The school librarian, the administration, and the faculty in this school have come together in a school-wide effort to build basic literacy. This sets into motion a powerful force to accomplish a very difficult and challenging task. Most notably, they have based their collaborative effort on a solid research base and they have pulled in the resources, the ideas, and pushed their own creativity to achieve a better result. It is also notable that while their initial alarm is low test-taking scores, they do not adopt a teach-to-the test strategy that might offer short-term gains. Instead, they opt for a longer-term effort that not only will sustain growth for the school, but also provide students with a magnificent life-long learning tool.

For a century, school librarians have been the all-too-silent partners of teachers and administrators in the battle for basic literacy. In the past decade, books have often taken a back seat to the exciting developments in technology with much spending being diverted toward machines. While we would not advocate less spending in technology, we would advocate more spending to keep the print collections of the school fresh, attractive, and current to give the nation's children books they "want to read." There are too many distractions for young people, too few students who speak English well, and too few schools who really care about literacy enough to mount a corrective effort. Victoria's letter demonstrates that basic literacy does not need a rocket scientist to develop, but it does require collaboration, commitment, change, money, and long-term focus and leadership. Quick fixes in education are no better than trying to patch up antiquated air traffic control systems or local voting procedures. There is a point when one more patch on the ragged jeans just won't work.

And Now the Research

Janet Lynne Tassell, Director of Learning and Assessment for North Spencer County School Corporation, files the following research report of the Heritage Hills Jr.-Sr. High School reading program:

When looking at the past Indiana Statewide Testing for Educational Progress (ISTEP+) results for our students, we found promising results that evidenced improvement in reading. Because of the many changes in the statewide test over the past few years, it is difficult to draw many of our desired conclusions. Thus, we decided, rather than comparing one group of students to another, we would follow whole groups of students as they progressed throughout their years of testing, allowing us to measure their growth at different points in their schooling. This provides a better indication of growth.

In looking at the graduating class of 2002, we found that the norm-referenced portion of the standardized test showed positive growth in the reading comprehension area. We were very interested in movement of students from the bottom quartiles to the upper quartiles in reading comprehension skills. From the eighth to the tenth grade we had an increase of students into the upper quartiles from the bottom quartiles. Furthermore, in "Language Expression" we found an increase in the upper quartiles and a large decrease in the lowest quartile as seen in the following:

Quartiles	8th Grade	10th Grade
1	42	55
2	42	48
3	32	34
4	37	12

The norm-referenced test results also showed that our students are maintaining reading comprehension levels close to grade level. The reading levels should be at or above: sixth -- 6.1, eighth grade -- 8.1, and tenth grade -- 10.1. At the 50th percentile, students should be reading at these reading levels. As seen in the following table, our data is especially impressive with our 50th percentile and bottom 25th percentile students:

Percentile	6th Grade	8th Grade	10th Grade
75th	12.4	12.7	12.9
50th	9.3	9.5	12.8
25th	6.6	7.8	10.1

From this analysis we have found growth in the area of English/language arts over the 1994-1999 testing results. However, our frustrations abound in our limitations of how we can compare data due to the inconsistencies of the test composition and report designs. Therefore, we were careful to utilize the limited but consistent data that could be gleaned over this time period.

In a survey conducted here in the spring of 2000, students and staff overwhelmingly indicated that the expanding classroom libraries are fundamental in increasing students' love and motivation of reading. Results from a fall 2000 parent survey show that 82% see their child reading for pleasure at home. Sixty-eight percent of the parents have noticed an increase in the time their child has spent reading in the last two to three years. Some of their comments include: "[My daughter] always talks about reading in the Read-In. When she gets home from school, she cannot wait to continue reading where she left off … I have noticed her enjoyment for reading has increased tremendously. Thank you so much for this program."

Comments on the Research

Not all schools or school districts are fortunate to have a person such as Janet Tassell who can track and do locally-based research, but research is a critical component of any major school-wide project. School librarians are wise to make connections between their programs and the research efforts of the school districts where they reside. In today's world it does not seem to be enough just to be a doer; one must be a documenter. The frustration of changing assessments does not seem to be going away. We all would wish that tests could measure both content knowledge as well as process skills (information literacy/knowing how to learn). The current political climate keeps jerking us all around and some school communities just can't seem to move forward. It is refreshing to see one district with its head on straight.

Appendix C

The Original Fast Facts

In 1999 Keith Lance published the first "Fast Facts" that reviewed the research from Colorado, Alaska, and Pennsylvania. This summary has never been updated but is reprinted here as an example of how to summarize research into a more understandable form. This document is available online at http://www.lrs.org and is reprinted here for the convenience of the reader.

FAST ⚡ FACTS
Recent Statistics from the Library Research Service

Proof of the Power
A First Look at the Results of the Colorado Study ... and More!

The Latest Statewide Studies

During 1998 and 1999, three statewide studies of the impact of school library media centers on academic achievement have been conducted. The forthcoming reports on these studies are:

- **Information Empowered: The School Librarian as an Agent of Academic Achievement in Alaska,**
- **Measuring Up to Standards: The Role of Library Information Programs & Information Literacy in Pennsylvania Schools**, and
- **How School Librarians Help Kids Achieve Standards** (a.k.a. *the second Colorado study* or *Colorado II*).

The Information Power Model & Previous Research Findings

The Information Power model developed by the American Association of School Librarians (AASL) focuses on three major themes for library media (LM) programs—collaboration, leadership, and technology—and three major roles for library media specialists (LMSs)—learning and teaching, information access and delivery, and program administration.

The findings of previous research on this topic can be summarized by LMS role:

Learning & Teaching

Previous research demonstrates that academic achievement of K-12 students is higher where the LMS:

- is part of a planning/teaching team,
- teaches information literacy independently, and
- works one-to-one with students in a flexibly scheduled program.

Information Access & Delivery

Previous research also associates higher academic achievement with:

- a quality collection of books and other materials selected to support the school's curriculum and used by both teachers and students,
- state-of-the-art technology that is integrated into the learning/teaching and information-seeking processes, and
- cooperation between library media centers (LMCs) and other libraries, especially public libraries.

CONTACT ABOUT THIS ISSUE

Keith Curry Lance – Director
Library Research Service
201 East Colfax Avenue, Suite 309
Denver, Colorado 80203-1799
Tel.: 303.866.6737
Fax: 303.866.6940
E-mail: lance_k@cde.state.co.us
Web site: www.lrs.org

Program Administration

Previous research has also established that higher academic achievement is associated with:

■ LM programs that are staffed to play an integral role in the school (minimally, at least one LMS with at least one aide),

■ principal support of the LM program and collaboration between classroom teachers and the LMS,

■ information technology that extends the reach of the LM program into the school's classrooms and labs, and

■ a well-organized, formally requested budget adequate to support these conditions.

Each of the three study reports will include a detailed analysis of the previous literature as well as an exhaustive bibliography.

Motivations for Further Research

With the above-mentioned facts well established by previous research, one might rightly ask why further research was necessary.

A prime motivation for the new studies was to confirm the findings of the original Colorado study, The Impact of School Library Media Centers on Academic Achievement. Both practitioners and policymakers want to know that those findings

■ can be replicated using standards-based tests,

■ hold up over time, and

■ apply to other states.

In addition, all three of the new studies seek to expand on the original Colorado study by demonstrating the value of

■ specific activities that define the LMS role,

■ principal and teacher support,

■ flexible scheduling, and

■ technology as part of LM programs.

Samples

Between them the three new studies involve over 800 schools in three states, and the participating schools serve both elementary and secondary grades—both middle and high school levels.

The Alaska study includes 211 of the state's 461 schools—46 percent of the schools serving the three tested grades: 4, 8, and 11.

The Pennsylvania study includes 435 of the state's 1,691 schools serving three tested grades: 5, 8, and 11. The 435 participating schools constitute an 87 percent response rate from a 500-case sample.

There are 200 schools in the new Colorado study. These participants constitute a 67 percent response rate from a 300-case sample of the state's 1,178 schools serving two tested grades: 4 and 7. (Statewide standards-based testing at the high school level has not yet begun.)

School Library Surveys

Alaska's school libraries were surveyed in Fall 1998. Counterpart surveys in Colorado and Pennsylvania were conducted in Spring 1999. While there were some minor differences among these surveys, all three were based on Colorado's 1998 questionnaire, and all three addressed five common sets of issues:

- staffing levels,
- time spent on a variety of staff activities,
- collection holdings by format,
- usage levels, and
- available technology and its functionality.

Available Data

In addition to original data collection via the above-mentioned surveys, all three studies also relied heavily on available data, including:

- state reading test scores (various grades indicated above),
- community characteristics, such as its
  - level of adult educational attainment,
  - socio-economic differences (e.g., income levels, poverty status), and
  - racial/ethnic demography.
- school characteristics, such as
  - teacher-pupil ratio,
  - teacher characteristics (e.g., percent with master's degrees, average years of experience, average salary), and
  - student characteristics (e.g., racial/ethnic demography, those eligible for the National School Lunch Program—an indicator of socio-economic status)

Successful Types of
Library Media Predictors

Four major types of library media program data were found to be predictors of academic achievement in at least two, if not all three, states:

- level of LM program development (e.g., staffing level, collection size, program expenditures),
- staff activities related to the Information Power themes of leadership, collaboration, and technology,
- levels of LM program usage, and
- technology (e.g., school-wide networks providing access to licensed databases as well as the Internet/World Wide Web).

Alaska Findings

The Alaska study yielded five major predictors of academic achievement:

- level of librarian staffing,
- time spent by librarians
  - delivering information literacy instruction to students
  - planning cooperatively with teachers, and
  - providing in-service training to teachers.
- a collection development policy that addresses the issue of challenges or requests for reconsideration of materials,
- the potential for Internet connectivity (i.e., computers with modem capability and telecommunications lines), and
- a relationship with the local public library.

Notably, this study could only demonstrate the efficacy of librarians, because there were too few cases of schools with both a librarian and an aide.

See Figure 1 for a graphic representation of the relationships among these variables and academic achievement in Alaska.

Pennsylvania Findings

The Pennsylvania study also yielded five major predictors of academic achievement:

- the presence of both librarians and support staff,
- the level of library expenditures (excluding staff salaries),
- the presence of rich collections of print and electronic information resources (i.e., books, periodical subscriptions, CD-ROM reference titles),
- the extent to which technology is utilized to extend the library information center's reach into the school's classrooms and labs (e.g., Access Pennsylvania, licensed databases, Internet/World Wide Web), and, pivotally,

■ the extent to which information literacy is integrated in the school's approach to standards and curriculum (e.g., time spent by library information specialists meeting with principals; teaching cooperatively and independently; attending faculty, curriculum committee, and standards committee meetings; managing information technology).

See Figure 2 for a graphic representation of the relationships among these variables and academic achievement in Pennsylvania.

Colorado Findings

Five sets of predictors of academic achievement were yielded by the second Colorado study:
■ library media program development,
■ leadership,
■ collaboration,
■ technology, and
■ flexible scheduling.

Library Media Program Development

As in the original Colorado study, a single factor encompasses all of the data about the library media program's level of development. Several characteristics of LM programs are strongly interrelated with each other, and, together, they constitute a positive, statistically significant predictor of academic achievement. A program's standing on this development factor is driven by
■ the number of LMS and total staff per 100 students,
■ the number of volumes per student as well as the number of print subscriptions and CD-ROM reference titles per 100 students, and
■ LM expenditures per student.

Leadership

One of the major themes of Information Power is leadership. Library media specialists who exhibit leadership are more likely to have a positive effect on academic achievement. In Colorado, indicators of such leadership include time spent by the LMS:
■ meeting with the principal,
■ participating in faculty meetings and serving on standards and curriculum committees, and
■ holding meetings of building and district level LM staff and participating in meetings of other LM professionals beyond the district (e.g., regional, state, and national conferences).

Collaboration

In Information Power, collaboration is billed above leadership, but the findings of this study indicate that leadership's impact on academic achievement is to be the prime mover behind collaboration with teachers. Where the LMS exhibits leadership, she or he is also more likely to:

■ plan cooperatively with teachers,
■ teach cooperatively with teachers as well as independently,
■ provide in-service training to teachers, and
■ manage the computer network that links the LMC, classrooms, and labs.

Technology

One of the strategic mistakes of the original Colorado study was to collect data on numbers of computers in or under the jurisdiction of the LMC alone. Of course, many computers used in instruction are located in classrooms and labs, and this time they were not left out. The only stipulation on which computers to count beyond those in the LMC was that they had to be networked to LM resources, such as the library catalog, licensed databases, and the Internet/World Wide Web. Statistical indicators of the importance of this kind of technology and the LM program's role in it include:

■ the number of computers per 100 students,
■ the number of computers providing access to licensed databases per 100 students, and
■ the number of Internet-accessible computers per 100 students.

Flexible Scheduling

Previous research indicates that students perform at higher levels when their access to the LMC is not limited to regularly scheduled class visits. Students should be free to visit the LMC as their learning needs dictate. Ideally, some of these visits would still be in whole class groups, but others would be as part of smaller groups and individually. In reality, a fairly common practice is to schedule classes for regular LMC visits to provide planning and meeting time for teachers. All too often, during these periods, the LMC staff are little more than babysitters. An interesting, unexpected finding of this study is that individual student visits to the LMC correlate with test scores, but group visits—at least, group visits of the sort most common now—do not.

See Figures 3 and 4 for graphic representations of the relationships between and among these predictors and academic achievement in Colorado. There are two figures in order to indicate differences in these relationships for grades 4 and 7.

Key Common Findings

While findings from the three states studied most recently vary somewhat, they share some key common findings:

- School library media specialists can and do exert a positive and significant effect on academic achievement.
- Principal support of the LM program and teacher collaboration with the LMS are critical to making the LM program an integral part of teaching and learning.
- For the LMS to be a pivotal player, support staff are essential. A professional LMS cannot do her or his job if tethered to the LMC.
- The LMS has a teaching role—both as a co-teacher of information literacy to students and as an in-service trainer of teachers.
- LM programs that contribute most strongly to academic achievement are those with the technology necessary to extend access to information resources beyond the LMC to classrooms and labs throughout the school.

Distinguishing Results

While the three studies share common findings, each also offers some distinguishing results.

- The Alaska study was the first to suggest the important role of the LMS as an information literacy teacher of students as well as an in-service training provider for teachers.
- The Pennsylvania study demonstrates that the synergy of LM staff, collections, and technology is most powerful where there is an integrated, collaborative approach to teaching information literacy.
- The Colorado study reveals that the relationship between leadership and collaboration is critical. Classroom teachers are more willing to collaborate with the LMS if she or he has taken the initiative to become an assertive, involved leader in the school. In addition, this study provides additional evidence linking flexibly scheduled LM programs with higher levels of academic achievement.

Controlling for School & Community Differences

As in the original Colorado study, each of these studies confirms that the relationships described above are not explained away by other school differences, such as:
- teacher-pupil ratio,
- teacher or student characteristics, and
- per pupil expenditures.

Likewise, these relationships cannot be explained away by community differences, such as
- adult educational attainment,
- socio-economic differences (e.g., income levels, poverty status), and
- racial/ethnic demography.

Recommended Actions

The combined weight of these three studies recommends several fairly obvious actions:

- Library media programs should be funded to have adequate professional and support staff, information resources, and information technology. Such conditions are necessary if not sufficient alone to generate higher levels of academic achievement.
- Library media specialists must assert themselves as leaders in their schools. Principals can do much to make this possible, including adopting policies and practices and communicating expectations that encourage LMSs to act as professional educators and classroom teachers to accept them as colleagues.
- The library media program cannot be limited to the library media center as a place. Just as LMSs must involve themselves in the design and delivery of instruction, technology must be used to make information resources available to teachers and students wherever they may be in the school.
- While Internet access is important, the LMS has an important role to play in ensuring that teachers and students have access to high-quality licensed databases from which current, authoritative information may be obtained.
- Wherever possible, schools should adopt policies of flexible scheduled access to the LMC. Available evidence indicates that LMCs that are reasonably accessible to students contribute more to academic achievement.

For More Information

For information about how to obtain copies of the reports for each of these studies, watch the Library Research Service web site, https://www.lrs.org, or contact the individual state library agencies. Also on the LRS web site, a PowerPoint presentation corresponding to this document is available. These slides were used in a session at the November 1999 joint conference of the American Association of School Librarians and the International Association for School Librarianship.

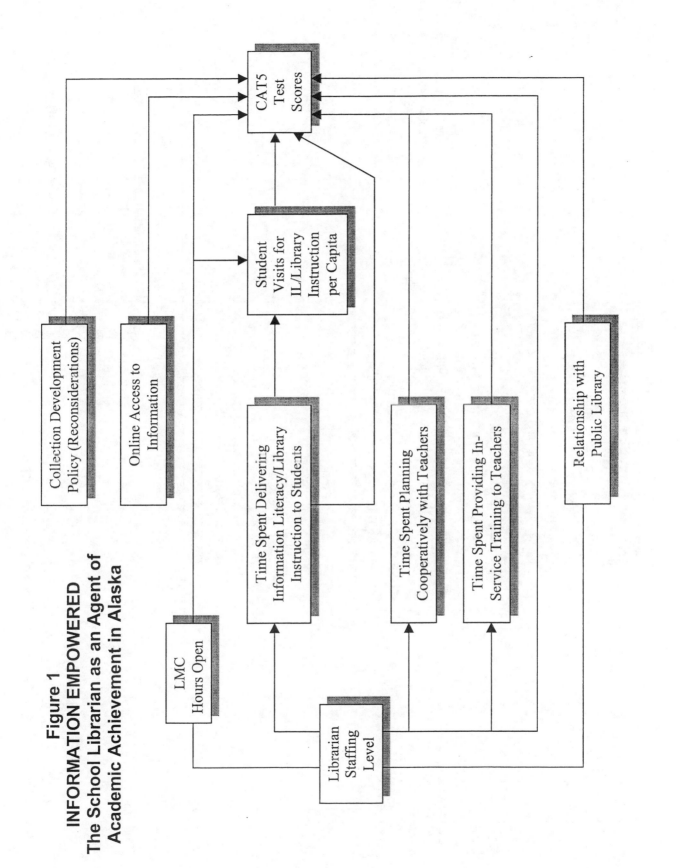

Figure 1
INFORMATION EMPOWERED
The School Librarian as an Agent of Academic Achievement in Alaska

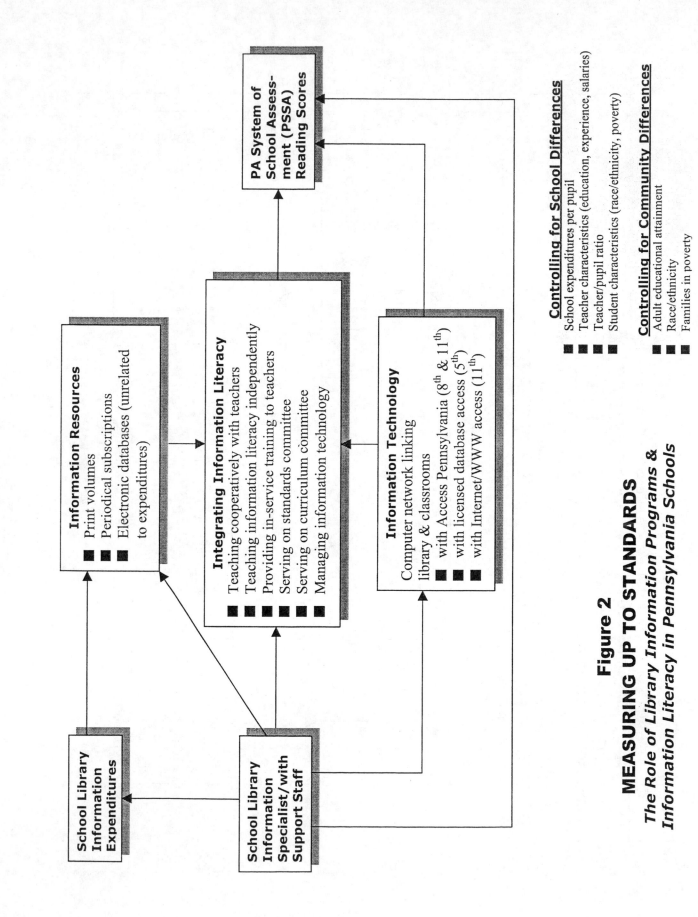

Figure 2

MEASURING UP TO STANDARDS

*The Role of Library Information Programs &
Information Literacy in Pennsylvania Schools*

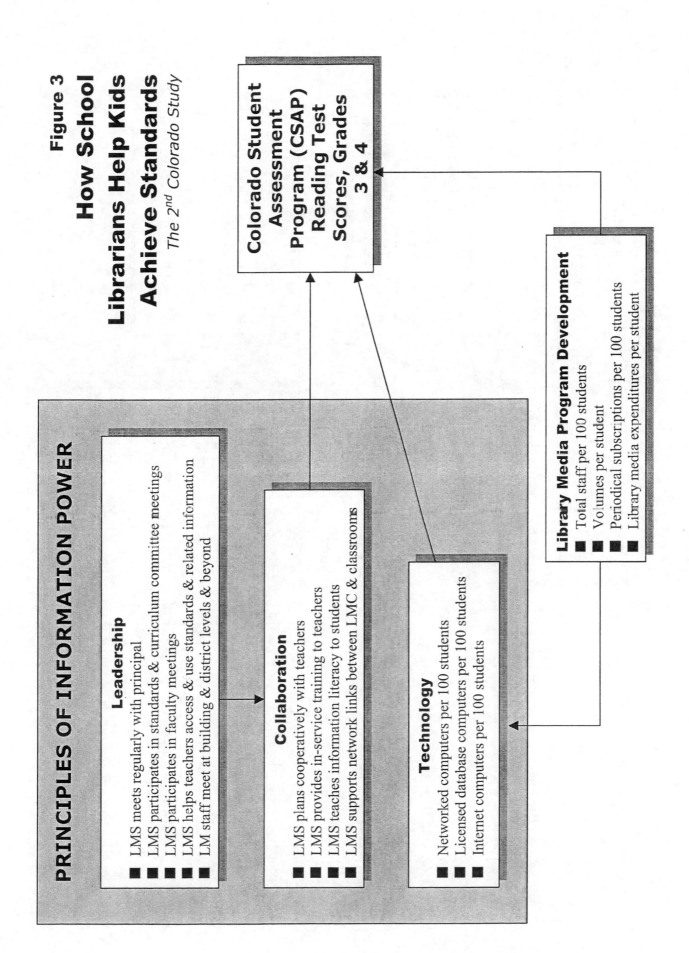

Figure 3
How School Librarians Help Kids Achieve Standards
The 2nd Colorado Study

Colorado Student Assessment Program (CSAP) Reading Test Scores, Grades 3 & 4

PRINCIPLES OF INFORMATION POWER

Leadership
- LMS meets regularly with principal
- LMS participates in standards & curriculum committee meetings
- LMS participates in faculty meetings
- LMS helps teachers access & use standards & related information
- LM staff meet at building & district levels & beyond

Collaboration
- LMS plans cooperatively with teachers
- LMS provides in-service training to teachers
- LMS teaches information literacy to students
- LMS supports network links between LMC & classrooms

Technology
- Networked computers per 100 students
- Licensed database computers per 100 students
- Internet computers per 100 students

Library Media Program Development
- Total staff per 100 students
- Volumes per student
- Periodical subscriptions per 100 students
- Library media expenditures per student

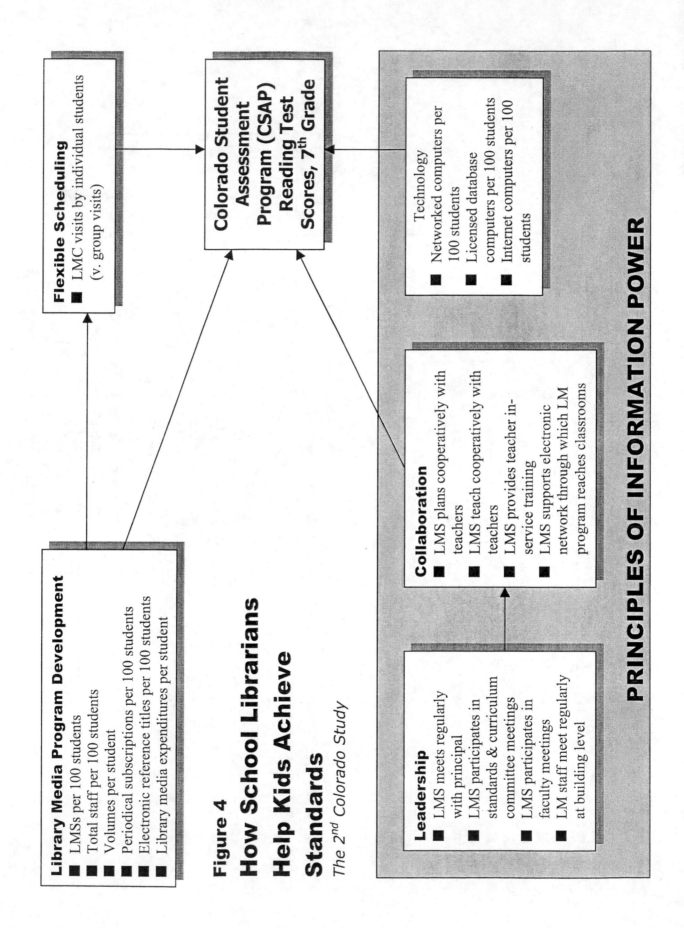

Flexible Scheduling
■ LMC visits by individual students (v. group visits)

Library Media Program Development
■ LMSs per 100 students
■ Total staff per 100 students
■ Volumes per student
■ Periodical subscriptions per 100 students
■ Electronic reference titles per 100 students
■ Library media expenditures per student

Colorado Student Assessment Program (CSAP) Reading Test Scores, 7th Grade

Technology
■ Networked computers per 100 students
■ Licensed database computers per 100 students
■ Internet computers per 100 students

Collaboration
■ LMS plans cooperatively with teachers
■ LMS teach cooperatively with teachers
■ LMS provides teacher in-service training
■ LMS supports electronic network through which LM program reaches classrooms

Leadership
■ LMS meets regularly with principal
■ LMS participates in standards & curriculum committee meetings
■ LMS participates in faculty meetings
■ LM staff meet regularly at building level

PRINCIPLES OF INFORMATION POWER

Figure 4
How School Librarians Help Kids Achieve Standards
The 2nd Colorado Study

Appendix D

The Alaska Study
Executive Summary and Handout

The following Alaska Summary brief entitled "Information Empowered" was published in 1999. It is followed by a handout summarizing the Alaska study. Both these documents are available online at http://www.lrs.org and are reprinted here for the convenience of the reader.

INFORMATION EMPOWERED

**The School Librarian as an Agent of
Academic Achievement in Alaska Schools**

Keith Curry Lance
Christine Hamilton-Pennell
Marcia J. Rodney
with
Lois Petersen
Clara Sitter

Alaska State Library
Juneau
1999

Executive Summary

This study is an assessment of the impact of Alaska school librarians on academic achievement in the state's public schools. It examines the direct relationship between such staffing and student performance, and identifies selected activities of library media staff that affect test scores. Other conditions of library media center operation—hours open, available technology, relationship with the public library, and selected policies—are also considered as potential predictors of academic achievement.

New Information Power Principles & Previous Research

This study's findings expand upon those of **The Impact of School Library Media Centers on Academic Achievement** (also known as "the Colorado study"), verify almost half a century of previous research on that topic, and demonstrate empirical support for the principles of **Information Power: Building Partnerships for Learning** (1998).

Methodologies

During the 1997-98 school year, library media centers in 211 Alaska public schools were surveyed about their staffing levels, hours of operation, staff activities, usage, technology, policies, and cooperation with public libraries. To the survey results, other data were added. For grades four, eight, and eleven, each school reported the percentage of students scoring below proficient, proficient, and above proficient on Version 5 of the California Achievement Tests (CAT5) of reading, language arts, and mathematics.

Using three analytical techniques—crosstabulation, comparison of means, and correlation—each library media program characteristic was assessed as a potential predictor of academic achievement. Relationships among potential library media predictors that might create indirect effects on academic achievement were also examined. After the direct and indirect effects of librarians on academic achievement were assessed, their effects relative to other school and community factors were analyzed via multiple regression.

Findings

School librarians are the "information empowered," because they play three critical roles in the learning community. They are teachers, information specialists, and administrators. In each of these roles, they empower students and teachers to meet high standards of academic achievement.

Following is a summary of positive, statistically significant relationships confirmed by this study:

Library Media Specialist Staffing

■ Test scores tend to be higher where there is
  - a librarian,
  - a full-time librarian rather than a part-time one,
  - a part-time librarian rather than no librarian at all.

Library Media Center Hours Open

■ Higher levels of librarian staffing lead to
  - longer LMC hours of operation,
  - higher levels of library media staff activity,
  - higher student usage, and consequently
  - higher test scores.

Staff Activities

■ The higher the level of librarian staffing, the greater the percentage of library media staff hours dedicated to
  - delivering library/information literacy instruction to students,
  - planning instructional units cooperatively with teachers, and
  - providing in-service training to teachers and other staff.

■ Regardless of level of librarian staffing, the more library media staff time devoted to these activities, the higher the test scores.

Library Media Program Usage

■ The more often students receive library/information literacy instruction in which library media staff are involved, the higher the test scores.

Partnerships, Technology & Policies

Test scores also tend to be higher where
■ there is a cooperative relationship between the LMC and the public library.
■ the library media program provides online access to information—particularly the facilities required to reach the Internet and the World Wide Web—and
■ the LMC has a collection development policy that addresses reconsideration of materials.

Controlling for Community and School Conditions

In addition, this study weighed the relative effects on academic achievement of library media specialist staffing, other school characteristics (i.e., per pupil spending, teacher-pupil ratio), and community conditions (i.e., adult educational attainment, Alaska Native population, poverty). While community conditions proved to have the strongest impact, the librarian-pupil ratio outweighed both per pupil expenditures and teacher-pupil ratio at the elementary level and the teacher-pupil ratio at the secondary level. Throughout the study, school size was controlled for by using ratios, such as the librarian-pupil ratio (i.e., typical weekly hours of librarian staffing per 100 students).

The small size of the data set and correlation between explanatory variables prevent our being able to assess the effect of library media services relative to other explanatory variables, while also controlling for community conditions. However, given these limitations, the data generally support the hypothesis that library services are beneficial for students in all communities.

In tackling these issues, this study broke new ground by taking recommended next steps beyond previous research. Its assessments of the efficacy of specific staff activities and online access to information are two examples of this accomplishment. This study also verifies that relationships to academic achievement found previously for school libraries in other states and communities are not anomalous, but apply equally to Alaska's school libraries. Like earlier studies, this one demonstrates that its key finding—the positive relationship between school librarians and test scores—cannot be explained away entirely by differences in school size, funding, and teacher staffing levels.

Test scores tend to be higher for all types of schools where

- there is a school librarian
- library staff spend more time delivering library/information literacy instruction to students
- collaborating with teachers on instructional units
- training teachers in information access
- students visit the school library more frequently

Full-time librarians are more likely to engage in key instructional activities than either part-time librarians or non-librarian staff.

Test scores tend to be higher for all types of schools where the library

- is open longer hours
- has a cooperative relationship with the public library
- provides online access to information via the Internet and the World Wide Web
- has a policy regarding selection and reconsideration of books and other materials

All of these relationships are both positive and statistically significant.

These relationships cannot be explained away entirely by differences in

- school size
- school funding
- teacher staffing levels

While community conditions such as the education level of adults (especially parents), absence of cultural and language barriers, and economic prosperity are important, these are variables over which schools have no control.

The work of a school librarian has also been shown to be an important factor in high student achievement levels, and this variable we CAN control.

Results from

INFORMATION EMPOWERED

The School Librarian as an Agent of Academic Achievement in Alaska

Want higher test scores?

A school librarian can make the difference!

About the Study

This study was conducted by the Library Research Service (Denver, Colorado) under contract to the Alaska State Library and with the cooperation and collaboration of staff of the

- Alaska State Library,
- Alaska Department of Education and Early Development, and
- Institute for Social and Economic Research, University of Alaska, Anchorage.

The sample for the study included 211 public elementary and secondary schools in Alaska that included grades four, eight, and eleven—those to which the California Achievement Tests, Version 5, were administered during the 1997/98 school year.

All sample schools participated in the 1998 Survey of School Library Media Centers in Alaska.

How a School Librarian Can Make a Difference

- keeping the library open longer

- providing more in-service to teachers

- collaborating with teachers

- delivering more library/information literacy instruction to students

- promoting more frequent student visits to the LMC

- building a stronger relationship with the public library

RESULTS:
Higher Test Scores

Appendix E

Colorado II Study
Executive Study and Handout

The following Colorado II Summary brief entitled "How School Librarians Help Kids Achieve Standards" was published in 2000. It is followed by a handout summarizing the Colorado study. Both these documents are available online at http://www.lrs.org and are reprinted here for the convenience of the reader.

How School Librarians
Help Kids Achieve
Standards

The Second Colorado Study

Keith Curry Lance
Library Research Service
Colorado State Library
Colorado Department of Education

Marcia J. Rodney
Library & Information Services Department
University of Denver

Christine Hamilton-Pennell
Library & Information Services Department
University of Denver
and
Mosaic Knowledge Works

Hi Willow Research & Publishing

April 2000

Executive Summary

Colorado Student Assessment Program (CSAP) reading scores increase with increases in the following characteristics of library media (LM) programs: LM program development, information technology, teacher/library media specialist (LMS) collaboration, and individual visits to the library media center (LMC). In addition, as participation increases in leadership roles, so does collaboration between teachers and LMSs. The relationship between these factors and test scores is not explained away by other school or community conditions. (See Figures 1 and 2, pp. 10-11.)

Library Media Program Development

CSAP reading test scores increase with increases in:
- LMS hours per 100 students (7th grade),
- total staff hours per 100 students,
- print volumes per student,
- periodical subscriptions per 100 students,
- electronic reference titles per 100 students (7th grade), and
- library media expenditures per student.

Information Technology

Where networked computers link library media centers with classrooms, labs, and other instructional sites, students earn higher CSAP reading test scores. These higher scores are particularly linked to the numbers of computers enabling teachers and students to utilize:

- LMC resources, either within the LMC or networked to the LMC,
- licensed databases, and
- Internet/World Wide Web.

Collaboration

A central finding of this study is the importance of a collaborative approach to information literacy. Test scores rise in both elementary and middle schools as library media specialists and teachers work together. In addition, scores also increase with the amount of time library media specialists spend as in-service trainers of other teachers, acquainting them with the rapidly changing world of information.

Test scores increase as library media specialists spend more time:
■ planning cooperatively with teachers (7th grade),
■ identifying materials for teachers,
■ teaching information literacy skills to students,
■ providing in-service training to teachers, and
■ managing a computer network through which the library media program reaches beyond its own walls to classrooms, labs, and offices (7th grade).

Flexible Scheduling

Students have greater freedom in middle school, and are often able to choose whether or not they visit their school's LMC and use the resources there or take them home. Choosing to visit the LMC as an individual, separate from a class visit, is also a strong indicator of higher test scores. Middle schools with high test scores tend to have LMCs that report a high number of individual visits to the LMC on a per student basis.

Indirect Effects

While not having a direct effect on test scores, leadership involvement on the part of the library media specialist (LMS) has a strong impact on whether or not the LMS is working closely with teachers and students. At both elementary and middle school levels, the more the LMS is involved in school and library media professional activities, the higher the level of collaboration. Collaboration, in turn, does have a direct impact on test scores.

Higher levels of collaboration result from:
■ meeting regularly with school administration,
■ serving on standards and curriculum committees,
■ working with faculty at school-wide staff meetings, and
■ meeting with library media staff at the building level.

At the elementary level, library media program development (levels of staffing, collections and expenditures) and technology are strong predictors of each other as well as of test scores. The seventh grade level sees a strong relationship between library media program development and flexible scheduling.

133

School & Community Differences

These predictors of academic achievement cannot be explained away by:
- school differences, including:
  - school district expenditures per pupil,
  - teacher/pupil ratio,
  - the average years of experience of classroom teachers, and
  - their average salaries; or
- community differences, including:
  - adult educational attainment,
  - children in poverty, and
  - racial/ethnic demographics.

How much will a school's test scores improve with specific improvements in its library media program? The answer depends on the library media (LM) program's current status, what it improves, and how much it is improved. When LM predictors are maximized (e.g., staffing, expenditures, and information resources and technology), CSAP reading scores tend to run 18 percent higher in fourth grade and 10 to 15 percent higher in seventh.

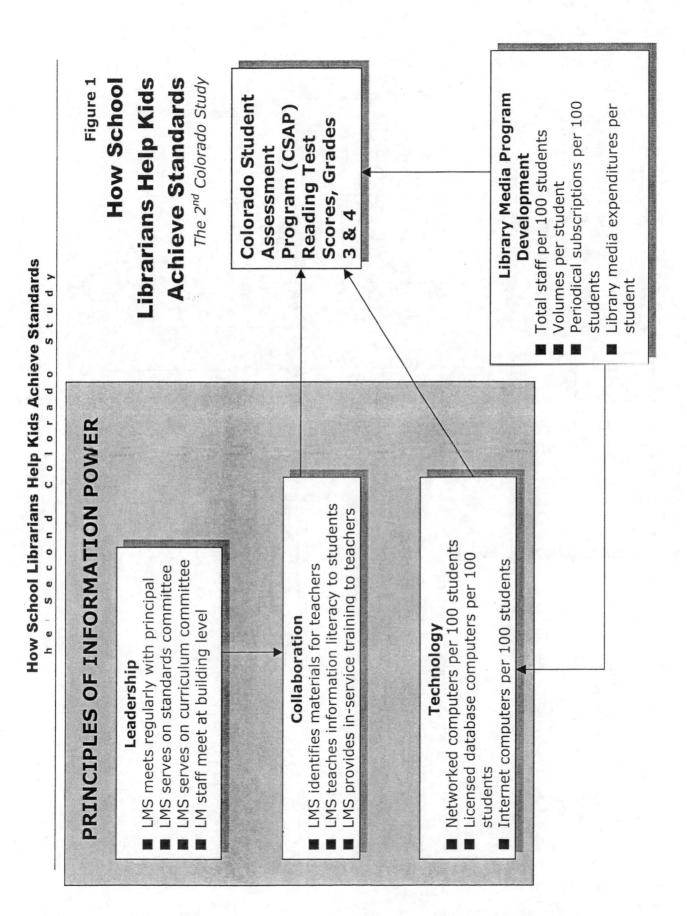

Figure 1

How School Librarians Help Kids Achieve Standards
The 2nd Colorado Study

PRINCIPLES OF INFORMATION POWER

Leadership
- LMS meets regularly with principal
- LMS serves on standards committee
- LMS serves on curriculum committee
- LM staff meet at building level

Collaboration
- LMS identifies materials for teachers
- LMS teaches information literacy to students
- LMS provides in-service training to teachers

Technology
- Networked computers per 100 students
- Licensed database computers per 100 students
- Internet computers per 100 students

Colorado Student Assessment Program (CSAP) Reading Test Scores, Grades 3 & 4

Library Media Program Development
- Total staff per 100 students
- Volumes per student
- Periodical subscriptions per 100 students
- Library media expenditures per student

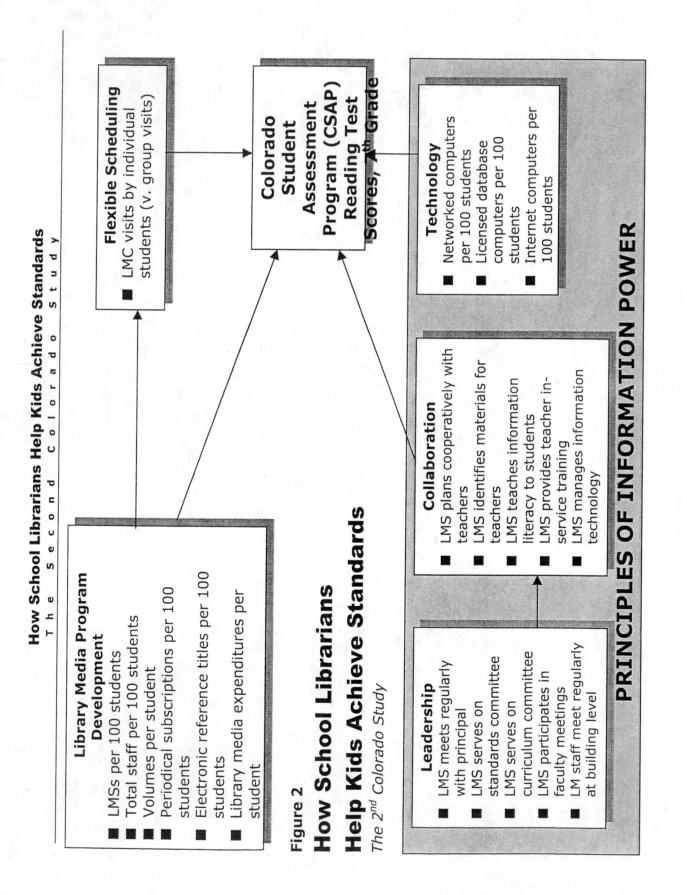

How School Librarians Help Kids Achieve Standards
The Second Colorado Study

Figure 2

How School Librarians Help Kids Achieve Standards
The 2ⁿᵈ Colorado Study

Library Media Program Development
- LMSs per 100 students
- Total staff per 100 students
- Volumes per student
- Periodical subscriptions per 100 students
- Electronic reference titles per 100 students
- Library media expenditures per student

Flexible Scheduling
- LMC visits by individual students (v. group visits)

Colorado Student Assessment Program (CSAP) Reading Test Scores, 7ᵗʰ Grade

Technology
- Networked computers per 100 students
- Licensed database computers per 100 students
- Internet computers per 100 students

Collaboration
- LMS plans cooperatively with teachers
- LMS identifies materials for teachers
- LMS teaches information literacy to students
- LMS provides teacher in-service training
- LMS manages information technology

Leadership
- LMS meets regularly with principal
- LMS serves on standards committee
- LMS serves on curriculum committee
- LMS participates in faculty meetings
- LM staff meet regularly at building level

PRINCIPLES OF INFORMATION POWER

How School Librarians
Help Kids Achieve
Standards
The Second Colorado Study

Keith Curry Lance
Library Research Service
Colorado State Library
Colorado Department of Education

Marcia J. Rodney
Library & Information Services Department
University of Denver

Christine Hamilton-Pennell
Library & Information Services Department
University of Denver &
Mosaic Knowledge Works

Other School Library
Impact Studies

For more information about recent research on the impact of school library media programs on academic achievement, visit the Library Research Service web site, http://www.lrs.org. Links are provided to:

- **The Impact of School Library Media Centers on Academic Achievement** (the original 1993 Colorado study),
- **Information Empowered:** *The School Librarian as an Agent of Academic Achievement in Alaska* (1999), and
- **Measuring Up to Standards:** *The Role of Library Information Programs & Information Literacy in Pennsylvania Schools*

Contact Information

Direct questions and comments about the Colorado study and requests for a speaker on this topic to:

Keith Curry Lance or Marcia J. Rodney
Library Research Service
201 E. Colfax Ave., Suite 309
Denver, CO 80203-1799
Tel.: 303-866-6737 – Fax: 303-866-6940
E-mail: klance@snl.net or mrodney@du.edu

Library Media Program Development
- staffing
- collections
- expenditures

Leadership
- meeting with principal
- serving on standards committees
- serving on curriculum committees
- holding LM staff meetings

Collaboration
- planning with teachers (7th)
- identifying materials for teachers
- teaching information literacy to students
- providing teacher in-service training
- managing computer network that links LMC and classrooms (7th)

Technology
- networked computers
- licensed databases
- Internet/Web

CSAP Reading Scores
(Grades 4 & 7)

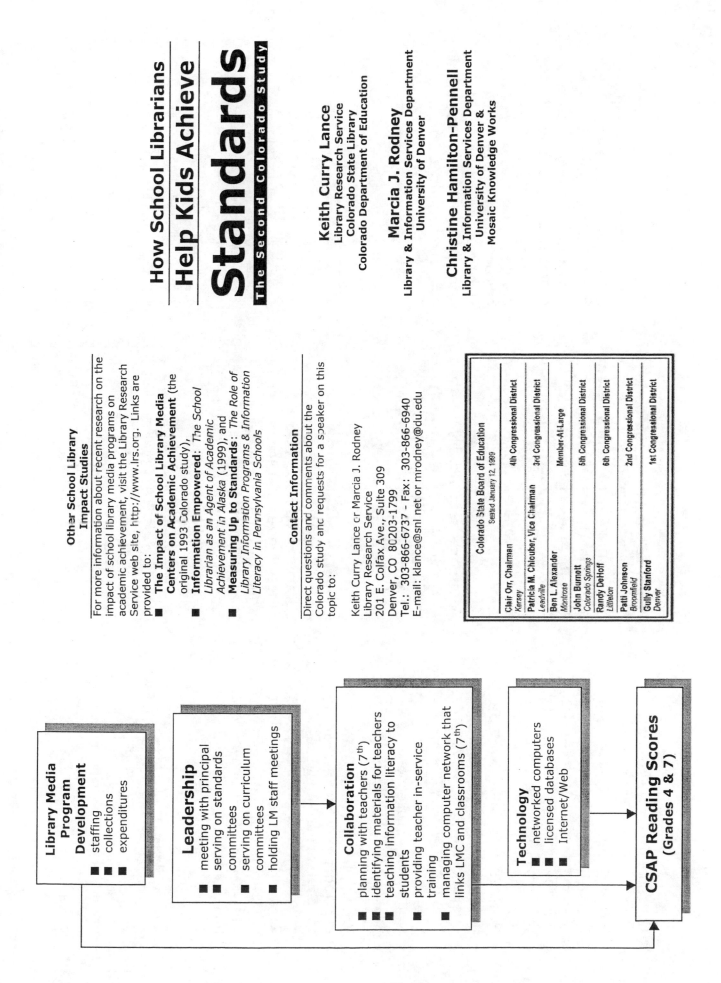

These predictors of academic achievement cannot be explained away by school differences, such as per pupil spending, teacher-pupil ratio, and other teacher characteristics (experience, salaries). Likewise, these predictors are not explained away by community differences, such as high adult educational attainment and low numbers of poor and minority children.

Colorado Student Assessment Program (CSAP) reading scores increase with improvements in library media programs. (Average percentage increases from lowest to highest rated LM programs: 4th/7th grade)

Schools with well-developed library media programs average 10-15%/18% higher reading scores. Well-developed programs are indicated by staffing level, collection size and age, and expenditures.

When library media staff collaborate with classroom teachers, reading scores average increases of 8%/18-21%. Key collaboration activities of library media staff are planning with teachers, teaching information literacy, and providing in-service training to teachers.

When schools have computer networks that extend the library media program's reach into classrooms and labs, reading scores rise 6-13%/18-25%. Such networks provide access to licensed databases and the World Wide Web.

When access to library media centers is scheduled flexibly, reading scores improve 13-22%. Flexible scheduling allows students to visit the LMC individually.

Collaboration activities are more likely to occur where the library media specialist is a school leader. She or he meets regularly with the principal, serves on standards and curriculum committees, and holds library media staff meetings.

The librarian presents lessons specifically geared to the Colorado State Standards. Through collaborative planning with teachers, each unit includes an assessment tool, such as a rubric made in consultation with each classroom or grade level.

Madeline Wood, Library Media Specialist
Samuels Elementary, Denver

Every grade level teacher meets and plans with our library media specialist to create and develop units that will improve student learning.

Gaynell C. Lawrence, Principal
Schmitt Elementary, Denver

The Library Media Center has become the center of the school. It is central to what goes on in the classroom. It's a busy place. Students come before and after school to use resources. Throughout the day, teachers come with entire classes, send small groups to work with the library media specialist, or send individuals to find information they need. Teachers come alone during planning time or before or after school to meet with the library media specialist, find resources, use the Internet, etc.

Phyllis Meyer
Teacher—Technology Resources
Baker Middle School
Denver

Appendix F

The Pennsylvania Study

Executive Summary and Handout

The following Pennsylvania Summary brief entitled "Measuring Up to Standards" was published in 2000. It is followed by a handout summarizing the Pennsylvania study. Both these documents are available online at http://www.lrs.org and are reprinted ehre for the convenience of the reader.

Summary Pages from *Pennsylvania Power!*

These pages were taken from *Pennsylvania Power!* by David V. Loertscher and Joyce Kasman Valenza (Hi Willow Research & Publishing, 2004). It is available from LMC Source at http://www.lmcsource.com.

Measuring Up to
Standards

**The Impact of School
Library Programs &
Information Literacy in
Pennsylvania Schools**

Keith Curry Lance
Marcia J. Rodney
Christine Hamilton-Pennell

Pennsylvania Citizens for Better Libraries
604 Hunt Club Drive
Greensburg, PA 15601

February 2000

*This research was supported with a Library Services and Technology Act (LSTA) grant
administered by the
Office of Commonwealth Libraries, Pennsylvania Department of Education*

Executive Summary

Pennsylvania school library programs can make a difference supporting the efforts of schools to measure up to standards. Pennsylvania System of School Assessment (PSSA) reading scores increase with increases in the following characteristics of school library programs: staffing, information technology, and integration of information literacy into the curriculum. In addition, as library staffing, information resources and information technology rise, so too does the involvement of school librarians in teaching students and teachers how to find and assess information. The relationship between staffing and test scores is not explained away by other school or community conditions. (See Figure 1, p. 9.)

Staffing

PSSA reading test scores increase with increases in:
■ school librarian staff hours; and
■ support staff hours.

Information Technology

Where networked computers link school libraries with classrooms, labs and other instructional sites, students earn higher PSSA reading test scores. These higher scores are particularly linked to the numbers of computers enabling teachers and students to utilize:
■ the ACCESS PENNSYLVANIA database;
■ licensed databases; and
■ Internet/World Wide Web.

Integrating Information Literacy

Information literate students know how to use information and ideas effectively. The "keystone" finding of this study is the importance of an integrated approach to information literacy teaching. For school library programs to be successful agents of academic achievement, information literacy must be an integral part of the school's approach to both standards and curriculum.

)Test scores increase as school librarians spend more time:
- teaching cooperatively with teachers;
- teaching information literacy skills independently;
- providing in-service training to teachers;
- serving on standards committee;
- serving on curriculum committee; and
- managing information technology.

Indirect Effects

In addition to its direct effect on academic achievement, higher levels of school library program staffing—especially certified school librarians — predict:
- higher expenditures;
- larger and more varied collections of information resources;
- increased access to information technology for teachers and students; and
- more integrated approaches to information literacy, standards and curriculum.

The more print and electronic information resources available through the school library, the greater amount of time spent by the school librarian on information literacy—that is, teaching students and teachers how to access and use such resources.

School & Community Differences

These predictors of academic achievement cannot be explained away by:
- school differences, including:
  - school expenditures per pupil;
  - teacher characteristics (education, experience, salaries);
  - teacher/pupil ratio; and
  - student characteristics (poverty, race/ethnicity), or
- community differences, such as:
  - adult educational attainment;
  - families in poverty; and
  - racial/ethnic demographics.

)

How Much Can Scores Rise With Good School Library Programs?

How much will a school's test scores improve with specific improvements in its school library program? The answer depends on the program's current status, what it improves, and how much it is improved. When all library predictors are maximized (e.g., staffing, library expenditures, information resources and technology, and information literacy activities of library staff), PSSA reading scores tend to run 10 to 15 points higher.

Measuring Up to Standards

The Impact of School Library Programs & Information Literacy in Pennsylvania Schools

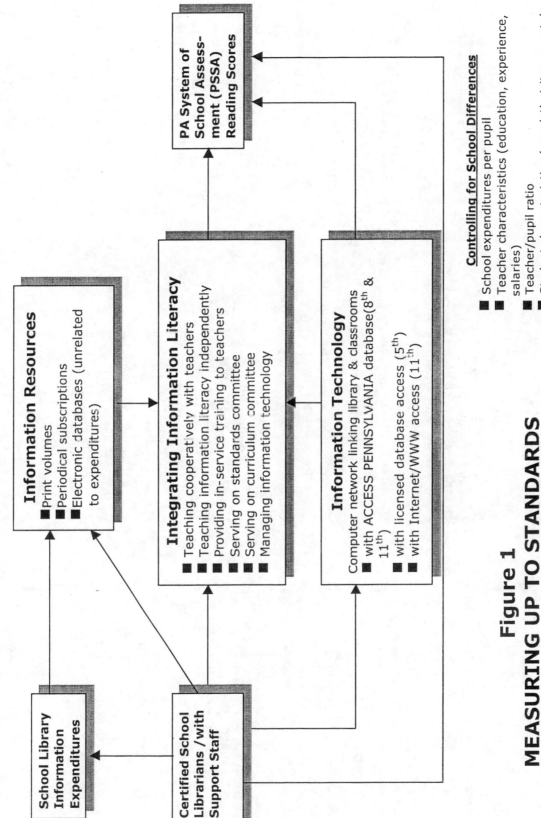

Figure 1

MEASURING UP TO STANDARDS

*The Impact of Library Information Programs &
Information Literacy in Pennsylvania Schools*

145 (Handout p9)

Measuring Up to Standards

The Role of Library Information Programs & Information Literacy in Pennsylvania Schools

Keith Curry Lance
Marcia J. Rodney
Christine Hamilton-Pennell

Pennsylvania Citizens for Better Libraries

Other School Library Impact Studies

For more information about recent research on the impact of school library information programs on academic achievement, visit the Library Research Service web site, http://www.lrs.org. Links are provided to:

- **The Impact of School Library Media Centers on Academic Achievement** (the original 1993 Colorado study),
- **Information Empowered:** *The School Librarian as an Agent of Academic Achievement in Alaska* (1999), and
- **How School Librarians Help Kids Achieve Standards** (2000).

Contact Information

Direct questions and comments about the Pennsylvania study and requests for a speaker on this topic to:

Keith Curry Lance or
Marcia J. Rodney
Library Research Service
201 E. Colfax Ave., Suite 309
Denver, CO 80203-1799
Tel.: 303-866-6737
Fax: 303-866-6940
E-mail: klance@sni.net or
mrodney@du.edu

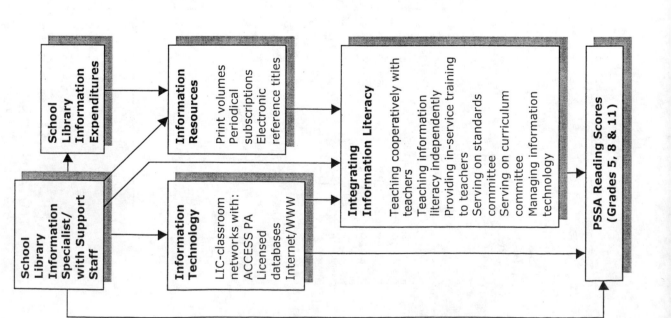

These predictors of academic achievement cannot be explained away by

School Differences

- School expenditures per pupil
- Teacher characteristics (education, experience, salaries)
- Teacher/pupil ratio
- Student characteristics (poverty, race/ethnicity)

Community Differences

- Adult educational attainment
- Families in poverty
- Racial/ethnic demographics

> When we open before school, students are poring over leisure reading. They've even asked if I would set up a cappucino bar.
> *Paul Scaer, JR Masterman School*

> A computer center ...a library ... teaching -- the result is a student body with good skills.
> *Annabel Grote,*
> *Upper Moreland High School*

With increases in staffing—especially LIS staffing—there are corresponding increases in

- Expenditures
- Information Resources
- Information Technology
- Integration of Information Literacy with Curriculum

In addition, increased integration of information literacy is associated with

- higher levels of staffing,
- larger collections of information resources, and
- information technology that takes the LI program closer to teachers and students

> Our library has become a "kid magnet" where students are engaged in active, authentic learning. *Patricia Kolencik, North Clarion High School*

> Teachers say to students when faced with a need for information: "have you asked the librarian, have you been to the library?" Teachers and librarians work together. *Lois McNicol, Garnet Valley High School*

Pennsylvania System of School Assessment (PSSA) reading scores increase with increases in:

Staffing

- School librarian staff hours
- support staff hours

Information Technology

Networked computers linking library & classrooms

- with ACCESS PENNSYLVANIA Database
- with licensed databases
- with Internet/World Wide Web

Integration of Information Literacy with the Curriculum

Time spent by school librarians...

- Teaching cooperatively with teachers
- Teaching information literacy independently
- Providing in-service training to teachers
- Serving on standards committee
- Serving on curriculum committee
- Managing information technology

What Every Parent Should Know About Pennsylvania School Library Programs And Achievement

In 2000, a major study conducted by Keith Curry Lance, Marcia J. Rodney, and Christine Hamilton-Pennell of Pennsylvania school library media programs discovered the following.

Basic Findings

Library Media Program Development

Pennsylvania reading test scores at the 5th, 8th, and 11th grade rise with increases in:

- School librarian and support staff hours.
- Networked computers linking school libraries with classrooms, labs, and other instructional sites taking advantage of the Access Pennsylvania Database, licensed databases, and the Internet.
- The amount of time librarians spend teaching cooperatively with teachers, teaching information literacy skills independently, providing inservice training to teachers, serving on standards committees, helping on curriculum committees, and managing information technology.

How much will a School's test scores with specific improvement in its school library program? The answer depends on the program's current status, what it improves, and how much it is improved. When all library predictors are maximized; e.g., staffing, library expenditures, information resources and technology, and information literacy activities of library staff; PSSA reading scores tend to run 10 to 15 points higher.[1]

Variables	Elementary Through High School		
	25 Highest scoring schools	25 Lowest scoring schools	Percent Difference (lowest to highest)
5th Grade Reading Scores (mean, see p. 54)	90.02	76.40	18%
Staffing Weekly librarian hours (mean, see p. 54)	34.31	29.36	17%
Weekly support staff hours (mean)	25.92	12.48	108%

Another way to see the differences

[1] Measuring up to Standards: The Impact of School Library Programs and Information Literacy in Pennsylvania Schools, by Keith Curry Lance, Marcia J. Rodney, and Christine Hamilton-Pennell, Pennsylvania Citizens for Better Libraries, 2000: (p. 6-8) Available at http://www.statelibrary.state.pa.us/libraries/lib/libraries/measuringup.pdf These findings cannot be explained away by school differences, including: school expenditures per pupil, teacher characteristics (education, experience, salaries), teacher/pupil ratio, and student characteristics (poverty, race, ethnicity) or community differences such as adult educational attainment, families in poverty, and racial/ethnic demographics.

8th Grade Reading Scores (Mean, see p. 55)	88.93	73.50	21%
Weekly librarian hours (mean, see p. 55)	38.40	37.63	2%
Weekly support staff hours (mean)	30.30	15.80	92%
11th Grade Reading Scores (Mean, see p. 56)	86.75	74.73	16%
Weekly librarian hours (mean, see p. 56)	45.06	43.25	4%
Weekly support staff hours (mean)	49.57	19.28	157%

Notice that the major difference comes when you add support staff to the professional staff. This gives the professional librarian time to concentrate on teaching and learning.

What librarians do that make a difference

From the Study (p. 58):

When you find a professional librarian with support staff, you are more likely to find:
- Teaching cooperatively with teachers
- Teaching information literacy independently
- Providing inservice training to teachers
- Serving on standards and curriculum committees
- Managing technology

Other differences of note (p. 52-53)

Reading Scores and the Best School Libraries

Students at the highest-scoring schools averaged reading scores in the upper 80's while their counterparts at the lowest-scoring schools averaged scores at the mid 70's.

School Library Expenditures

Higher achieving schools often spend twice as much – more – on their school library programs as lower achieving schools…affecting the size of the school library program's collection of information resources.

Information Technology

The most dramatic statistical difference between lower and higher achieving schools is in the area of information technology networked to the school library:

Elementary: 40-50 computers vs. 6-10
High School: 75-100 computers vs. 20-25

Appendix G

The Oregon Study
Handout

The following Oregon handout entitled "Good Schools Have School Librarians" was published in 2001. This document is available on the web at http://www.oema.net/Oregon_Study/OR_study.htm and is reprinted here for the convenience of the reader.

GOOD

Schools Have School
LIBRARIANS

Oregon School Librarians Collaborate to
Improve Academic Achievement

Keith Curry **LANCE**
Marcia J. **RODNEY**
Christine **HAMILTON-PENNELL**

Published with funds granted by the
Oregon State Library under the Library
Services Technology Act State
Administered Program, P. L. 104-208

**Oregon Educational Media Association
2001**

Other School Library
Impact Studies

For more information about recent research on the impact of school library media programs on academic achievement, visit the Library Research Service web site, http://www.lrs.org. Links are provided to:

- **The Impact of School Library Media Centers on Academic Achievement** (the original 1993 Colorado study),

- **How School Librarians Help Kids Achieve Standards:** *The Second Colorado Study* (2000),

- **Information Empowered:** *The School Librarian as an Agent of Academic Achievement in Alaska* (2nd edition, 2000), and

- **Measuring Up to Standards:** *The Role of Library Information Programs & Information Literacy in Pennsylvania Schools* (2000)

Contact Information

Direct questions and comments about this research to:

Keith Curry Lance
Library Research Service
201 E. Colfax Ave., Suite 309
Denver, CO 80203-1799
Tel.: 303-866-6737
Fax: 303-866-6940
E-mail: keithlance@earthlink.net

Oregon schools with the best reading scores tend to have stronger library media programs than schools with the lowest scores.

At most grade levels, when the confounding effects of poverty are taken into account, library media programs exert a measurable impact on test scores while other school variables, such as per pupil expenditures and teacher-pupil ratio, do not.

Inspiration Point

When librarians are available full-time, students learn that the librarian is the person who can help them with all sorts of things as they work to meet their learning goals. Students are inspired by the types of presentations a teacher-librarian can provide and are often inspired to try new methods themselves. It's most rewarding when a student asks, "Can you show me how to do what you just did?"
Garnetta Wilker, Librarian, Lake Oswego Junior High School

"Wow- there are some great new books here. I can't wait to read them. Can I check one out now?"
Student, Lake Oswego Junior High School

"This is our library. It's the place where you can find everything you need."
Student giving a tour to new seventh grade students, Lake Oswego Junior High School

---

School library media programs in Oregon schools exert a positive and statistically significant impact on academic achievement.

Successful LM programs have

- professional and support staff,
- library media specialists who are involved in teaching and learning as well as information access and delivery,
- diverse collections in multiple formats,
- high levels of individual and group visits to the LMC,
- information technology that extends throughout the school, and
- expenditures that support these efforts.

The impact of LM programs on Oregon reading scores at elementary and secondary levels cannot be explained away by other school and community conditions.

Teach the Teacher

As a mentor I have been working with three elementary schools in our district. I have made presentations about the OSLIS Website to the teachers in each o the schools. Wow! It was like givin candy to a baby! Teachers who are often the first to go home stayed way beyond my allotted time exploring all the options. They thanked us for such a wonderful site.

Then I was invited to two of the schools to participate in their grou planning for their collaboration projects. Again I was delighted with everyone's excitement. All three schools will be completing their projects this year.

Char Wisely, Media Specialist Abraham Lincoln Elementary Medford

Appendix H

The Iowa Study

Handout

The following Iowa handout entitled "Make the Connection" with its accompanying brief preliminary report was published in 2002. This document is available on the web at http://www.aea9.k12.ia.us/download/04/aea_statewide_study.pdf and is reprinted here for the convenience of the reader.

Summary from *Iowa Power!*

These pages were taken from *Iowa Power!* by David V. Loertscher and Sharron McElmeel (Hi Willow Research & Publishing, 2004). It is available from LMC Source at http://www.lmcsource.com.

Make the Connection

Quality School Library Media Programs Impact Academic Achievement in Iowa

Marcia J. RODNEY
Keith Curry LANCE
Christine HAMILTON-PENNELL

2002

Other School Library Impact Studies

For more information about recent research on the impact of school library media programs on academic achievement, visit the Library Research Service web site, http://www.lrs.org. Links are provided to:

- **The Impact of School Library Media Centers on Academic Achievement** (the original 1993 Colorado study),
- **How School Librarians Help Kids Achieve Standards:** *The Second Colorado Study* (2000),
- **Information Empowered:** *The School Librarian as an Agent of Academic Achievement in Alaska* (2nd edition, 2000), and
- **Measuring Up to Standards:** *The Role of Library Information Programs & Information Literacy in Pennsylvania Schools* (2000)
- **Good Schools have School Librarians:** *Oregon School Librarians Collaborate to Improve Academic Achievement* (2001)

Contact Information

Direct questions and comments about this research to

Marcia J. Rodney
Information Consultant
527 W. Ash Ct.
Louisville, CO 80027
Tel.: 303-673-9082
E-mail: mrodney@earthnet.net

Iowa schools with a higher percentage of the best reading scores tend to have stronger library media programs than schools with the lowest percentage of good scores.

. . . .

At Iowa elementary schools, when the confounding effects of poverty are taken into account, library media programs exert a measurable impact on test scores while other school variables, such as per pupil expenditures and teacher-pupil ratio, do not.

. . . .

At Iowa middle schools, no matter what overall per pupil spending is, library media services have a positive impact on test scores, while teacher-pupil ratio and teacher experience do not.

. . . .

At Iowa high schools, the more time library media specialists spend motivating students to read, the higher their test scores are.

DIGGING INTO THE PAST BRINGS UP RICHES

I collaborated with the 5th-6th grade social studies teacher to create our "Decades" research project. Students were introduced to the past hundred years with a two-day PowerPoint presentation, browsing stations with books organized by decades, and historic photographs on the Library of Congress American Memory Project Web site.

Students then chose topics of interest, and took research notes with guidance from both the teacher and me. Next, I taught students how to transform their research into PowerPoint presentations. Students presented their projects to the class, and also listened to elderly guest speakers who gave first-hand accounts of living through the earlier part of the century. Finally, I presented booktalks to students on historical fiction from the past hundred years, so that students could continue to extend their interests through recreational reading. Parents have been impressed by students' PowerPoint projects.

Anne Marie Kraus
Library Media Specialist
Roosevelt Elementary School
Iowa City, Iowa

School library media programs in Iowa schools exert a positive and statistically significant impact on academic achievement.

Successful library media programs at elementary, middle, and high schools have one important element in common:

the certified Library Media Specialist

When you find a Library Media Specialist, you're also more likely to find

☞ collaborative teaching

☞ effective reading motivation

☞ students who've been taught how to find and evaluate information

☞ more books, magazines, tapes, and electronic reference works for students to explore

☞ more students using the library's print and online resources, both in the library and by networking to it

---

RACE YOU TO THE BOOKS!

Sustained Silent Reading was instituted at the high school two years ago. I applied for a grant to purchase hundreds of high interest paperbacks, nearly two per student, to be placed in the classrooms for easy access. The books are in attractive baskets and may be exchanged for different titles whenever the students wish.

Students select which books go in their room's baskets. Students were so excited the first time they saw 500+ new paperbacks that they argued over which room got to go next. When I wanted to buy the second batch of books, I asked the kids what books they wanted. I should have tape recorded them -- they wanted or did not want. In other words, they cared.

Teachers MUST read along with kids, of course. The football coach told me this was the first time he completed a book since he was in college. He read Harry Potter first, and thought his reading skills had really improved significantly. He told me, "Next time Aurilee calls me to read the scripture in church, I'm going to tell her 'sure'."

Virginia Miehe, Library Media Specialist
West Liberty High School
West Liberty, Iowa

Make the Connection

**Quality School Library Media Programs
Impact Academic Achievement in Iowa**

Preliminary Results

Preliminary results are in on the Iowa study of the impact of school libraries on academic achievement.

Elementary Level

Fourth grade reading scores tend to rise with:

- weekly hours of professional librarian staffing (both total and per 100 students);
- library staff time spent planning and teaching with teachers and managing networked computers;
- the number of library books per student, the number of magazine and newspaper subscriptions (both total and per student), and the number of videos per student; and
- the number of books and other items used in the library per 100 students.

Middle School Level

Eighth grade reading scores tend to increase with:

- the school library's weekly hours of operation,
- weekly hours of professional librarian staffing per 100 students,
- the number of individual library visits for information literacy instruction per student,
- the number of group visits per 100 students, and
- the number of books and other items used in the library per 100 students.

High School Level

Eleventh grade reading scores tend to improve with:

- weekly hours of professional librarian staffing per 100 students, and
- weekly staff hours spent offering reading incentive activities for students (total and as a percent of total staff hours).

Relative Impact of School Library Development, Other School & Community Characteristics

At the elementary school level, where the variation in library conditions was sufficient to analyze, it was determined that the level of development of the school library (i.e., its staffing and collections) explains almost 2.5 percent of the variation in reading scores. Two other sets of factors were taken into account when assessing the impact of the school library: key characteristics of the community and the school.

Not surprisingly, the variables that outweighed the school library's impact were poverty and race/ethnicity. A third socio-economic variable, adult educational attainment, was narrowly outranked by the school library in its impact on test scores. Combined, these community variables explained almost a third of test score variation. Interestingly, when these community factors and the school library were taken into account, characteristics of the school (i.e., the education level of the school's teachers, the teacher-pupil ratio, overall per pupil spending on education) explained no additional variation.

Additional Information

Stay tuned for the final report which will also identify characteristics of school libraries run by professional librarians. Professional librarian staffing correlated with test scores at all school levels.

This study replicates research conducted in Alaska, Colorado, Massachusetts, Oregon, Pennsylvania, and Texas.

What Every Parent Should Know About Iowa School Library Programs And Achievement

In 2002, a major study conducted by Marcia J. Rodney, Keith Curry Lance, and Christine Hamilton Pennell of Iowa school library media programs discovered the following.

Basic Findings

Library Media Program Development

Iowa reading test scores at the fourth and eighth grade rise with increases in:

- Weekly LMS staff hours per 100 students,
- Total weekly LM staff hours per 100 students,
- Print volumes per student, and
- Periodical subscriptions per 100 students

Whatever the current level of development of a school's library media program, these finding indicate that incremental improvements in its staffing and collections will yield incremental increases in reading scores.[2]

Variables	Elementary Through High School		
	25 highest scoring schools	25 lowest scoring schools	Percent Difference (lowest to highest)
4th Grade Reading Scores (Percent proficient & above)	84.43	42.32	99%
Staffing Librarian's hours per 100 students	7.99	4.91	68%
Total library staff per 100 students	17.14	15.06	14%
8th Grade Reading Scores (Percent proficient & above)	65.94	48.96	35%
Librarian's hours per 100 studnets	11.74	8.23	43%
Total library staff hours per 100 students	22.36	19.33	16%
11th Grade Reading Scores (Percent proficient & above)	89.79	52.63	71%
Librarian's hours per 100 students	10.27	6.91	49%
Total library staff hours per 100 students	20.11	16.99	18%

Another way to see how people make a difference

[2] *Make the Connection: Quality School Library Media Programs' Impact on Academic Achievement in Iowa* by Marcia J. Rodney, Keith Curry Lance, and Chritine Hamilton-Pennell. Iowa Area Education Agencies, 2002. available at: www.davidvl.org under "research." This finding holds up whether school district expenditures per pupil are high or low; the teacher/pupil ratio; the percentage of classroom teachers with masters degrees; the number of children in poverty, racial or ethnic demographis; or, adult educational attainment.

From the Study:

What librarians do that makes a difference:

When you find a professional librarian, you are more likely to find:

- Collaborative teaching
- Effective reading motivation
- Students who have been taught how to find and evaluate information
- More books, magazines, tapes, and electronic reference works for students to explore
- More students using the library's print and online resources, both in the library and by networking to it.

Iowa schools with a higher percentage of the best reading scores tend to have stronger library media programs than schools with the lowest percentage of good scores.

At Iowa elementary schools, when the confounding effects of poverty are taken into account, library media programs exert a measurable impact on ttest scores whil other school variables, such as per pupil expenditures and teacher-pubil expenditures and teacher-pupil ratio, do not.

At Iowa middle schools, no matter what overall per pupil spending is, library media services have a positive impact on test scores, while teacher-pupil ratio and teacher experience do not.

At Iowa high schools, the more time library media specialists spend motivating students to read, the higher their test scores are.

Appendix I

The Michigan Study
Handout

The following Michigan handout entitled "The Impact of Michigan School Librarians on Academic Achievement: Kids Who Have Libraries Succeed" was published in 2003. This document is available on the web at http://www.mame.gen.mi.us/MI_Study/MI_Study.html and is reprinted here for the convenience of the reader.

The Impact of Michigan School Librarians on Academic Achievement: Kids Who Have Libraries Succeed

Marcia J. **RODNEY**
Keith Curry **LANCE**
Christine **HAMILTON-PENNELL**

2003

Other School Library Impact Studies

For more information about recent research on the impact of school library media programs on academic achievement, visit the Library Research Service web site, http://www.lrs.org. Links are provided to:

- **The Impact of School Library Media Centers on Academic Achievement** (the original 1993 Colorado study)
- **How School Librarians Help Kids Achieve Standards: *The Second Colorado Study*** (2000)
- **Information Empowered:** *The School Librarian as an Agent of Academic Achievement in Alaska* (2nd edition, 2000)
- **Measuring Up to Standards:** *The Role of Library Information Programs & Information Literacy in Pennsylvania Schools* (2000)
- **Good Schools have School Librarians:** *Oregon School Librarians Collaborate to Improve Academic Achievement* (2001)

Contact Information

Direct questions and comments about this research to:

Marcia J. Rodney
RSL Research Group
527 W. Ash Ct.
Louisville, CO 8C027
E-mail: mrodney@rslresearch.com

Michigan schools with a higher percentage of the best reading scores tend to have <u>more school librarian hours per student</u> than schools with the lowest percentage of good scores.

....

At Michigan elementary schools, reading test scores tend to rise as <u>students spend more time in the library and library staff spend more time <u>teaching students, working with teachers and developing collections.</u></u>

....

At Michigan middle schools, reading test scores usually rise as <u>more computers throughout the entire school are networked to library resources, including Access Michigan.</u>

....

At Michigan high schools, reading test scores generally rise as <u>the library is open more hours, with more professional staffing, more books, and more students visiting the library on their own.</u>

FASTER OFF THE SHELF

A student was asked if she was finding everything she needed. Her reply was that this was the third day that she had been looking on the Internet for information on "cloning" but she just couldn't find anything for her research paper. I determined that the real problem was that she was finding too much information and was overwhelmed. We told her that we had a book on cloning that might be helpful. When we placed it in her hand, she exclaimed, "wow, a whole book on cloning! This is great, can I use it?"

We told her not ONLY could she USE it she could actually TAKE IT HOME with her for 3 weeks. She was so excited, and said that she was going to tell her friends that we had books on stuff like this that they could use (novel idea those libraries). We felt like missionaries who had just brought food and water to the survivor on a deserted island!! She could now go home and do her work instead of staying after school!!

Shirley Dudek
Library Media Specialist
L'Anse Creuse High School
Harrison Township

School library media programs in Michigan schools exert a <u>demonstrably positive and statistically significant impact</u> on reading test scores.

The impact of school library services on academic achievement cannot be explained away by:

<u>school differences</u>
- **overall per pupil school spending**

- **the teacher/pupil ratio**

<u>community differences</u>
- **the percentage of children living in poverty**

- **the percentage of children belonging to racial/ethnic minority groups**

- **the percentage of adults who graduated from high school.**

THE HEART OF THE SCHOOL

It's lunchtime, a busy time in the library. There is the usual group catching up on the daily news and a student telling me about his latest success in his genealogy research. Some are putting together the jigsaw puzzle while others compete in a friendly game of chess. The computers are filled with students printing assignments and searching the Internet. Someone checks out a paperback and another requests an interlibrary loan. It's not quiet by any means! It's a gathering place. It's comfortable and welcoming.

Students stop me in the hall to discuss what they are reading. They don't wait until the yearly survey to tell me about a new author or series they think we should add to our collection. Though I arrive at school 45 minutes before school starts, there are always students waiting to get in and an hour and a half after school I often have to send them home so I can lock up.

Has it made a difference in the students' test scores? Studies indicate that it should. Has it made a difference in their school lives? I would like to think so.

Patti Colvin
Manton School Libraries
Manton

Appendix J

The Illinois Study
Fact Sheet and Handout

The following Illinois fact sheet entitled "Powerful Libraries Make Powerful Learners: The Illinois Study" was published in 2005. It is followed by a handout summarizing the Illinois study. Both of these documents are available online at http:www.islma.org/resources.htm and are reprinted here for the convenience of the reader.

This study was funded by the Illinois School Library Media Association with additional funding from an FY 04 LSTA Grant from the Illinois State Library, Jesse White, Secretary of State and State Librarian, and a grant from the 21st Century Information Fluency project of the Illinois Mathematics & Science Academy. The study is endorsed by the Illinois State Board of Education.

The Study
- Conducted during the fall of 2003
- Data gathered from 657 Illinois schools, grades kindergarten through twelfth were represented
- Data gathered on hours of operation, staff and their activities, library collection and educational technology, total library expenditures, and several types of library usage
- Statistical analysis compared school library and academic achievement indicators: 5th & 8th grade ISAT reading and writing scores; 11th grade PSAE reading scores; and 11th grade ACT scores
- Test performance was compared for schools that were stronger & weaker on each library variable (median and above vs. below)
- School and community variables were accounted for: household income; per pupil spending; teacher-pupil ratio, students' race/ethnicity
- Study is the 14th of its kind and confirms findings from all the other state studies

Higher Achievement is Associated With:
- More hours of flexible scheduling
- Higher staffing levels
- More weekly hours of librarian staffing
- More staff time spent on selected activities
- Larger & more current collections
- School libraries more accessible via technology
- More money spent on libraries
- Higher usage of middle and high school libraries

The evidence produced by this study indicates that Illinois school libraries contribute measurably to the academic achievement of students as reflected by their test scores. At all grade levels, test scores tend to be higher:
- where access to school libraries is more flexibly scheduled,
- where school libraries are staffed more fully,
- where school librarians spend more time collaborating with classroom teachers,
- where larger collections are available,
- where educational technology is more widely available to augment the local collection and, generally, to extend access to online resources into the classroom,
- where school libraries are better funded, and
- where students use school libraries, both individually and in groups, to learn and practice the information literacy skills they will need to excel on tests and as lifelong learners.

These links between high-quality school library programs and academic achievement cannot be explained away as mere artifacts of community socio-economic factors (i.e., household income, race/ethnicity) or certain key school conditions (per pupil spending, teacher-pupil ratio). Indeed, sometimes taking these contextual variables into account reveals a greater impact by school libraries or librarians that was previously masked by those other variables. *In short, the findings of this study and its predecessors support the belief that powerful libraries - and librarians - do, indeed, make powerful learners.*

Research Finding #1: Schools with better-staffed libraries have more students who succeed on tests.

Research Finding #2: High Schools with computers that connect to library catalogs and databases average 6.2% improvement on ACT scores.

Research Finding #3: Students that visit the library more frequently receive improved reading and writing scores.

Research Finding #4: Students with access to larger, more current book collections achieve higher reading, writing, and ACT scores.

Developed for ISLMA by Jane A. Sharka. © 2005 Illinois School Library Media Association. In addition to this fact sheet, a summary of *Powerful Libraries Make Powerful Learners* research may be found at http://www.islma.org/resources.htm.

The Recommendations

Several recommendations for action relating to Illinois schools are offered on the basis of this study's findings:

- **Access to school libraries should be scheduled as flexibly as possible.** Local conditions sometimes limit the extent to which flexible scheduling can be adopted. Vested interests in existing schedules sometimes make it difficult to make such changes. But, the evidence supports a policy of flexible scheduling to maximize the benefits to students and teachers of school library programs.

- **A high-quality school library, at any grade level, requires at least one librarian plus support staff.** It is through collaboration with classroom teachers that school librarians affect the academic achievement of students. It is when visiting school libraries that students benefit from their usage. For both of these sets of activities to occur, both types of library staff are needed.

- **Computers that provide access to library resources - in the library or elsewhere in the school - should be available to facilitate student performance.** When library and educational technology programs are coordinated, library resources can be available to students and teachers when and where the resources are needed. Computers outside the library, but connected to library resources, extend the reach of the library program beyond its own walls. At the same time, the results of this study suggest that print collections of books and periodicals remain important resources, and that their currency is especially important.

- **School libraries should be funded to maintain their traditional collections as well as expand their reach beyond the library's walls via educational technology.** School libraries must purchase and continue to purchase the information resources required to support instruction in their schools, whether it is available in print or online.

- **Last, but not least, students achieve academically when their visits to libraries bring them into contact with librarians as teachers and co-teachers.** Clearly, visits to libraries impact academic achievement most when libraries are being used as classrooms, study spaces, training facilities, and research

centers. School libraries and librarians should not merely support instruction in their schools; they should be integral to it.

So what?

If you are a teacher...
- Meet with your librarian often to collaborate on how best to work information literacy into your classroom and curriculum.
- Take your students to the library - often - and co-teach with your librarian those critical research skills (information literacy).
- Invite your librarian into your classroom to share new resources and how to use them with your students.
- Tell your librarian about resources that would benefit your students with their homework.

If you are an administrator...
- Ensure librarians are members of technology and curriculum committees in order for Information Literacy to be an integral part of all curriculum decisions.
- Facilitate flexible scheduling in buildings whenever and wherever possible.
- Consider librarians and libraries as ESSENTIAL to academic improvement, not as "frills" that are expendable when finances are tight.
- Make sure your libraries have funding to purchase current resources and technologies - print and non-print. Weed collections regularly and replace resources afterwards.

If you are a parent or community member...
- Volunteer in your school's library. Your assistance can provide extra time for library staff to work with teachers and students.
- Encourage your parent/teacher organization to support the library with extra funds or fundraiser projects.

If you are a Board of Education member...
- Guarantee a significant level of funding for library resources and staffing regardless of school enrollment at all levels.
- Visit your schools' libraries. Ask about the role of the librarian related to information literacy.
- Ask questions about library connections to curriculum developments and projects.
- Support collaboration (financial & personnel) for integration of library resources and programs and technology infrastructures.

Developed for ISLMA by Jane A. Sharka. © 2005 Illinois School Library Media Association. In addition to this fact sheet, a summary of *Powerful Libraries Make Powerful Learners* research may be found at http://www.islma.org/resources.htm.

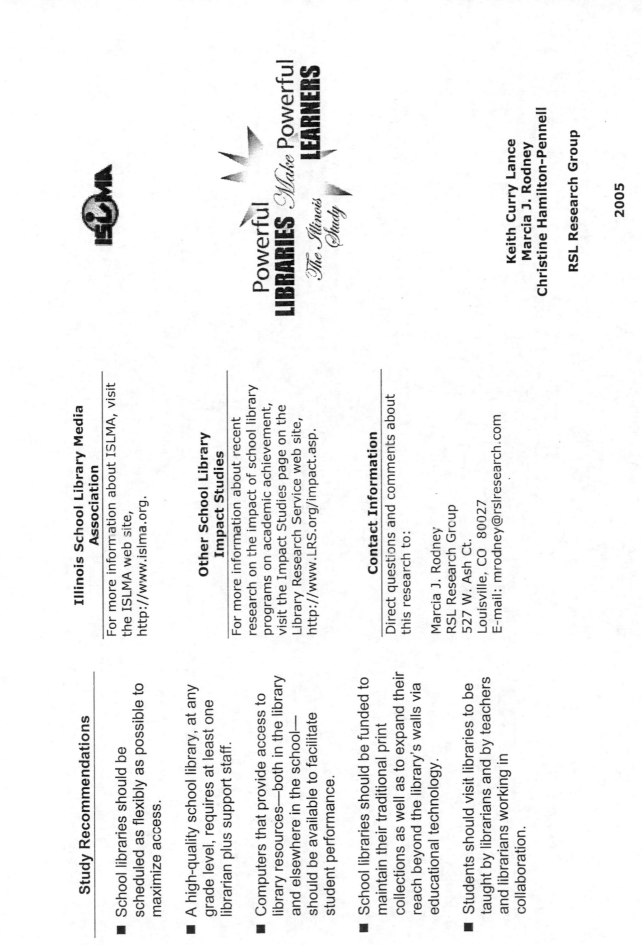

Study Recommendations

- School libraries should be scheduled as flexibly as possible to maximize access.

- A high-quality school library, at any grade level, requires at least one librarian plus support staff.

- Computers that provide access to library resources—both in the library and elsewhere in the school—should be available to facilitate student performance.

- School libraries should be funded to maintain their traditional print collections as well as to expand their reach beyond the library's walls via educational technology.

- Students should visit libraries to be taught by librarians and by teachers and librarians working in collaboration.

Illinois School Library Media Association

For more information about ISLMA, visit the ISLMA web site, http://www.islma.org.

Other School Library Impact Studies

For more information about recent research on the impact of school library programs on academic achievement, visit the Impact Studies page on the Library Research Service web site, http://www.LRS.org/impact.asp.

Contact Information

Direct questions and comments about this research to:

Marcia J. Rodney
RSL Research Group
527 W. Ash Ct.
Louisville, CO 80027
E-mail: mrodney@rslresearch.com

Keith Curry Lance
Marcia J. Rodney
Christine Hamilton-Pennell

RSL Research Group

2005

School Library Usage

Elementary schools with libraries that circulate more books and other items (median = 570 loans per week) average 6% higher reading and 11% higher writing scores.

Middle schools have higher writing scores and high schools, higher ACT scores when their libraries receive more group visits per week, especially for information literacy instruction have higher.

Grade Level	Median weekly group visits (for info literacy)	Average score improvement
Middle	18 (8)	10%
High	16 (10)	9%

These comparisons illustrate the dimensions of school library programs that correlate positively and statistically significantly with student test scores. The overwhelming majority of these relationships persist regardless of the school's per pupil spending, teacher-pupil ratio, or student race/ethnicity. Many of the relationships remain even when household income is taken into account.

> *The Media Center is the hub of all media in the building – video, print, technological, etc. – with one main library and two attached computer labs.* Kyle Schumacher, Principal, Deer Path Middle School East, Lake Forest

> *The IRC is an effective place for students to meet to complete group projects. It is a central location with all of the resources needed.* Penny Swartz, Coordinator, Niles West High School IRC, Skokie

School Library Collections & Educational Technology

Schools with larger library book collections have higher test scores. The test varies by grade level.

Grade Level	Median volumes	Average score improvement
Elementary	9,000	8% (reading)
Middle	8,722	14% (writing)
High	11,554	4% (ACT)

Schools in which library resources are more readily available via school computers have higher test scores. The test varies by grade level.

Grade Level	Library-connected computers per 100 students	Average score improvement
Elementary	11	6% (reading)
Middle	14	8% (writing)
High	23	4% (ACT)

School Library Expenditures

Schools that spend more on their libraries have higher reading and other scores at all grade levels.

Grade Level	Median library spending	Average score improvement Reading	Writing (* ACT)
Elementary	$4,500	5%	10%
Middle	$6,250	9%	13%
High	$10,255	12%	7%

Flexible Scheduling of School Libraries

Schools with libraries more available for flexible scheduling have higher reading and other scores at all grade levels.

Grade Level	Median flexible hours	Reading	Writing (* ACT)
Elementary	16	10%	11%
Middle	30	5%	
High	35	6%	5% *

School Library Staff & Their Activities

Schools with more weekly hours of library staffing have higher reading and other scores at all grade levels.

Grade Level	Median staff hours	Reading	Writing (* ACT)
Elementary	42	13%	17%
Middle	49	8%	18%
High	70	7%	5%*

The more library staff hours, the more likely librarians are identifying materials for teachers, planning and teaching with them, and motivating students to read.

> *We use a flexible delivery model and have found our [library] to be the literacy hub of our building.* Denise Welter, Principal, Landmark School, McHenry

> *This is the best school library I have ever been in, and ... it wouldn't be nearly as good if [the librarian] didn't have a full day here.* 8th grade student, Lombard Middle School, Galesburg

Appendix K

The Texas Study

Summary from *Texas Power!*
The following pages were taken from *Texas Power!* by David V. Loertscher and Keith Curry Lance (Hi Willow Research & Publishing, 2004). It is available from LMC Source at http://www.lmcsource.com.

What Every Parent Should Know About Texas School Librarians

By Keith Curry Lance

What do you as a parent know about the role of the school librarian in your child's education? What should you know?

There are three important facts about school librarians.

- School librarians make a measurable contribution to improving the academic achievement of Texas students.[3]
- School librarians pursue a variety of activities that contribute to improving student performance.[4]
- Texas schools need more school librarians, and those with librarians alone need more library aides.[5]

School librarians make a measurable contribution to improving the academic achievement of students.

If you compare students in schools with and without librarians, the percentage of students meeting or exceeding academic standards is more than 10 percent higher for schools with librarians. For schools with librarians, an average of 89.3 percent of students meets minimum reading standards; for schools without librarians an average of 78.4 percent of students meets those standards. Thus, for example, in a typical classroom of 30 students, three more students would be expected to "pass" the test if the school had a librarian.

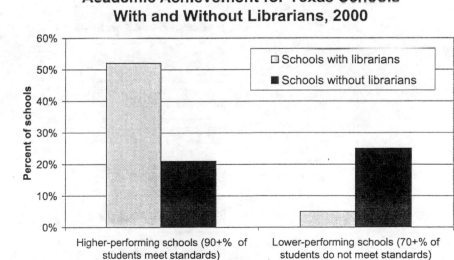

Academic Achievement for Texas Schools With and Without Librarians, 2000

TAAS benchmark

---

[3] This fact is derived from Texas School Libraries: Standards, Resources, Services, and Students' Performance, prepared by Ester G. Smith of EGS Consulting for the Texas State Library and Archives Commission, April 2001. The measure of academic achievement utilized in that 2001 study was the Texas Assessment of Academic Skills (TAAS) reading test. That test has been succeeded by the TAKS test.

[4] This fact is supported in part by the Texas study as well as by similar studies conducted in Alaska, Colorado, Iowa, Michigan, New Mexico, Oregon, and Pennsylvania, among other states.

[5] This fact is documented by the 2001 Texas study. It is also based on the new standards for Texas school libraries that will take effect in 2004.

Notably, however, this difference is suppressed by the fact that TAAS scores were artificially inflated since the test was scored as one of "minimum" competency. A truer picture of the discrepancy is easily drawn by setting specific high benchmarks for the percentage of students meeting minimum TAAS standards. If the bar is set at 90 percent or more of students meeting or exceeding reading standards, 52 percent of schools with librarians, compared with only 21 percent of schools without librarians, "pass." Conversely, if a low bar is set at 70 percent or more of students not meeting reading standards, only five percent of schools with librarians do so poorly, compared with more than a quarter of schools without librarians.

> ## School librarians pursue a variety of activities that contribute to improving student performance.

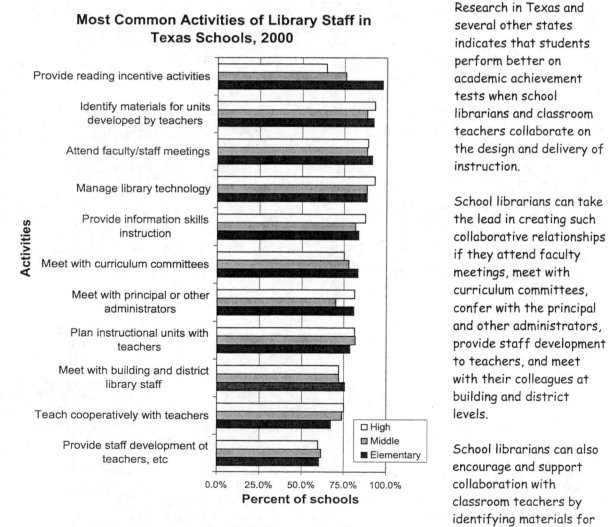

Most Common Activities of Library Staff in Texas Schools, 2000

Research in Texas and several other states indicates that students perform better on academic achievement tests when school librarians and classroom teachers collaborate on the design and delivery of instruction.

School librarians can take the lead in creating such collaborative relationships if they attend faculty meetings, meet with curriculum committees, confer with the principal and other administrators, provide staff development to teachers, and meet with their colleagues at building and district levels.

School librarians can also encourage and support collaboration with classroom teachers by identifying materials for teacher-designed units, managing library technology, and providing reading incentive programs for students.

Texas schools need more school librarians, and those with librarians alone need more library aides.

Percent of Texas School Libraries With Only One Staff Member, 2000

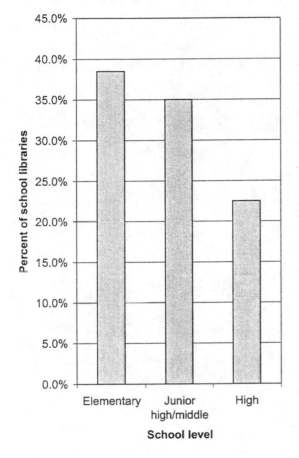

New state standards for school libraries require that every school library have at least one full-time librarian and at least one half-time library aide to be recognized as "acceptable." Exemplary" school libraries are required to have 1.5 librarians and 1.5 library aides.

Based on these requirements, most libraries in Texas schools with more than 500 students are understaffed.

Under state standards, staffing requirements increase with school enrollment.

New Campus-Level Library Staffing Standards

Enrollment	Exemplary	Acceptable
0-500	1.5 librarians 1.5 aides	1 librarian 0.5 aide
501-1,000	2 librarians 2 aides	1 librarian 1 aide
1,001-2,000	3 librarians 3 aides	1 librarian 1.5 aides
2,001+	3 librarians 3 aides (plus 1 more of each per 700 students)	2 librarians 2 aides

In 2000, 38.5 percent of elementary schools, 35 percent of middle/junior high schools, and 22.5 percent of high schools had libraries with only one staff member.

In 2004, as new standards for school libraries take effect in Texas, it is likely that many fewer schools will be judged as "acceptable" or "below standard"rather than "exemplary" in library staffing.

If your school does not have a library staffed at the levels prescribed above, contact your superintendent, your principal, and your child's teachers. Ask them to provide the additional staffing needed to make your child's school library an "exemplary" one, knowing that this is one of the demonstrated ways in which the quality of your child's education can be improved.

Appendix L

The Florida Study

Making the Grade

The summary and complete report of the Florida study can be found in *Making the Grade: The Status of School Library Media Centers in the Sunshine State and How They Contribute to Student Achievement* by Donna J. Baumbach (Hi Willow Research & Publishing, 2003). Available from LMC Source at http://www.lmcsource.com.

Summary from *Florida Power!*

The following pages are from *Florida Power!* by David V. Loertscher and Donna Baumbach (Hi Willow Research & Publishing, 2004). It is available from LMC Source at http://www.lmcsource.com.

What Every Parent Should Know About Florida School Library Media Programs

A recent study[1] showed that school library media programs are active, vital contributors to teaching and learning in Florida's K-12 schools. Findings from this and numerous other studies on the impact of school library media centers are consistent. School library media programs positively impact student achievement when:

> A professionally trained, full-time certified library media specialist leads the program
> Adequate support staff is present
> School library media collections are strong in quantity, in quality and in variety
> Students have access to resources beyond the library media center
> Literacy, information literacy and technological literacy are taught
> Students use the library media center and its resources
> Technology is available

At the **elementary level**, FCAT scores[2] are higher where:	At the **middle school** level, FCAT scores are higher where:	At the **high school** level, FCAT scores are higher where:
• There is a certified library media specialist • There are more paid staff • Circulation is higher • There are more books and videos • There are more computers in the library media center and more Internet access • There are more non-print materials	• There are more certified library media specialists • The media center is open more hours each week • There are more videos in the collection • There are more electronic reference materials • There are more computers in the library media center and more Internet access	• The library media center is staffed more hours each week • There are more certified library media specialists • There are more paid library staff members • There are more interlibrary loans • There is more usage of technology in the library media center • There are more computers and more Internet access

FCAT and ACT scores are significantly higher where there is higher usage of the library media center. Usage increases with:

> The number of certified, university trained library media specialists
> The total number of staff hours per student
> The number of networked computers per student
> The number of books, periodical subscriptions, videos and software packages per student
> Library media expenditures per student

[1] *Making the Grade: The Status of School Library Media Centers in the Sunshine State and How They Contribute to Student Achievement* by Donna Baumbach, University of Central Florida. Summary available online at http://www.sunlink.ucf.edu/makingthegrade.
[2] Florida Comprehensive Assessment Test (FCAT) reading scores; from data *in Making the Grade*

What Every Parent Should Know About Florida School Library Media Specialists

What do you as a parent know about the role of the school library media specialist and library media program in your child's education? What should you know?

Here are three important facts about Florida's school library media specialists:

1. School library media specialists make a measurable contribution to improving the academic achievement of Florida students.[1]
2. Certified school library media specialists, experienced teachers with additional hours of specialization and advanced degrees, pursue a variety of activities that contribute to improving student performance.[2]
3. Florida schools need more university-trained, certified school library media specialists, and those with school library media specialists need additional library clerks and volunteers.[3]

If you compare students in higher scoring schools where there is at least one certified school library media specialist and additional staffing totaling more than 80 hours per week with similar schools whose staffing is less than 80 hours per week, the percentage of students meeting or exceeding academic standards is higher at all grade levels where there is more staffing. [4]

However, not all Florida school have a certified library media specialist! Only 80% of Florida's public elementary schools and less than 80% of combination schools (K-12, 6-12, etc.) have a certified school library media specialist.   Library media specialists are critical to elementary students! At a time when students are learning to read, to locate information to meet their school and personal needs, and to use technology and information systems, schools who think they cannot afford a certified library media specialist really cannot afford to be without them if they are preparing students for middle school, high school and beyond!

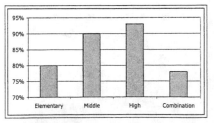

Percentage of Florida Public Schools with at Least One Certified Library Media Specialist

Over 25% of all Florida school library media specialists and 40% of high school library media specialists will be retiring in the next several years, so more of our schools may be without trained school library media specialists. How can this happen when there is more information, more technology and more emphasis on learning and student achievement? Don't let it happen in your school.

---

[1] This fact is derived from *Making the Grade: The Status of School Library Media Centers in the Sunshine State and How They Contribute to Student Achievement*, by Donna J. Baumbach, University of Central Florida. The measure of academic achievement utilized in this 2003 study was the reading portion of the Florida Comprehensive Assessment Test (FCAT).
[2] Florida Department of Education Certification Requirements for Educational Media
[3] This fact is documented by the 2003 Florida study *(Making the Grade.)*
[4] Baumbach, D. *Making the Grade: : The Status of School Library Media Centers in the Sunshine State*

Appendix M

The Ohio Study
Fact Sheet

The following Ohio fact sheet entitled "Student Learning Through Ohio School Libraries" was published in 2003. This document is available on the web at http://www.oelma.org/studentlearning.htm and is reprinted here for the convenience of the reader.

Student Learning Through Ohio School Libraries

The Ohio Research Study Fact Sheet
December 15, 2003
http://www.oelma.org/studentlearning.htm

The research study, *Student Learning through Ohio School Libraries*, was funded by the State Library of Ohio through a Library Services and Technology Act (LSTA) grant from the federal Institute of Museum and Library Services (IMLS) to the Ohio Educational Library Media Association (OELMA), and was coordinated through Leadership for School Libraries (L4SL), a coalition of OELMA, INFOhio (the state K-12 network), the Ohio Department of Education and The State Library of Ohio. The research was undertaken by Dr. Ross J. Todd and Dr. Carol C. Kuhlthau of Rutgers University and the Center for International Scholarship in School Libraries (CISSL). The study sought to understand **how students benefit from school libraries** through elaborating "conceptions of help" and providing some measure of the extent of these "helps," as perceived by students and faculty.

The Study
- Conducted from October, 2002 through December, 2003
- Looked at 39 effective school libraries across Ohio
- Collected information through two web-based surveys with 48 questions & one open-ended critical incident
- Surveyed 13,123 students in Grades 3 to 12 and 879 faculty
- Largest study to date of how the school library helps students learn

When effective school libraries are in place, students do learn. 13,000 students cannot be wrong.

The Results
99.44% of the sample (13,050 students) indicated that the school library and its services, including roles of school librarians, have helped them in some way, regardless of how much, with their learning.

Collectively, the data show that effective school libraries in Ohio are dynamic rather than passive agents of learning. The findings indicate that the effective school library helps the strongest as a *resource agent* and a *technical agent*, providing access to information resources necessary for students to complete their research assignments and projects successfully. However, the qualitative responses show that the school library's strength is not just as a passive information supply and exchange agency. Clearly helpful is the library's part in engaging students in an active process of building their own understanding and knowledge – the library as an *agent for individualized learning, knowledge construction and academic achievement.*

Correspondingly, the instructional intervention by the school librarian goes beyond teaching students how to use technology tools to access and evaluate information, but also provides instruction in how to use these tools effectively and reflectively to create products.

The study shows that an effective school library, lead by a credentialed school librarian who has a clearly defined role in information-centered pedagogy, plays a critical role in facilitating student learning for building knowledge. This instructional intervention role, centering on the development of information literacy, affords Ohio students significant opportunities to learn and to succeed with their research. What this conveys is the notion of an effective school library in Ohio as not just an *information place*, but also as a *knowledge space* where students develop the appropriate information literacy scaffolds to enable them to engage with information and build new knowledge. An effective school library is not just *informational*, but *formational*.

The Implications and Recommendations
The successes of the school libraries in this study show what can be focused on and improved in any school, and they provide useful benchmarks for measuring improvement. The study identifies some essential *informational, transformational* and *formational* building blocks for effective school libraries in Ohio's schools to play a leading role as *dynamic agents of learning*. Key building blocks are:

- Resources
- Technological infrastructure
- Reading resources
- Information literacy
- Technological literacies
- Reading engagement

As a result of the Ohio research study, it is recommended that:

- *all school library programs provide instructional intervention, through a credentialed school librarian, which centers on the development of information literacy skills for inquiry learning*
- *all school libraries, including elementary schools, be staffed with credentialed school librarians who have educational certification and who engage in collaborative instructional initiatives to help students learn and achieve*
- *all school librarians have a clearly defined role as information-learning specialist, with expertise*
  - as an instructional designer who creates and delivers information literacy instruction at class, group and individual levels;
  - as an educational partner-leader who mutually collaborates, negotiates, and plans with school administrators, teachers, students and parents to implement information literacy instruction in the curriculum;
  - as a school library program administrator who mutually negotiates, plans and implements a whole-school library program which articulates the integration of information, transformations and formation, as well as the managerial and organizational dimensions of the role; and
  - as a partner-leader in the provision of learning-oriented professional development targeted to whole-school success of learning goals.
- *all school libraries provide a learning-centered space supported by a strong technology infrastructure*
- *all stakeholders engage in sustained and action-oriented discussions in the context of continuous improvement of the necessary resources, technology and staffing requirements needed to maximize the learning opportunities through school libraries.*

In Ohio, the provision of opportunities to learn through effective school libraries is critical to ensure that no student is left behind.

The essential foundations for an effective school library in Ohio's schools are identified in the model below. All Ohio schools are encouraged to strive for excellence through continuous improvement of school libraries. These building blocks for excellence are not to be perceived as independent blocks; rather, as elements that work together in integrated and iterative ways to bring about student achievement.

The Ohio School Library as a Dynamic Agent of Learning
ESSENTIAL LEARNING FOUNDATIONS

INFORMATIONAL The Resource Base	TRANSFORMATIONAL Learning-Teaching Intervention
Resources: Current, multi-perspective, multi-format resources with readability levels aligned with the local curriculum, and supporting Ohio's academic content standards. **Technological infrastructure:** State-of-art technology to acquire, organize, produce, and disseminate information, and function as a gateway to information. **Reading resources:** Reading materials targeted beyond informational curriculum needs – personal pursuits, pleasure/leisure reading.	**Information literacy:** Development of information literacy for engagement with information in all its forms in the context of curriculum needs, content strands and subject knowledge creation processes for effective engagement and utilization of information. **Technological literacies:** Development of media and technological skills, which include critical thinking skills and communication competencies; as well as the appropriate and ethical use of technology for information access, retrieval, production, and dissemination via electronic resources, networks, and the Internet. **Reading engagement:** Development of approaches to promote and encourage reading for academic achievement and life-long learning through participation in national and state reading celebrations and initiatives; reading to students, promoting literature, reinforcing reading skills, and encouraging independent reading for personal enjoyment; engaging in a range of activities to foster sustained love of reading.

FORMATIONAL
Student Expectations and Achievement

Knowledge creation: Students achieve through being able to define problems, frame questions, explore ideas, formulate focus, investigate, analyze and synthesize ideas to create own views, evaluate solutions and reflect on new understandings.

Knowledge use: Students develop transferable skills for sustaining knowledge creation beyond the classroom.

Knowledge production: Students can use technology and information tools to produce new knowledge and demonstrate achievement. They create information products that accurately represent their newly developed understanding.

Knowledge dissemination: Students can communicate ideas using oral, written, visual and technological modes of expression – individually or in teams.

Knowledge values: Students are ethical, responsible users of information who accept responsibility for personal decisions and information actions. They demonstrate concern for quality information and value different modes of thought.

Reading literacy: Students have high levels of reading literacy. They become independent, life-long sustained readers.

© 2004 Ross J. Todd, Carol C. Kuhlthau and OELMA. In addition to this fact sheet, a summary of the *Student Learning through Ohio School Libraries* research may be found at **http://www.oelma.org/ studentlearning.htm**. Dissemination supported by the Institute for Library and Information Literacy Education (www.illie.org) through the Institute for Museum and Library Services (IMLS).

Appendix N

The Minnesota Study

Executive Summary

The following Minnesota Summary brief entitled "Check It Out!: The Results of the School Library Media Program Census" was published in 2003. This document is available online at http://metronet.lib.mn.us/survey/index.cfm and is reprinted here for the convenience of the reader.

Summary from *Minnesota Power!*

The next pages are taken from *Minnesota Power!* by Anne Hanson, Doug Johnson, and David V. Loertscher (Hi Willow Research & Publishing, 2004). It is available from LMC Source at http://www.lmcsource.com.

Check It Out!

The Results of the School Library Media Program Census

Executive Summary

January 2003

Minnesota School Library Media Programs

Metronet • 1619 Dayton Ave. • St. Paul MN 55104 • 651-646-0475

How Do You Check Out a School Library Media Center?

Learning Opportunities

✓ Do most of the teachers and classes use the library media center's resources?

✓ Do students have access to the library media center and library media specialist throughout the school day?

✓ Do teachers and the library media specialist collaborate to coordinate what is taught in the media center and classroom?

✓ Do teachers encourage student use of the media center's resources?

✓ Do students' research projects use a variety of technologies to locate and use information?

Information and Reading Resources

✓ Does the media center have a current (less than 10 years old) and varied collection? (10-15 items per student or 5000 volumes, whichever is greater.)

✓ Does the media center have a wide variety of new books and other print materials that encourage and support reading and learning?

✓ Is the library media center energetic and inviting? Does it include:
  • A reference area?
  • A storytelling/book talk area?
  • An instructional area?
  • Displays and collections of student work?

✓ Does the media center have multiple, up-to-date technologies that provide guided access to:
  • The Internet?
  • An automated card catalog?
  • Multimedia production capabilities?
  • On-line and multimedia resources?

Availability, Programs, Policies

✓ Is the media center available before and after school?

✓ Is the media center large enough for individuals and classes to use at the same time?

✓ Is there a professional library media specialist who:
  • Teaches the information process?
  • Understands the uses of technology?
  • Selects and uses a wide variety of materials?

✓ Is the media program funded to maintain a level of materials and personnel that make a difference in student achievement?

You can learn more about media centers using the data from schools that responded to the census. Data is available by individual school and district at http:/www.metronet.lib.mn.us/survey/index.cfm.

A more detailed checklist is available at MEMO Library/Media Center Report Card www.memoweb.org.

A quality school library is kid friendly and kid centered.

Check It Out! The Census Results

Fifty years of research has shown the power of school library media programs on student learning. What did the Census show about Minnesota's programs?

This study began with the premise that a well-funded, well-staffed school library media center can have a positive impact on student achievement regardless of the economic and social factors in the school and community. The more assets a school's library media program has—current collection of books and other materials, licensed media specialist, support staff, computers, Internet access, licensed databases, knowledgeable principal, and collaborative teachers—the more likely its students will score higher on standardized tests.

Metronet used a combination of an online census to collect statistical information and site visits to determine if Minnesota's school library media programs have the resources needed to impact achievement.

So, how do Minnesota school library media programs check out? Many strong, effective media programs operate in all parts of the state. A few are truly outstanding; many are excellent. However, an even greater number do not meet even the minimum *Minnesota Standards for Effective School Library Media Programs* in the key areas—staffing, teaching, collection, and funding. These key findings tell the story.

Library Media Specialists Make a Difference

- Schools with above average reading scores have school library media specialists (LMS) that work more hours. In the 633 Minnesota schools with above average reading scores on the Minnesota Comprehensive Assessment and Basic Standards Test, 423 (66.8%) had a media specialist who worked 36 hours a week or more.

- School media centers are open an average of 28.4 hours per week—the range of hours open is 1 and 43. The smaller the school, the fewer hours a media specialist is available for students.

Lots of Old Books

- Minnesota students are using books that are older than they are—and in some cases, older than their teachers. The average copyright date of materials at all grade levels is 1985. An *average* date of 1985 means there are a lot of old books in media centers.

- Average per pupil spending for books in elementary schools is $9.35, about 50% of the average cost of one book.

- There is a statistically significant relationship between higher reading scores and larger school media center budgets at the elementary level.

Commitment and Investment Make the Difference.

- Geography and size of the district do not have an impact on the quality of the program. Districts of all sizes that have made their media programs a priority have effective programs.

- The skill and training of the media specialist, level of professional and support staff, size of the collection and budget, the support of the principal, and the size of the school determine the effectiveness of the program.

The leaders of tomorrow will be those who know where to find information, how to evaluate it, and how to use it. School library media programs help create tomorrow's leaders, but the programs need professional staff and resources to make a difference for Minnesota students.

Check It Out!
Do Our School Library Media Programs Pass the Test?

You can find the Minnesota answers and much more in the Final Report on the results of the school library media program census at www.metronet.lib.mn.us.

1. What is the average copyright date of books in Minnesota school library media centers?

   A. 1999
   B. 1952
   C. 1985
   D. 1992
   E. 1970

Hint—Ronald Reagan was President

Many books in the media center are older than this year's senior class!

2. If you were using a history book with a copyright date of 1985, which of the following events would you find in that book?

   A. Mikhail Gorbachev becomes Premier of the Soviet Union.
   B. Space shuttle Challenger explodes.
   C. Bombing of federal building in Oklahoma City
   D. Fall of the Berlin Wall.
   E. Collapse of the Soviet Union; Baltic States gain independence.
   F. South Africa votes to end rule by white minority.
   H. None of the above

Most kids today didn't even watch these on TV. Where will they read about these events?

3. If your assignment is to research a prominent American, which of the following books are you likely to find on the shelves of your school library?

   A. *Iacocca: An Autobiography*, Lee Iacocca 1985
   B. *Me: Stories of My Life*, Katharine Hepburn 1991
   C. *An American Life: An Autobiography*, Ronald Reagan 1990
   D. *It Doesn't Take a Hero: The Autobiography*, Gen. H. Norman Schwarzkopf 1992
   E. *White House Years*, Henry Kissinger 1979
   F. *Personal History*, Katharine Graham 1997

Remember—the average copyright is 1985! (1983 for high schools)

What about the Internet? If you "Google" Lee Iacocca, you get 25,000 hits. Ronald Reagan— 45,000. How do you know the best ones? Ask the media specialist!

4. How many books per pupil does the average elementary school media center have?

Lots of books, but they're old! →

A. 16
B. 6
C. 36 *(circled)*
D. 44

Extra Credit:
In Middle Schools – _29_
In High Schools – _27_

5. How much does the average media center spend annually on books per pupil? Circle the right answer.

	High	Middle	Elementary
A	$9.35	$7.35	$4.50
B	$10.50	$8.50	$7.00
C	$11.29 *(circled)*	$10.44 *(circled)*	$9.35 *(circled)*
D	$21.10	$25.00	$18.75

See the connection here?

Elementary school media centers spend less than the cost of one book per pupil per year!

6. What was the average price of a book in 1985 and 2001:

	1985	2001
Children's Book	$11.61	$16.55
Young Adult Book	$14.56	$19.15

7. Which of the following make a difference in how effective a school library media program is for student learning?

A. A licensed media specialist in charge of the program.

B. A supportive and knowledgeable principal.

C. Teachers who understand and use the media program to enhance student learning.

D. Up-to-date technology and access to fee-based information sources and the Internet.

E. A district level media coordinator.

F. All of the above. *(circled)*

How is your media center doing—does it have all of these things?

"We need professional media specialists to teach students how to use resources. High School Principal

Check It Out!
How Do Our School Library Media Programs Stack Up

These elements make a difference in student learning and achievement! The more of these things in a school, the better students do.

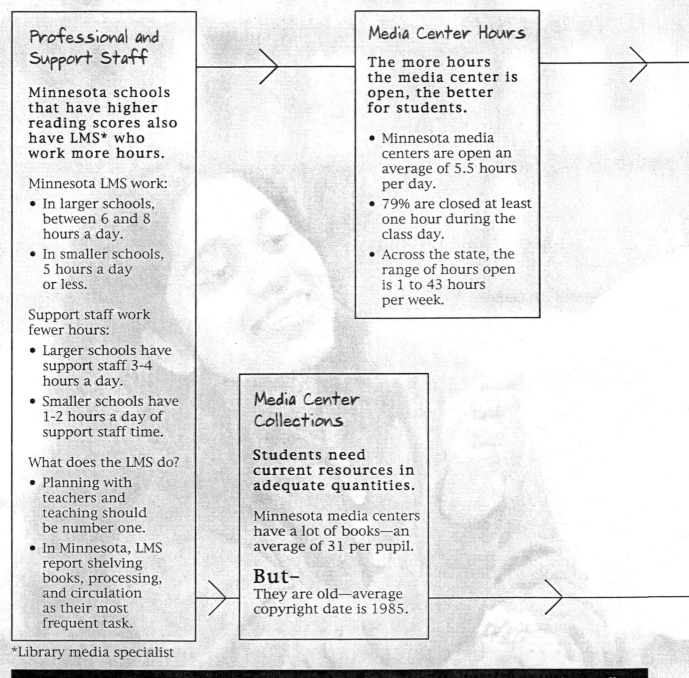

Professional and Support Staff

Minnesota schools that have higher reading scores also have LMS* who work more hours.

Minnesota LMS work:
- In larger schools, between 6 and 8 hours a day.
- In smaller schools, 5 hours a day or less.

Support staff work fewer hours:
- Larger schools have support staff 3-4 hours a day.
- Smaller schools have 1-2 hours a day of support staff time.

What does the LMS do?
- Planning with teachers and teaching should be number one.
- In Minnesota, LMS report shelving books, processing, and circulation as their most frequent task.

Media Center Hours

The more hours the media center is open, the better for students.

- Minnesota media centers are open an average of 5.5 hours per day.
- 79% are closed at least one hour during the class day.
- Across the state, the range of hours open is 1 to 43 hours per week.

Media Center Collections

Students need current resources in adequate quantities.

Minnesota media centers have a lot of books—an average of 31 per pupil.

But–
They are old—average copyright date is 1985.

*Library media specialist

> ## "We know what to do; we need the resources to do it."
> ### Elementary School Principal

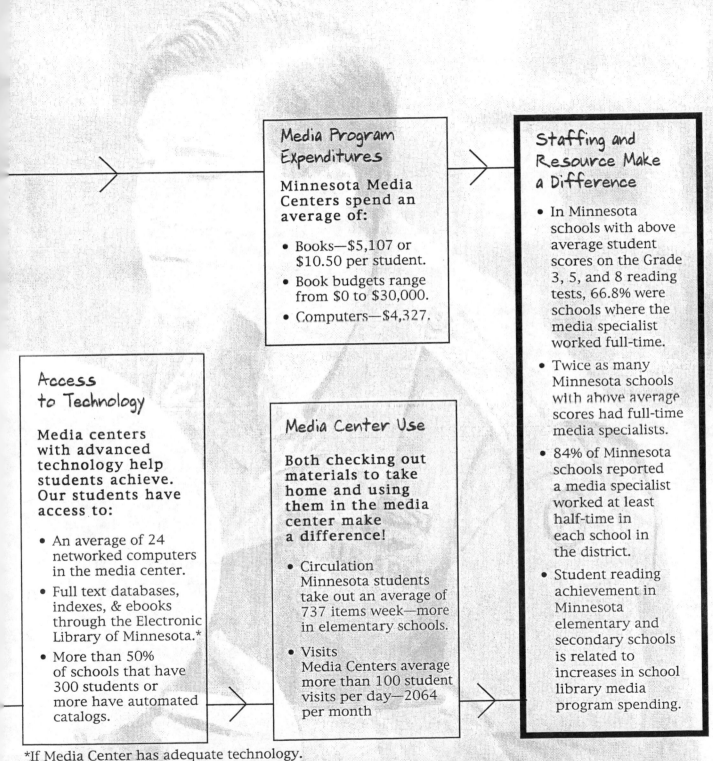

Media Program Expenditures

Minnesota Media Centers spend an average of:

- Books—$5,107 or $10.50 per student.
- Book budgets range from $0 to $30,000.
- Computers—$4,327.

Staffing and Resource Make a Difference

- In Minnesota schools with above average student scores on the Grade 3, 5, and 8 reading tests, 66.8% were schools where the media specialist worked full-time.

- Twice as many Minnesota schools with above average scores had full-time media specialists.

- 84% of Minnesota schools reported a media specialist worked at least half-time in each school in the district.

- Student reading achievement in Minnesota elementary and secondary schools is related to increases in school library media program spending.

Access to Technology

Media centers with advanced technology help students achieve. Our students have access to:

- An average of 24 networked computers in the media center.
- Full text databases, indexes, & ebooks through the Electronic Library of Minnesota.*
- More than 50% of schools that have 300 students or more have automated catalogs.

Media Center Use

Both checking out materials to take home and using them in the media center make a difference!

- Circulation
  Minnesota students take out an average of 737 items week—more in elementary schools.

- Visits
  Media Centers average more than 100 student visits per day—2064 per month

*If Media Center has adequate technology.

"It is a hopeful sign that some districts have made a commitment to media programs." Site Visitor

Checking It Out! Best Practices

These programs demonstrate good school library media program practices.

1. Northern Lights Library Network

Lincoln High School, Thief River Falls ISD 564

"This was a busy, busy media center, attractive and inviting, with self-help directions available, but a professional never too busy to help when asked."

- Program is an essential and integral part of the standards and curriculum.

- Team effort, involving the media specialist, paraprofessional, independent study students, and student library assistants.

- Relationship with the teaching staff is pleasant and productive.

- Students use the center independently as well as under the direction of the teacher.

- Principal and LMS think they are exemplary in all Standards areas except for the book budget.

2. Metronet

Valley View Elementary School, Bloomington ISD 271

"This energetic media program emphasizes books and literature."

- One full-time media person, one educational aide, and one tech support person.

- Principal believes that media people should have autonomy to run their program.

- Up-to-date book collection and technology; both integrated into classroom activities.

- Media specialist works collaboratively with classroom teachers.

3. Southcentral Minnesota Inter-Library Exchange

West High School, Mankato ISD 7

"One of our best visits. The principal, media specialist, and media secretary all showed pride in their jobs and media center accomplishments."

- Full-time media secretary plus a full-time district media technician and media coordinator.

- Media specialist is extremely responsive to teachers. Kids like him too.

- Book budget has been substantial and continues.

- LMS (library media specialist) has great support from and rapport with teaching staff and administration.

- Both principal and media specialist feel the media program is exemplary in some Standards and minimum in very few.

4. Southwest Area Multicounty Multitype Interlibrary Exchange

Pipestone Junior/Senior High, Pipestone-Jasper School ISD 2689

"Principal commented that if you don't have the staff, you don't have a program!"

- Unique program that is a combined public/school library facility. Many years of cooperation make it work smoothly.

- Good relationship between media specialist and administration results in financial and program support.

- Well-stocked, well-used facility.

- Positive atmosphere resulting in active use of the media center.

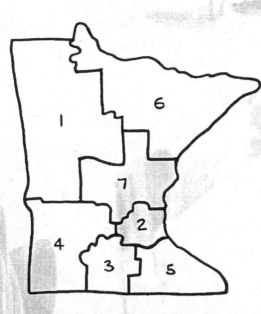

6. North Country Library Cooperative
Ely Junior/Senior High School, Ely ISD 696

"This library media program is a splendid example of what can be accomplished when the staff and administration have a vision, work cooperatively to make a plan, and implement the plan."

- Well-planned, bright and cheerful facility designed to be easily monitored by the staff.

- Program integrated into the school curriculum beginning in the elementary grades continuing through high school.

- Demands of the high school library limits time LMS has for elementary library.

- Cooperation between the local public library and the school library on the Accelerated Reader Program.

- Principal and media specialist developed a six-year plan to improve and update the media centers, now in year six of the plan.

5. Southeast Library System
Kenyon-Wanamingo Elementary School, Kenyon-Wanamingo ISD 2172

"The obvious strength of this program is the staff who have the full support and hearty appreciation of the principal."

- Media center is bright and colorful with space for quiet reading.

- Adequate selection of print materials and the largest non-print collection we saw.

- Doing well this year, but cutting staff for next school year. Principal and media specialist both concerned about loss of service.

- Principal would like to see improvement in technology. Budget cuts will slow this improvement.

- Media center is open one evening and one morning a week for six weeks during the summer for a reading program.

7. Central Minnesota Library Exchange
Milaca Secondary School (Grades 7-12), Milaca ISD 912

"This visit proved to me that an ideal secondary media center program can exist. The media specialist is a great example of how providing information gets support!"

- Library media specialist is a respected and strong advocate for her program.

- LMS works with teachers to plan and provide learning experiences for students that involve research skills, problem solving, and communication.

- Keeps the administration informed of the achievements and the needs of the media program and its impact on student learning.

- LMS work with administration resulted in $40,000 for the collection. Unfortunately, it was reduced because of budget cuts, but the work of the media specialist did make a difference.

"These comments from the site visitors show vibrant and effective school library media programs in all regions."

Check It Out! Recommendations

Information *is* power in this new century. More that ever, students need to learn information literacy and research skills for their academic work and to become productive adults in the future. School library media specialists can lead the way in teaching these skills to our students, but they need the resources to maintain effective programs.

Minnesota school library media programs are showing signs of long-term neglect in many districts. It will take a commitment at state and local levels to build media center collections, hire qualified staff, and provide the budget to support the programs.

More information on these recommendations and the Census results can be found in *Checking It Out: The Results of the Minnesota School Library Media Program Census Final Report.*

Recommendations

1. Principals, teachers, parents, and other administrators need to raise their expectations for media programs and the results they expect from these programs based on the research on the impact of school library media programs on student achievement and *Standards for Effective School Library Media Programs 2000*.

2. All school districts need to make a commitment to a full-time professional media specialist and adequate para-professional staffing in every school building to ensure all students learn information literacy and research skills—and develop a love of reading.

3. Minnesota needs to make immediate state and local investments in school library media program print collections so they meet the Standard of current—books less than 10 years old. This is a long-term commitment to resource building.

4. The Legislature and the Department of Children, Families, & Learning (CFL) need to recognize the importance of school library media programs in improving student achievement. Staff is needed at the state level to help districts develop strong media programs based on the *Standards for Effective School Library Media Programs 2000*.

5. The Legislature, CFL, and local districts must commit to maintaining and developing statewide resources and services to provide student access to what they need to succeed. This includes continued state support of telecommunications costs and maintenance and development of resources that expand access and availability statewide.

6. All stakeholders must work to eliminate the digital divide in Minnesota public schools. All students need access to up-to-date technology and training in how to use it.

7. The Department of Children, Families, & Learning should continue data collection on school library media programs to provide on-going measurement of program development.

8. Library media specialists and their supporters must become vocal advocates for all school library media programs. They must document and disseminate information on the impact of media programs on student achievement.

"I think it is possible to tell what kind of school it is by what the media center is like. I want an active library where students are encouraged to use many different kinds of resources. This cannot be achieved without professional staff to provide help and supervision, an adequate budget to buy books and other resources, and support staff so the media specialist has time to plan and work with teachers. Every student deserves this kind of media center."

Junior/Senior High School Principal
Southwest Minnesota

Metronet
1619 Dayton Avenue • Saint Paul, Minnesota 55104
651.646.0475
www.metronet.lib.mn.us

This Metronet project was funded by the Institute of Museum and Library Services under the provisions of the Library Services and Technology Act (LSTA), administered as a grant by the state library agency, Library Development and Services, the Department of Children, Families, & Learning.

This document and the full report are available in PDF format at
http://metronet.lib.mn.us/survey/index.cfm

What Every Parent Should Know About Minnesota School Libraries

In 2003, Metronet published a study of Minnesota school libraries titled *Check It Out!: The results of the School Library Media Program Census.*. Here is a reprint of their executive summary:[6]

Key Findings

In Minnesota schools with above average student scores on the Grade 3, 5, and 8 reading tests, 66.8% were schools where the media specialist worked full-time. Twice as many schools with above average scores had full-time media specialists. Student reading achievement in elementary and secondary schools is related to increases in school library media program spending.

• Correlation analysis shows that elementary students' MCA (Minnesota Comprehensive Assessment) scores are significantly related to library budgets for books and materials, particularly at the fifth grade level. The larger the library budget is for books and electronic materials, the higher students' reading achievement is.

• The average copyright for all books in Minnesota schools is 1985. In high schools, the average age is 1983. Minnesota students are using books for research and study that are older than they are, and in some cases, older than their teachers.

Highlights

Census Findings

• Minnesota lags behind in spending for books for its school library media programs. Average annual spending for books in Minnesota school library media centers is $5,107. In the North Central region of the U.S., which includes Minnesota, the average amount spent on books annually is $6,700, over 30% higher than Minnesota's spending. Minnesota school library media centers spend an average of $9.35 per pupil for books at the elementary level, $10.44 at the middle school level, and $11.29 at the high school level.

• Minnesota school library media centers own an average of 31 books per pupil. This exceeds the highest level in the *Minnesota Standards for Effective School Library Media Programs 2002* for collection size. The average copyright date of 1985, however, suggests that many of these collections are old due to lack of weeding.

• Media specialists are the most common workers in school library media programs. 84% of the responding schools report one licensed media specialist works in the media

---

[6] Baxter, Susan J. and Ann Walker Smalley. *Check It Out! Results of the School Library Media Program Census.* St. Paul MN: Memonet, 2003. The entire report and an executive summary document can be printed out in pdf format at http://metronet.lib.mn.us/survey/index.cfm An update will be available late 2004. Reproduced here by permission.

center; 5% report two media specialists work in the media center.

· Support staff works an average of 18.6 hours per week in a media center. The smaller the school, the less likely support staff is available.

· Hours worked for licensed and clerical staff increased with the school size in almost all cases. The smaller the school, the fewer hours a media specialist has to spend with students.

· Media specialists report their most frequent activity is "other library activities" such as shelving books, circulation of materials, materials processing, and related tasks. These tasks are considered to be support tasks and do not require a licensed media specialist to perform them.

· In descending order of reported frequency, media specialists spend time on: managing and troubleshooting computer and technical problems, teaching information skills to students, collection development, and assisting students with Internet skills. 68% of library media specialists report their most frequent activity is "collaborating with teachers."

· The average elementary library media specialist provides 58 prep coverage periods per month. Prep coverage is less common at the high school level, where the average number of prep coverage periods is five.

· School library media centers have an average of more than of 100 visits by students per day, more than 2,064 visits per month. 737 items are checked out per average week. This does not reflect the materials that are used within the library media center.

· School size affects the number of networked computers in the media center, the presence of an automated library catalog, and access to statewide electronic resources from home. The smaller the school, the less likely there will be an automated cataloged or remote access to media center and statewide electronic resources.

· 1,172 schools responded to the online School Library Media Program Project Census, an unprecedented 82% response rate. In 217 districts every school responded. 74 districts had at least some schools respond. In 45 districts, no school responded.

Site Visit Findings

· 131 elementary and secondary schools were visited as part of the project to determine the impact of less quantifiable elements such as the role of the principal and of the atmosphere of the media center on program effectiveness.

· The site visits confirmed the census findings: large collections of old, worn books, many programs run by part-time library media specialists or non-licensed staff, increasing workloads for media specialists including technology support, classroom teaching, and other duties, and the widespread responsibility of elementary media specialists for prep time coverage for teachers.

· The more knowledgeable and supportive a principal is about school library media program, the greater the chance that an effective school library media program will be in place in the school.

· The more hours a licensed school library media specialist works in the media program, the more effective the program.

• Many school library media specialists have too few resources to maintain an effective school library media program. Site visitors found effective programs in all areas of the state.

• There is a digital divide in Minnesota schools, both across districts and within districts. Access to up-to-date technology varied widely.

• Schools with technology integration specialists and/or professional media specialists involved in planning with teachers on using technology to enhance curriculum make better use of their technology investment to improve student learning. In these schools, curriculum drives the technology investment.

• The presence of district level support for school library media programs makes a difference in the effectiveness of school library media programs. In districts with media coordinators or similar positions, students were more likely to have access to resources and materials and to be taught information literacy skills.

• Implementation of computerized reading programs such as Accelerated Reader and Reading Counts are having an impact on media center budgets and usage.

Recommendations

• Principals, teachers, parents, school boards, and other administrators need to raise their expectations for media programs and the results they expect from these programs based on the research on the impact of school library media programs on student achievement and *Minnesota Standards for Effective School Library Media Programs 2000*.

• All school districts need to make a commitment to a full-time professional media specialist and adequate paraprofessional staffing in every school building to ensure all students learn information literacy and research skills—and develop a love of reading.

• Minnesota needs to make immediate state and local investments in school library media program print collections so they meet the Standard of current—books less than 10 years old. This will require a long-term commitment to resource building.

• The Legislature and Department of Children, Families & Learning (CFL) need to recognize the importance of school library media programs in improving student achievement by hiring staff at the state level to assist school districts develop effective library media programs based on *Minnesota Standards for Effective School Library Media Programs 2000*.

• The Legislature, CFL, and local districts must commit to maintaining and developing statewide resources and services to provide student access to what they need to succeed, including continued state support of telecommunications costs and maintenance and development of resources that expand access and availability statewide.

• All stakeholders must work to eliminate the digital divide in Minnesota public schools. All students need access to up-to-date technology in media centers, computer labs, and classrooms and training in how to use it.

• The Department of Children, Families & Learning should continue data collection on school library media programs to provide on-going measurement of program development.

• Library media specialists and their supporters must become vocal advocates for all school library media programs and document and disseminate information on the impact of media programs on student achievement.

Appendix O

The Missouri Study
Executive Summary

The following Missouri Summary brief entitled "Show Me Connection: How School Library Media Center Services Impact Student Achievement" was published in 2003. This document is available online at http://dese.mo.gov/divimprove/curriculum/librarystudy/libraryresearch.pdf and is reprinted here for the convenience of the reader.

Show Me Connection:

How School Library Media Center Services Impact Student Achievement

2002-2003

Prepared by:
Quantitative Resources, LLC
Jamie Miller
Jinchang Want, Ph.D.
Lisa Whitacre, M.S.

Prepared for:
MO Department of Elementary and Secondary Education
Missouri State Library

March 2003

Executive Summary

The Weighted Average Missouri MAP index scores from the Missouri Assessment Program (MAP) rose with the availability of School Library Media Center Services. The relationship between the School Library Media Center Services and student achievement was not negated by other school or community demographics.

When other conditions were taken into account, the development of School Library Media Center Services alone accounted for up to 11% of the variation in the Weighted Average Missouri MAP index. Generally, its importance falls below that of demographic differences, which consistently demonstrated stronger affects at about 40% of the variation in the Weighted Average Map Index.

School & Community Differences

The impact of the development of School Library Media Center Services on student achievement cannot be negated by:

School differences, including:
- Free and reduced lunch rate,
- Percentage of black/African American; or
- Teacher education/certification.

Community differences, including:
- Percent of poverty,
- Median household income; or
- Educational level attainment.

School Library Media Center Services

The following characteristics of School Library Media Center Services should be the focus of a school district or building that has a desire to impact student achievement:
- Library Usage
- Summer Reading Program
- Library Access

The complete affects of School Library Media Center Services on student achievement are summarized in Figure 1 on the following page.

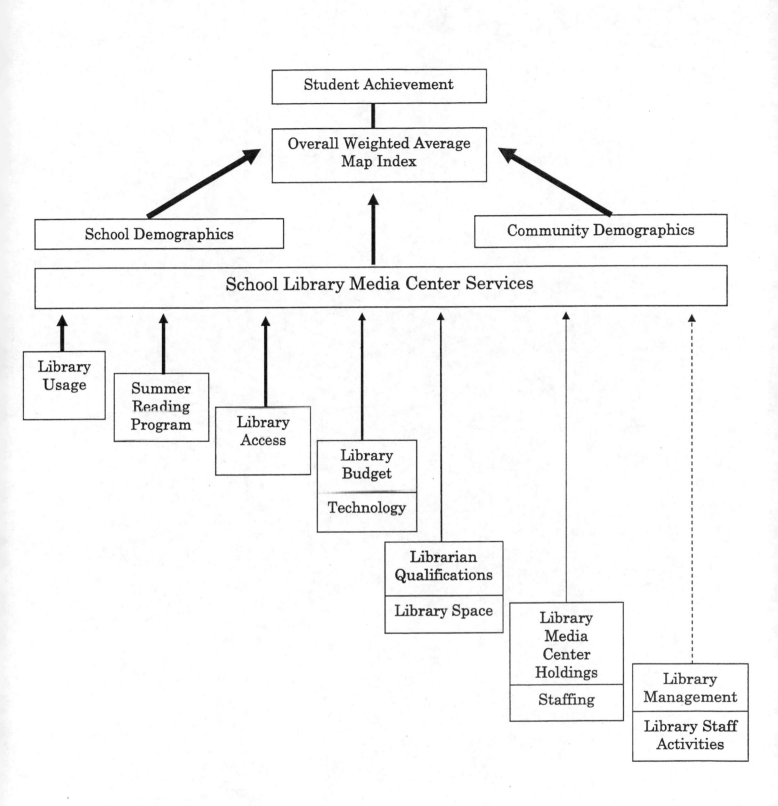

4

Appendix P

The New Mexico Study
Executive Summary

The following New Mexico Summary brief entitled "How School Libraries Improve Outcome for Children" was published in 2002. This document is available online at http://www.stlib.state.nm.us/files/NMStudyforDistribution.pdf and is reprinted here for the convenience of the reader.

How School Libraries
Improve Outcomes for Children

The New Mexico Study

Keith Curry Lance
Marcia J. Rodney
Christine Hamilton-Pennell

New Mexico State Library
Santa Fe, New Mexico
June, 2002

Executive Summary

New Mexico achievement test scores rise with the development of school library programs. The relationship between school library development and test scores is not explained away by other school or community conditions at the high school level. There was insufficient variation in librarian staffing to make similar claims for the elementary and middle school levels.

School Library Development

New Mexico achievement test scores tend to rise with increases in:
- school librarian and total library staff hours per 100 students;
- print volumes per student;
- periodical subscriptions, video materials, and software packages per 100 students; and
- school library expenditures per student.

Whatever the current level of development of the school library program, these findings indicate that incremental improvements in its staffing, collections, and funding will yield incremental increases in reading scores. The only caveat is that school library spending cannot exert a positive influence on academic achievement if it comes at the expense of other school programs.

School & Community Differences

The impact of school library development on academic achievement at the high school level cannot be explained away by:
- school differences, including:
  - the percentage of classroom teachers with master's degrees,
  - teachers' average years of experience, and
  - the teacher/pupil ratio, or
- community differences, including:
  - the percentage of schoolchildren living in poverty,
  - the percentage of schoolchildren belonging to racial/ethnic minority groups, and
  - the percentage of adults who graduated from high school.

When these other conditions are taken into account, school library development alone accounts for 7.9 percent of variation in average achievement scores among high schools. This figure takes into account community socio-economic status (SES), which explains 42.0 percent of variation in high school test scores. It also considers other school conditions that explain no additional variation beyond the 50.0 percent attributable to the combination of community SES and school library development factors.

Similar conclusions could not be drawn from such analyses at elementary and middle school levels, due to a lack of variation in school library staffing at those school levels. (Most elementary schools lacked a full-time librarian; most middle schools had precisely one full-time librarian.)

School Librarians & Strong School Libraries

School librarians exert a complex web of effects on the school library programs. Findings about these effects are summed up in the following description of a strong school library.

A strong school library program is one
- that is adequately staffed, stocked and funded. Minimally, this means one full-time librarian and one full-time aide. The relationship, however, is incremental; as the staffing, collections, and funding of school library programs grow, reading scores rise.

- whose staff are actively involved leaders in their school's teaching and learning enterprise. A successful school librarian is one who has the ear and support of the principal, serves with other teachers on the school's standards and curriculum committees, and holds regular meetings of the library staff. Students succeed where the school librarian participates with classroom teachers and administrators in making management decisions that encourage higher levels of achievement by every student.

- whose staff have collegial, collaborative relationships with classroom teachers. A successful school librarian is one who works with a classroom teacher to identify materials that best support and enrich an instructional unit, is a teacher of essential information literacy skills to students, and, indeed, is a provider of in-service training opportunities to classroom teachers. Students succeed where the school librarian is a consultant to, a colleague with, and a teacher of other teachers.

- <u>that embraces networked information technology.</u> The school library of today is no longer a destination; it is a point of departure for accessing the information resources that are the essential raw material of teaching and learning. Computers in classrooms, labs and other school locations provide networked access to information resources—the library catalog, electronic full text, licensed databases, locally mounted databases, and the Internet. Students succeed where the school library program is not a place to go, apart from other sites of learning in the school, but rather an integral part of the educational enterprise that reaches out to students and teachers where they are.

How School Libraries Improve Outcomes for Children:
The New Mexico Study

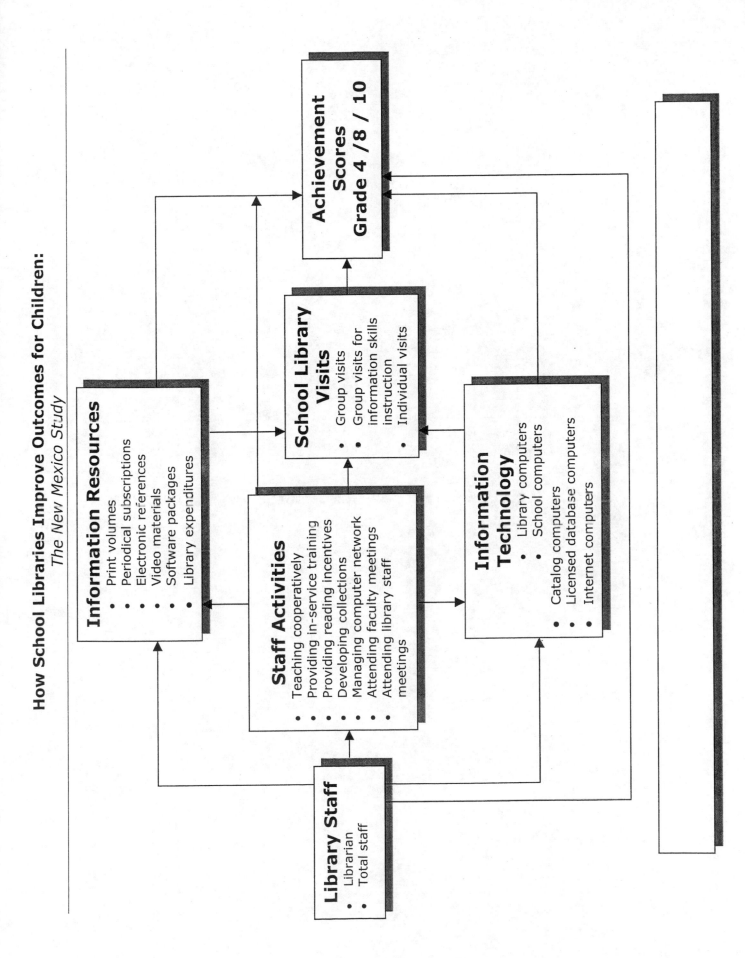

Appendix Q

The Indiana Study

Handout

The following Indiana handout entitled "Helping Students Achieve: Indiana School Library Media Specialists at Work" was published in 2004. This document is available online at http://www.ilfonline.org/Units/Associations/aime/Data/index.htm and is reprinted here for the convenience of the reader.

Summary from *Indiana Power!*

These pages are from *Indiana Power!* by Connie Champlin, David V. Loertscher, and Nancy A.S. Miller (Hi Willow Research & Publishing, 2004). It is available from LMC Source at http://www.lmcsource.com.

The role of the library media specialist in schools has been changing and evolving for decades. Gone are the days of someone who merely checked books out all day; instead the library media specialist is an active participant in teaching and learning in the school. Three recent surveys conducted through Indiana University looked at the role the library media specialist plays in Indiana Schools.

"Library quality, both in terms of better staffing and better collections, is related to reading achievement."

— Dr. Stephen Krashen, Professor Emeritus, University of Southern California (*The Power of Reading*, 2004)

Quality Checklist

Does your library media program:

✓ Have a **full-time** library media specialist (LMS) with a **full-time** clerk?

✓ Have a full-time LMS who co-plans, **co-instructs**, and co-evaluates?

✓ Have a library media **budget** that meets or exceeds the national average in expenditures?

✓ Have a **flexible instructional schedule** with open access and resources available 24/7?

✓ Have a full-time LMS who plans and participates in school, district, and state-wide **professional** development?

✓ Have a full-time LMS and a comprehensive collection that supports **reading**?

If you answered <u>YES</u> to all of the above questions, then you have a high quality library media program!

Read on for more details!

Check out the data!

Does your library media program:

Have a full-time library media specialist (LMS) with a full-time clerk?

*F*ull-time, certified school library media specialists (LMS) who are supported with full-time clerical assistance enhance their schools' academic programs (AIME and Indiana University, 2004) :
♦ A full-time LMS is more involved in the planning,

presentation, and evaluation of activities aligned with Indiana's Academic Standards.
♦ Students in buildings with a full-time LMS have greater access to electronic resources and higher involvement with technology and multimedia production.
♦ Elementary schools served by a full-time LMS are twice as likely to be involved in meaningful reading activities than ones which only have a part-time or no library media specialist.
♦ Resource collections managed by full-time LMS are more up-to-date, popular, and relevant to the curriculum.

A certified elementary school library media specialist, with experience for at least three years on a full-time basis at the same school, and who performs information access and administrative services at a proficient to exemplary level, is a <u>strong positive predictor</u> of a learning environment in which 6th grade students score well above average on all language arts portions of the ISTEP exam.—Indiana University, 2004

Does your library media program:

Have a full-time LMS who plans and participates in school, district, and state-wide professional development?

A large majority of full-time school library media specialists are involved in professional development leadership activities in their school, district, or state. In 2003, for example, full-time library media specialists were almost twice as likely to be involved as a member or as the chair of a school leadership team. Because they

"Direct [positive] correlation can be made between student achievement and school library programs led by library media specialists whose dual teaching certification uniquely qualifies them to provide leadership in the school for achieving school Mission, Objectives, and Strategies."
— Dr. Blanche Woolls, Professor, San Jose State University, 2004

work with every teacher in the building, school library media specialists have the global

perspective of the school. This makes them excellent candidates to lead school improvement initiatives.
   Full-time library media specialists are also more likely to mentor new library media specialists or classroom teachers, create monthly communication to staff, meet with their administrator to keep open lines of communication, and offer in-service workshops to their fellow teachers.

Does your library media program:

Have a library media budget that meets or exceeds the national average in expenditures?

♦ Indiana elementary schools expend 36% to 56%　the national average per student.
♦ Indiana middle/junior high schools expend 32%　the national average per student.
♦ Indiana senior high schools expend 57%　the national average per student.

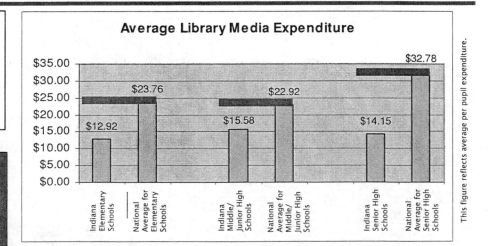

Average Library Media Expenditure

This figure reflects average per pupil expenditure.

*T*he purchase price for a typical library book has more than doubled since 1990, while the local funding for purchase of library books has not increased. In 1980, most Indiana schools provided enough local funding to acquire at least one new library book per student. Today that local investment ratio is one new library book for every three students and in some Indiana high schools, the ratio has dropped to one new library book for every five students.

Does your library media program:

✓ Have a flexible instructional schedule with open access and resources available 24/7?

What do administrators want from media specialists? They want their teachers to have incredible teaching opportunities. They want their students to have remarkable learning experiences...and let's not forget higher test scores. The good news is: it will all happen in your media center with appropriate, quality staffing. A full-time library media specialist supported by a full-time clerical assistant is necessary in order to provide adequate services that effectively enhance student and teacher academic performance. Larger schools, of course, require more library media professionals who can provide a wide diversity of skills.

The chance of having 24-hour access to multiple collections in an online catalog, resource lists, professional development, homework help, reference sources, and web quests are greatly increased with a full-time library media specialist. Perhaps most importantly, a library media specialist greatly increases the chance of a school utilizing appropriate online databases including INSPIRE, a fantastic resource funded by Indiana residents (www.inspire.net). State funded access to INSPIRE saves each public school in Indiana thousands of dollars annually.

INSPIRE
Indiana Virtual Library

Does your library media program:

✓ Have a full-time LMS who co-plans, co-instructs, and co-evaluates?

In studies replicated in more than a dozen states from 1993 to 2003, each study found a positive correlation between student achievement and an effective library media specialist (LMS) who extensively collaborates (co-plans, co-teaches, co-instructs) with teachers (The Colorado Library Research Service).

Exemplary performance levels for teaching promoted by

> Up to 20 percent more of sixth graders in an Indiana elementary school with a full-time, experienced LMS who performs at exemplary professional levels will pass <u>all</u> of the language arts ISTEP exam sections than in elementary schools where the LMS is not highly involved in professional roles.
> — Indiana University, 2004

the American Association for Librarians target indicators (ALA 1999):

♦ The library media program is a catalyst for intellectual inquiry.
♦ The school schedule ensures time for teachers and the LMS to regularly meet at common planning times, to plan instructional units, learning strategies, and activities.
♦ The district encourages the LMS to work collaboratively with administrators and teachers in planning, developing, and writing curriculum.
♦ Teaching is facilitative, collaborative, and creative. Reflection and authentic assessment are built into all instructional units.

Does your library media program:

✓ Have a full-time LMS and a comprehensive collection that supports reading?

Between 1997 and 2002 the Indiana General Assembly provided $13 million that public school libraries used to update their book collections; during those years book circulation increased sharply. Following the loss of these state funds, the acquisition of new library materials and book circulation declined. Indiana remains well below the national average in the amount of money spent on library materials (Indiana University CEEP, 2004).

> Full-time elementary school library media specialists involved over twice as many students and teachers in meaningful reading promotion activities such as the Young Hoosier Book Award and Read Aloud Books Too Good to Miss, than situations where the library media specialist serves on a part-time basis or there is no certified media specialist employed for that building.
> — Indiana University, 2004

Additional data and resources may be found at http://www.ilfonline.org/Units/Associations/aime/Data/index.htm

For further information on the research studies referenced, contact Dr. Daniel Callison, Professor and Executive Associate Dean, IU-Indianapolis. Phone — (317) 278-2376 E-Mail — callison@iupui.edu

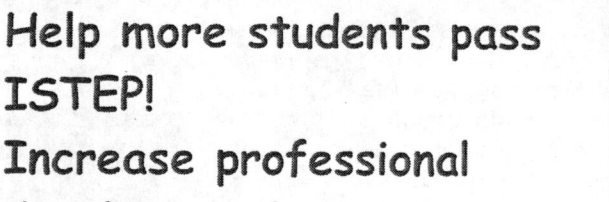

The Professional Organization for School Library Media Specialists

Association for Indiana Media Educators

941 E. 86th Street, Suite #260
Indianapolis, Indiana 46240

"A substantial body of research since 1990 shows a positive relationship between school libraries and student achievement. The research studies show that school libraries can have a positive impact on student achievement — whether such achievement is measured in terms of reading scores, literacy, or learning more generally. A school library program that is adequately staffed, resourced, and funded, can lead to higher student achievement regardless of the socioeconomic or educational levels of the community."
— School Libraries Work (Scholastic Research, 2004)

- Help more students pass ISTEP!
- Increase professional development!
- Increase reading ability!
- Help your teachers and students achieve more!

Helping Students Achieve:
Indiana School Library Media Specialists @ Work

How Does Indiana Compare to the Nation in School Libraries?

In March 2004, the Federal Government released the report: *The Status of Public and Private School Library Media Centers in the United States: 1999-2000*. available at:
http://nces.ed.gov/pubs2004/2004313.pdf>http://nces.ed.gov/pubs2004/2004313.pdf
While the data are old (federal wheels grind slowly), it is the most recent national statistics we have. How did Iowa compare to the nation that year? The following table summarizes some of the most important findings:

Characteristic	Source	Indiana	Nation
Public schools that claim to have a library	p. 4	97.5%	91.6%
Private schools in the U.S. that claim to have a library	p. 6	Not Reported	62.8%
Public schools that have a certificated librarian	p. 8	76.8%	75.2%
Number of schools with a full time librarian at the school	p. 18	24.3%	60.5%
School libraries with paid library aides	p. 22	36.1%	71.6%
Average library expenditures (books and multimedia)	p. 28	$8,151	$8,729
Average number of books in the library	p. 28	11,393	10,232
Average library circulation of materials per week	P. 46	598	605

Conclusions:
- Indiana has many, many schools that do not have a full-time librarian. This means that many schools share a librarian with another school or several schools. Why is that a problem? David Loertscher conducted dissertation research in Indiana in 1973 in the school libraries of Indiana and found that the most frustrated professionals were those that serve more than one school. These librarians are unable to develop a full reading or information literacy program in any of their schools. Which is better when there is money to hire only a half-time person? In spite of the equity arguments, it would seem better to hire a full-time person who could really make a difference in one school but leave the other one vacant. At least half the children/teachers would flourish rather than everyone suffering. Equitable policies are the best action.
- Spending on materials is below the national average.
- Collections of books are above the national average but no measure was taken of copyright date so that the collections could be quite old in one school and current in another.
- Circulation is at the national average, but not high enough to give a major boost to literacy.

Good advice for every parent and grandparent:
- A school library with lots of books and a professional librarian makes a difference to your child's/grandchild's education.
- Find out if your school actually has a professional librarian and good budgets to buy materials you child wants to read.
- Even in hard times, if you cut the library, you decrease your child's chances of succeeding in school.
- Advocate for a great school library. Young minds are this nation's future, your Social Security, Medicare, and the best hope for a sound national future.

Appendix R

The North Carolina Study Brochure

The following North Carolina brochure entitled "Libraries Do Make A Difference in North Carolina Public Schools" was published in 2003. It is available in the book *An Essential Connection: How Quality School Library Media Programs Improve Student Achievement in North Carolina* by Robert Burgin and Pauletta Brown Bracy (Hi Willow Research & Publishing, 2004). This is available from LMC Source at http://www.lmcsource.com.

An Essential Connection:
How Quality School Library Media Programs Improve
Student Achievement in North Carolina

Robert Burgin

Pauletta Brown Bracy

With assistance from Kathy Brown

RB Software & Consulting

http://www.rburgin.com

June 2003

Executive Summary

School library programs in North Carolina elementary, middle school, and high schools have a significant impact on student achievement – as measured by scores on standardized reading and English tests.

Scores on standardized reading and English tests in the schools included in this study tended to increase when libraries in the schools:

- ✓ Were staffed more hours during the school week
- ✓ Were open more hours during the school week
- ✓ Had newer books
- ✓ Spent more money per 100 students on books and other print materials like magazines and newspapers
- ✓ Spent more money per 100 students on electronic access to information (e.g., online database searching, Internet access)
- ✓ Were more likely to subscribe to online periodical services
- ✓ Were more likely to subscribe to CD ROM services

These findings are consistent with those of earlier studies in Alaska, Massachusetts, Colorado, Pennsylvania, Oregon, Texas, Iowa, and California, all of which found similar links between student achievement and the quality of school library programs.

Appendix S

Trade Books and Reading Achievement

Scholastic prepared the following research review entitled "Scholastic Trade Books: Research on the Use of Trade Books to Improve Reading Achievement" for its trade book division that actually competes with its library division. The review lists positive studies for obvious reasons but is a review that works not just for classroom libraries but also for the centralized school library, which is the only realistic entity in the school that can provide rotating non-fiction collections to support classroom libraries and to motivate children to read more non-fiction. This brochure is available at http://teacher.scholastic.com/products/paperbacks/pdfs/Research.pdf.

Research and Results

SCHOLASTIC

CLASSROOM LIBRARIES WORK!

The Benefits of Classroom Libraries that Include Trade Books

Research Foundation

• A common feature of effective reading programs is student access to a wide variety of appealing trade books and other reading materials. (Cullinan, 2000)

• Highly effective literacy educators create print-rich classroom environments filled with lots of high-quality, diverse reading materials. (Morrow & Gambrell, 2000)

• Results of the 1992 National Assessment of Educational Progress (NAEP) indicate that fourth graders who report reading nonfiction books, storybooks, and magazines are more proficient readers than those who read only one or two types of text. (Dreher, 1999)

• Adolescents and young adults need ... access to a sufficient number of books in the classroom on topics that are relevant to the students. (Krisch et al., 2002)

• When classrooms are filled with trade books and teachers encourage free reading, children's reading achievement, comprehension, and attitudes toward reading improve. (Fielding, Wilson, & Anderson, 1989)

Research Implications

Children learning to read need access to meaningful and personally interesting books. Without real engagement with meaningful books, children will not become readers. Effective teachers of reading understand the critical relationship between access to books and reading achievement. They recognize that the availability of reading material is related to how much children read, and that how much children read is related to how well they read. Because a rich and supportive literacy environment is critical to reading success, they provide their students with a rich and extensive classroom library filled with a diverse selection of interesting trade books.

Effective teachers of reading incorporate diverse trade books into their reading curriculum, introducing their students to the wide range of genres, authors, and topics. These teachers know that students who read a diverse range of reading materials are more proficient readers than those who read a narrower selection of texts. A well-stocked classroom library ensures that students will have access to a wide selection of diverse trade books.

The Benefits of Trade Books For Culturally Diverse Students and English Language Learners

Research Foundation

• Trade books are powerful instructional tools for meeting the needs of a variety of students with diverse learning styles. (Flippo, 1999)

• The same language-rich, language-integrated environment that helps native speakers acquire literacy...will also help ESL students add English to their home language. (Piper, 1998)

• Language flourishes best in a language-rich environment. Second language learners need to be exposed to meaningful literacy activities...It is vital for teachers to make reading and writing appealing and significant to the children. (McLaughlin, 1995)

• When the content of texts is familiar and interesting to English-language learners, they are more successful in reading. (Brisk & Harrington, 2000)

Research Implications

Effective teachers of reading understand that children from culturally diverse backgrounds learn best when the classroom environment is respectful of their linguistic, social, and cultural heritage. These teachers surround their students with culturally appropriate and relevant trade books that capitalize on the background knowledge and experiences that their students bring to school. By connecting these children with meaningful multicultural books they can relate to, teachers validate and build on their students' cultural and world knowledge. A rich classroom collection of multicultural trade books, acknowledges the background experience of culturally diverse students, bridges the gap between home and school, and enhances their engagement in reading.

Research suggests that the acquisition of English as a second language is enhanced by native language use. Thus, effective teachers provide English language learners with trade books in both languages.

The Benefits of Reading Practice with Trade Books

Research Foundation

- Wide and frequent reading of trade books increases a student's reading achievement. (Cipielewski & Stanovich, 1992)

- Increased frequency, amount, and diversity of reading activity increases reading achievement. (Guthrie et al., 1996)

- The volume of independent, silent reading students do in school is significantly related to gains in reading achievement. (Cunningham & Stanovich, 1996)

- Providing time for independent reading in schools has a positive impact on reading comprehension, vocabulary development, spelling, written style, oral/aural language, and control of grammar. (Krashen, 1993)

- "Reading a lot" is one of the most powerful methods of increasing fluency, vocabulary, [and] comprehension. (Stanovich, 1993)

- Adolescent and young adults' engagement in reading, including the amount of time they spend on reading and the diversity of materials they read, is closely associated with performance and reading ability. (Krisch et al., 2002)

- Students who read widely and frequently are higher achievers than students who read rarely and narrowly. (Guthrie et al., 1999)

- Fourth graders in the United States do better academically when they ... have greater access to books and other reading materials in their environment. (National Center for Education Statistics, 2000)

- Reading volume ... significantly affects ... general knowledge of the world, overall verbal ability, and academic achievement. (Shefelbine, 2000)

- Because time spent reading is tied to reading and writing competence, many students who do not read in their free time eventually lose academic ground even if they are not initially remedial readers. (Mullis, Campbell, & Farstrup, 1993)

Research Implications

Children who read voluntarily and extensively practice their reading skills, and reading practice is essential for children to become proficient readers. Research demonstrates a strong correlation between high reading achievement and large amounts of independent reading. Effective reading programs should therefore include independent reading of a wide variety of reading materials, including trade books.

Effective teachers of reading recognize that students need to read a lot to practice and refine their reading skills, and they provide their students with blocks of time within the school day to read books beyond their textbooks. They also encourage their students to read outside of the school day and year, as research shows that even proficient readers eventually exhibit academic declines if they do not read in their free time. They promote independent reading outside of the school by such means as daily at-home reading assignments, setting high expectations for their students, providing summer reading lists, encouraging parent involvement, and working with community groups to provide access to books.

While the best predictor of reading success is the amount of time spent reading, reading achievement is also influenced by the frequency, amount, and diversity of reading activities. Effective teachers of reading engage their students in reading for a variety of purposes—for pleasure, for exploration, and for information to perform a task. These teachers recognize that not all students enter reading through the same door, so they provide them with a wide range of meaningful reading activities, including those that promote social interaction with their peers.

Effective teachers of reading know that diverse readers span a range of reading interests and abilities and need access to a wide variety of engaging books in their immediate environment to meet their reading needs. They stock their classroom library with a large number of trade books, reflecting different genres, topics, authors, and reading levels. By providing access to a rich classroom library, teachers promote greater amounts of reading, increased reading frequency, and more diverse reading experiences among their students, thus helping them to attain greater levels of reading achievement.

"Increased frequency, amount, and diversity of reading activity increases reading achievement."

–Guthrie, et al., 1996

The Benefits of Trade Books in Relation to Reading Comprehension

Research Foundation

- The single most valuable activity for developing children's comprehension is reading itself. The amount of reading that children do is shown to predict the growth in reading comprehension across the elementary school years even after controlling for entry-level differences. (California Department of Education, 1996)

- Students who read actively and frequently improve their comprehension of text as a consequence. (Cipielewski & Stanovich, 1992)

- The amount of reading is a strong predictor of reading comprehension, outweighing intelligence, economic background, and gender. (Reutzel & Gikkubgsworth, 1991)

- The best strategy for developing comprehension is for teachers to require students to read a significant amount of age-appropriate materials. (Honig, 1996)

- An abundance of interesting books in the classroom promotes the use of comprehension strategies. (Guthrie et al, 2000)

Research Implications

Because effective teachers of reading recognize that teaching skills and strategies in the context of real reading assists their students in polishing and integrating their newly acquired reading skills, they give their students extended reading practice with books of their own choosing. These teachers understand that to improve reading skills, students need direct instruction followed by meaningful practice with appropriate text. Thus they allocate a substantial amount of time each day for free voluntary reading. To facilitate their students' independent reading, they stock their classroom with engaging trade books, representing a wide variety of genres, topics, authors, and reading levels to accommodate individual reading needs.

The more children read, the more they build their background knowledge, which in turn strengthens their ability to comprehend. Effective teachers of reading facilitate the expansion of background knowledge by providing frequent and varied opportunities for their students to interact with a variety of trade books.

Effective teachers of reading know that comprehension is enhanced by reflection and social interaction. Therefore, they provide their students with multiple opportunities to respond to their reading and interact with their peers through a variety of activities such as book clubs and discussions. Student interaction in discussions promotes their ability to think critically and promotes a deeper understanding of what they have read.

The Benefits of Trade Books in Relation to Vocabulary

Research Foundation

- Vocabulary growth is heavily influenced by the amount and variety of material children read. (Snow, Burns, & Griffin, 1998)

- Children expand their vocabularies by reading extensively on their own. The more children read, the more their vocabularies grow. (Armbruster, Lehr, & Osborn, 2001)

- Children learn an average of 4,000 to 12,000 new words each year as a result of book reading. (Anderson & Nagy, 1992)

- Independent reading is a major source of vocabulary growth. (Nagy & Anderson, 1984)

Research Implications

According to the research, the majority of vocabulary growth occurs not as a result of direct instruction, but as the result of reading voluminously. Effective teachers of reading know that for students to own a word, they need to see the word used in meaningful contexts a multitude of times. By reading voluminously, students are exposed frequently and often to words in meaningful contexts, thus increasing their opportunities to learn new words. Even a moderate amount of daily independent reading of trade books has a positive impact on increasing vocabulary. Students at all levels who read independently acquire new words as the result of reading more.

Effective teachers of reading facilitate increased vocabulary growth by promoting increased independent reading of trade books, both in and out of school. As books are rich in academic words, the extended reading of trade books not only increases vocabulary in terms of quantity, but it also enhances vocabulary in terms of quality.

Increased vocabulary knowledge helps students understand what they read, and reading comprehension is enhanced when students understand the meaning of words. Thus there is a reciprocal benefit to independent reading of trade books—vocabulary growth and reading comprehension.

The Benefits of Reading Trade Books Aloud

Research Foundation

- The most important activity for building the knowledge and skills ... required for reading is that of reading aloud to children. (Adams, 1990)

- Reading to children...increases their knowledge of the world, their vocabulary, their familiarity with written language ... and their interest in reading. (Armbruster, Lehr, & Osborn, 2001)

- Reading out loud to children is a proven way to develop vocabulary growth and language expansion and plays a causal role in developing both receptive and expressive language capabilities. Reading out loud can also enhance children's background knowledge of new concepts that may appear in both oral and written language. (Lyon, 2002)

- Children ... who are read aloud to daily score significantly better on measures of vocabulary, comprehension, and decoding ability. (Bus, van Ijzendoorn, & Pelligrini, 1995)

- You can help your students become more fluent readers by providing them with models of fluent reading. (Armbruster, Lehr, & Osborn, 2001)

Research Implications

Research shows that the opportunity for students to listen to books read aloud benefits their oral and written language and is strongly correlated to successful literacy development. Effective teachers of reading know that reading aloud encourages reading engagement, builds comprehension and vocabulary, and promotes fluency development. Thus they read aloud frequently in class. A rich classroom library representing a variety of reading levels supports teachers in reading aloud books that promote reading growth.

Effective teachers of reading know that reading aloud books that are more difficult than their students are able to read independently bridges the gap for those students with limited language experiences in their background. Thus, a rich and varied classroom library filled with diverse trade books representing a variety of different reading levels, genres, authors, topics, and cultures can be an equalizer for students of diverse backgrounds and limited language experiences.

Reading aloud to students allows teachers to model reading strategies. Effective teachers of reading understand that the modeling of reading strategies through reading aloud supports readers in learning how to make meaning from diverse types of text, such as informational and narrative texts. To this end, these teachers read aloud from a varied array of trade books that introduce students to the different genres and types of text. A well-stocked classroom library filled with a wide variety of trade books provides depth and breadth in terms of the number and type of books for modeling strategies by reading aloud.

The Role of Motivation in Trade Books

Research Foundation

- There are three potential stumbling blocks that are known to throw children off course on the journey to skilled reading. The third obstacle ... [is] the absence or loss of an initial motivation to read or failure to develop a mature appreciation of the rewards of reading. (Snow, Burns & Griffin, 1998)

- Access to books through classroom and school libraries ... motivates students to read. (Gambrell, Codling, & Palmer, 1996)

- Motivation and reading development are fostered when children are immersed in a book-rich environment, engaged in interactions with others about books, and given the responsibility for making decisions about what, when, and how they read. (Gambrell, 1996)

- Student ownership of literacy is increased when students have access to a diverse range of interesting and appealing books representing a variety of genres. (Au & Aslam, 1996)

Research Implications

Research demonstrates that the availability of books is a key factor in reading development. When students are immersed in book-rich environments, motivation to read is high. Effective teachers of reading increase their students' motivation to read by increasing the number and diversity of high-interest trade books available in the classroom. These teachers promote student choice in the selection of books to read and assist their students in finding books matched to their appropriate level of challenge.

A key to teaching all children to read is engagement in an exciting literate atmosphere that stimulates and supports reading. Effective teachers recognize that students need both skill and desire to read if they are to develop as proficient readers. They facilitate engagement in reading by modeling their own love of reading, reading aloud, book talking, providing access to a wealth of trade books, engaging students in a variety of activities with diverse texts, including daily independent reading of self-selected trade books, and providing book-related incentives that recognize students for their reading and emphasize the value of reading.

The Benefits of Trade Books in Relation to Fluency

Research Foundation

- Fluency develops as a result of many opportunities to practice reading with a high degree of success. (Armbruster, Lehr, & Osborn, 2001)

- Independent reading is a major source of reading fluency. (Allington, 2001)

- Adequate progress in learning to read beyond the initial level depends on sufficient practice in reading to achieve fluency with different kinds of texts. (Snow, Burns, & Griffin, 1998)

Research Implications

Research suggests that the independent reading of trade books is essential to increasing fluency. Effective teachers of reading know that fluency develops from an abundance of reading practice with books the reader can read with success. Through the process of reading an abundance of books at their independent reading level, students become more fluent at reading, thus gaining competence and confidence as readers. To encourage reading practice, effective teachers of reading initiate an independent reading program and provide their students with access to enjoyable trade books at their independent reading level. A well-stocked classroom library provides students access to trade books representing a variety of genres, topics, authors, and reading levels, thus ensuring each student the opportunity to experience reading success.

Effective teachers of reading understand that when reading to develop fluency, students need to read books that are neither too hard nor too easy for them. Text that is too hard impedes comprehension, and text that is too easy does not promote vocabulary growth. Effective teachers know the reading levels of their students and the reading levels of the trade books in their classroom, so that they can match their students to texts that can be read with success, thus assisting their students to grow as readers. Matching students to text is critical to establishing an optimal learning environment for reading.

Effective teachers of reading recognize that fluency varies with the type and readability of the text. These teachers strive to provide their students with a wide range of reading experiences with books representing a variety of genres and writing styles. A large and varied classroom library supports student interaction with diverse books.

"Fluency develops as a result of many opportunities to practice reading with a high degree of success."

–Armbruster, Lehr, & Osborn, 2001

References—Alphabetical by Category

The Benefits of Classroom Libraries that Include Trade Books

Cullinan, B. (2000). "Independent Reading and School Achievement." *School Library Media Research,* 3. http://www.ala.org/aasl/SLMR/, Volume 3.

Dreher, M.J. (1998/1999). "Motivating Children to Read More Nonfiction." *The Reading Teacher,* 42, 414–417.

Fielding, L.G., Wilson, P.T., & Anderson, R.C. (1989). "A New Focus on Free Reading: The Role of Trade Books in Reading Instruction." In Raphael, T. E. & Reynolds, R., eds. *Contexts of Literacy.* White Plains, NY: Longman.

Krisch, I., deJong, J., LaFontain, D., MacQueen, J., Mendelovits, J., and Moneur, C. (2002). *Reading for Change: Performance and Engagement Across Countries: Results from PISA 2000.* Paris, France: Center for Educational Research, Organization for Economic Co-operation and Development.

Morrow, L.M., & Gambrell, L.B. (2000). "Literature-based Reading Instruction." In Kamil, M., Mosenthal, P., Pearson, P.D., & Barr, R., eds. *Handbook of Reading Research* (Vol. 3, pp 563–586). Mahwah, NJ: Erlbaum.

The Benefits of Trade Books for Culturally Diverse Students and English Language Learners

Brisk, M.E. and Harrington, M.M. (2000). *Literacy and Bilingualism: A Handbook for ALL Teachers.* Mahwah, NJ: Erlbaum.

Flippo, R.F. (1999). *What Do the Experts Say?: Helping Children Learn to Read.* Portsmouth, NH: Heinemann.

McLaughlin, B. (1995). "Fostering Second Language Development in Young Children: Principles and Practices." National Center for Research on Cultural Diversity and Second Language Learning.

Piper, T. (1998). *Language and Learning: The Home and School Years.* Upper Saddle River, NJ: Prentice Hall.

The Benefits of Reading Practice With Trade Books

Anderson, R., Wilson, P., & Fielding, L. (1988). "Growth in Reading and How Children Spend Their Time Outside of School." *Reading Research Quarterly,* 23: 285–303.

Cipielewski, J. & Stanovich, K. (1992). "Predicting Growth in Reading Ability from Children's Exposure to Print." *Journal of Experimental Child Psychology,* 54: 74–89.

Cunningham, A. & Stanovich, K. (1996). "What Reading Does for the Mind." *American Educator,* 22: 8–15.

Guthrie, J.T., Wigfield, A., Metsala, J.L., & Cox, K.E. (1999). "Motivational and Cognitive Predictors of Text Comprehension and Reading Amount." *Scientific Studies of Reading,* 3: 231–256.

Guthrie, J.T., Van Meter, P., McCann, A. Wigfield, A., Bennett, I., Poundstone, C., Rice, M., Faibisch, F., Hunt, B., & Mitchell, A. (1996). "Changes in Motivations and Strategies during Concept-Oriented Reading Instruction." *Reading Research Quarterly,* 31: 306–322.

Krashen, S. (1993). *The Power of Reading: Insights from the Research.* Englewood, CO: Libraries Unlimited.

Krisch, I., deJong, J., LaFontain, D., MacQueen, J., Mendelovits, J., and Moneur, C. (2002). *Reading for Change: Performance and Engagement Across Countries: Results from PISA 2000.* Paris, France: Center for Educational Research, Organization for Economic Co-operation and Development.

Mullis, I., Campbell, J. & Farstrup, A. (1993). *NAEP 1992: Reading Report Card for the Nation and the States.* Washington, DC: U.S. Department of Education.

National Center for Education Statistics. (2000). *The Nation's Reading Report Card: Fourth-grade Reading 2000.* Washington, D.C: National Center for Education Statistics.

Shefelbine, J. (2000). *Reading Voluminously and Voluntarily.* New York: The Scholastic Center for Literacy & Learning.

Stanovich, K.E. (1993). "Does Reading Make You Smarter? Literacy and the Development of Verbal Intelligence." In Reese, H., ed. *Advances in Child Development and Behavior,* Vol. 25. San Diego, CA: Academic Press.

Stanovich, K.E. & Cunningham, A.E. (1993). "Where Does Knowledge Come From? Specific Associations Between Print Exposure and Information Acquisition." *Journal of Educational Psychology,* 85: 211–230.

The Benefits of Trade Books in Relation to Reading Comprehension

California Department of Education. (1996). *Teaching Reading: A Balanced Comprehensive Approach to Teaching Reading in Pre-Kindergarten Through Grade Three.* Sacramento, CA: California Department of Education.

Cipielewski, J. & Stanovich, K. (1992). "Predicting Growth in Reading Ability from Children's Exposure to Print." *Journal of Experimental Child Psychology,* 54: 74–89.

Guthrie, J.T., Schafer, W.D., Vaon Secker, C., & Alban, T. (2000). "Contributions of Integrated Reading Instruction and Text Resources to Achievement and Engagement in Statewide School Improvement Program." *Journal of Educational Research,* 93: 211–226.

Honig, B. (1996). *Teaching Our Children to Read: The Role of Skills in a Comprehensive Reading Program.* Thousand Oaks, CA: Corwin Press.

Reutzel, D.R. & Gikkubgsworth, P.M. (1991). "Reading Time in School: Effect on Fourth Graders' Performance on a Criterion-referenced Comprehension Test." *Journal of Educational Research,* 84: 170–176.

The Benefits of Trade Books in Relation to Vocabulary

Anderson, R.C. & Nagy, W.E. (1992). "The Vocabulary Conundrum." *American Educator,* 14–18, 44–46.

Armbruster, B.B., Lehr, F., & Osborn, J.M., eds. (2001). *Put Reading First: The Research Building Blocks for Teaching Children to Read.* Washington, DC: The National Institute for Literacy.

Nagy, W. & Anderson, R. (1984). "How Many Words Are There in Printed School English?" *Reading Research Quarterly,* 19: 304–330.

Snow, C.E., Burns, S.M., & Griffin, P., eds. (1998). *Preventing Reading Difficulties in Young Children.* Washington, DC: National Academy Press, 314.

The Benefits of Reading Trade Books Aloud

Adams, Marilyn J. (1990). *Beginning to Read: Thinking and Learning About Print.* Cambridge, MA: MIT Press.

Armbruster, B.B., Lehr, F., & Osborn, J.M., eds. (2001). *Put Reading First: The Research Building Blocks for Teaching Children to Read.* Washington, DC: The National Institute for Literacy.

Bus, A., van Ijzendoorn, M.H., & Pelligrini, A. (1995). "Joint Book Reading Makes for Success in Learning to Read: A Meta-Analysis On Intergenerational Transmission Of Literacy." *Review of Educational Research,* 65: 1–21.

Lyon, G. Reid. (2002). "Overview of Reading and Literacy Research." In Patton, S. and Holmes, M., eds. *Keys to Literacy.* Washington, DC: Council for Basic Education.

The Role of Motivation in Trade Books

Au, K.H. & Asam, C.L. (1996). "Improving the Literacy Achievement of Low-Income Students of Diverse Backgrounds." In Graves, M.F., van den Broek, P., & Taylor, B.M., eds. *The First R: Every Child's Right to Read,* 199–223. New York: Teachers College Press.

Gambrell, L.B. (1996). "Creating Classroom Cultures that Foster Reading Motivation." *The Reading Teacher,* 50: 1.

Gambrell, L.B., Codling, R.M. & Palmer, B.M. (1996). *Elementary Students' Motivation to Read.* (Reading Research Report #52). Athens, GA: National Reading Research Center.

Snow, C.E., Burns, S.M., & Griffin, P., eds. (1998). *Preventing Reading Difficulties in Young Children.* Washington, DC: National Academy Press, 314.

The Benefits of Trade Books in Relation to Fluency

Armbruster, B.B., Lehr, F., & Osborn, J.M., eds. (2001). *Put Reading First: The Research Building Blocks for Teaching Children to Read.* Washington, DC: The National Institute for Literacy.

Snow, C.E., Burns, S.M., & Griffin, P., eds. (1998). *Preventing Reading Difficulties in Young Children.* Washington, DC: National Academy Press, 314.

References—Complete Alphabetical Listing

Allington, R. (2001). *What Really Matters For Struggling Readers: Designing Research-Based Programs*. New York: Addison-Wesley.

Adams, Marilyn J. (1990). *Beginning to Read: Thinking and Learning About Print*. Cambridge, MA: MIT Press.

Allington, R. (2001). *What Really Matters For Struggling Readers: Designing Research-Based Programs*. New York: Addison-Wesley.

Anderson, R., Wilson, P., & Fielding, L. (1988). "Growth in Reading and How Children Spend Their Time Outside of School." *Reading Research Quarterly, 23:* 285–303.

Anderson, R.C. & Nagy, W.E. (1992). "The Vocabulary Conundrum." *American Educator, 14–18,* 44–46.

Armbruster, B.B., Lehr, F., & Osborn, J.M., eds. (2001). *Put Reading First: The Research Building Blocks for Teaching Children to Read*. Washington, DC: The National Institute for Literacy.

Au, K.H. & Asam, C.L. (1996). "Improving the Literacy Achievement of Low-Income Students of Diverse Backgrounds." In Graves, M.F., van den Broek, P., & Taylor, B.M., eds. *The First R: Every Child's Right to Read,* 199–223. New York: Teachers College Press.

Brisk, M.E. and Harrington, M.M. (2000). *Literacy and Bilingualism: A Handbook for ALL Teachers*. Mahwah, NJ: Erlbaum.

Bus, A., van Ijzendoorn, M.H., & Pelligrini, A. (1995). "Joint Book Reading Makes for Success in Learning to Read: A Meta-Analysis On Intergenerational Transmission Of Literacy." *Review of Educational Research,* 65: 1–21.

California Department of Education. (1996). *Teaching Reading: A Balanced Comprehensive Approach to Teaching Reading in Pre-Kindergarten Through Grade Three*. Sacramento, CA: California Department of Education.

Cipielewski, J. & Stanovich, K. (1992). "Predicting Growth in Reading Ability from Children's Exposure to Print." *Journal of Experimental Child Psychology,* 54: 74–89.

Cullinan, B. (2000). "Independent Reading and School Achievement." *School Library Media Research,* 3. http://www.ala.org/aasl/SLMR/, Volume 3.

Cunningham, A. & Stanovich, K. (1996). "What Reading Does for the Mind." *American Educator,* 22: 8–15.

Dreher, M.J. (1998/1999). "Motivating Children to Read More Nonfiction." *The Reading Teacher,* 42: 414–417.

Fielding, L.G., Wilson, P.T., & Anderson, R.C. (1989). "A New Focus on Free Reading: The Role of Trade Books in Reading Instruction." In Raphael, T.E. & Reynolds, R., eds. *Contexts of Literacy.* White Plains, NY: Longman.

Flippo, R.F. (1999). *What Do the Experts Say?: Helping Children Learn to Read*. Portsmouth, NH: Heinemann.

Gambrell, L.B. (1996). "Creating Classroom Cultures that Foster Reading Motivation." *The Reading Teacher,* 50: 1.

Gambrell, L.B., Codling, R.M. & Palmer, B.M. (1996). *Elementary Students' Motivation to Read*. (Reading Research Report #52). Athens, GA: National Reading Research Center.

Guthrie, J.T., Schafer, W.D., Vaon Secker, C., & Alban, T. (2000). "Contributions of Integrated Reading Instruction and Text Resources to Achievement and Engagement in Statewide School Improvement Program." *Journal of Educational Research,* 93: 211–226.

Guthrie, J.T., Van Meter, P., McCann, A. Wigfield, A., Bennett, I., Poundstone, C., Rice, M., Faibisch, F., Hunt, B., & Mitchell, A. (1996). "Changes in Motivations and Strategies during Concept-Oriented Reading Instruction." *Reading Research Quarterly,* 31: 306–322.

Guthrie, J.T., Wigfield, A., Metsala, J.L., & Cox, K.E. (1999). "Motivational and Cognitive Predictors of Text Comprehension and Reading Amount." *Scientific Studies of Reading,* 3: 231–256.

Honig, B. (1996). *Teaching Our Children to Read: The Role of Skills in a Comprehensive Reading Program*. Thousand Oaks, CA: Corwin Press.

Krashen, S. (1993). *The Power of Reading: Insights from the Research*. Englewood, CO: Libraries Unlimited.

Krisch, I., de Jong, J., LaFontain, D., MacQueen, J., Mendelovits, J., and Moneur, C. (2002). *Reading for Change: Performance and Engagement Across Countries: Results from PISA 2000*. Paris, France: Center for Educational Research, Organization for Economic Co-operation and Development.

Lyon, G. Reid. (2002). "Overview of Reading and Literacy Research." In Patton, S. and Holmes, M., eds. *Keys to Literacy.* Washington, DC: Council for Basic Education.

McLaughlin, B. (1995). "Fostering Second Language Development in Young Children: Principles and Practices." National Center for Research on Cultural Diversity and Second Language Learning.

Mullis, I., Campbell, J. & Farstrup, A. (1993). *NAEP 1992: Reading Report Card for the Nation and the States*. Washington, DC: U.S. Department of Education.

Morrow, L.M., & Gambrell, L.B. (2000). "Literature-based Reading Instruction." In Kamil, M., Mosenthal, P., Pearson, P.D., & Barr, R., eds. *Handbook of Reading Research* (Vol. 3, pp 563–586). Mahwah, NJ: Erlbaum.

Nagy, W. & Anderson, R. (1984). "How Many Words Are There in Printed School English?" *Reading Research Quarterly,* 19: 304–330.

National Center for Education Statistics. (2000). *The Nation's Reading Report Card: Fourth-grade Reading 2000*. Washington, D.C.: National Center for Education Statistics.

Piper, T. (1998). *Language and Learning: The Home and School Years*. Upper Saddle River, NJ: Prentice Hall.

Reutzel, D.R. & Gikkubgsworth, P.M. (1991). "Reading Time in School: Effect on Fourth Graders' Performance on a Criterion-referenced Comprehension Test." *Journal of Educational Research,* 84: 170–176.

Shefelbine, J. (2000). *Reading Voluminously and Voluntarily*. New York: The Scholastic Center for Literacy & Learning.

Snow, C.E., Burns, S.M., & Griffin, P., eds. (1998). *Preventing Reading Difficulties in Young Children*. Washington, DC: National Academy Press, 314.

Stanovich, K.E. (1993). "Does Reading Make You Smarter? Literacy and the Development of Verbal Intelligence." In Reese, H., ed. *Advances in Child Development and Behavior,* Vol. 25. San Diego, CA: Academic Press.

Stanovich, K.E. & Cunningham, A.E. (1993). "Where Does Knowledge Come From? Specific Associations Between Print Exposure and Information Acquisition." *Journal of Educational Psychology,* 85: 211–230.

ITEM #439937 10M   03/04

Appendix T

The Scholastic Research Review of School Libraries and Achievement

Scholastic also commissioned a review of the research of school libraries and disseminated the following pamphlet entitled "School Libraries Work." Terry Young, its author, plans to revise this brochure in the fall of 2005. Watch the Scholastic website for a reproducible copy. This review is available online at http://www.scholasticlibrary.com/download/slw_04.pdf.

Research Foundation
Paper

School Libraries Work!

Table of Contents

Preface:
School Libraries Work!

The School Library Is Critical
to the Learning Experience
and Student Academic Achievement.

The school library has long been regarded as the cornerstone of the school community—a learning hub integral to teaching and learning. By providing teachers and students with a full range of print and electronic resources to support learning, the school library impacts student achievement.

A substantial body of research since 1990 clearly demonstrates the importance of school libraries to students' education. Whether student achievement is measured by standardized reading achievement tests or by global assessments of learning, research shows that a well-stocked library staffed by a certified library media specialist has a positive impact on student achievement, regardless of the socio-economic or educational levels of the community.

This research foundation paper brings together position statements from a variety of organizations and findings from nearly a decade of empirical studies that cite the measurable impact of school libraries and library media specialists on learning outcomes. As you will see, school libraries administered by certified library media specialists are a powerful force in the lives of America's children.

School Libraries are Much More Than Books

The Impact of School Libraries and Library Media Specialists on Student Academic Achievement.

Summary:

School libraries are much more than books. They are a learning hub with a full range of print and electronic resources that support student achievement. The school library is a gathering place for people of all ages and interests to explore and debate ideas. The library media specialist, working collaboratively with all teachers, helps students develop a love of reading, become skilled users of ideas and information, and explore the world through print and electronic media resources.

The Program

SCHOOL LIBRARY PROGRAMS INFLUENCE LEARNING OUTCOMES AND STUDENT ACHIEVEMENT WHEN:

- Library media specialists collaborate with classroom teachers to teach and integrate literature and information skills into the curriculum.

- Library media specialists partner with classroom teachers on projects that help students use a variety of resources, conduct research, and present their findings.

- Library media specialists are supported fiscally and programmatically by the educational community to achieve the mission of the school.

(continued)

LIBRARY MEDIA SPECIALISTS ARE CRUCIAL
TO THE TEACHING AND LEARNING PROCESS:

- They teach skills and strategies students need to learn and achieve.

- They are partners in educating students, developing curricula, and integrating resources into teaching and learning.

- They teach the skills students need to become effective users of ideas and information.

- They seek, select, evaluate, and utilize electronic resources and tools and instruct teachers and students in how to use them.

The Place
SCHOOL LIBRARIES ARE PLACES OF OPPORTUNITY:

- Where all students can strive for and achieve success

- Where quality collections are provided, in print and online, that support the curriculum and address a variety of learning needs

- Where students develop a love of reading and literature

- Where library media specialists help students explore the world around them through print and electronic media

- Where students can work individually or in small groups on research and collaborative projects

—*American Library Association. (2003)*. Toolkit for School Library
Media Programs. *Chicago: American Library Association*

"Libraries must purchase a sufficient number of new books per student, and they must make a concentrated effort to replace older materials for each classroom and school library on an annual basis."

— *"Providing Books and Other Print Materials for Classroom and School Libraries."*
A Position Statement of the International Reading Association, *1999*.

Certified School Library Media Specialists and School Libraries Are Vital to High Achieving Schools.

DIRECT CORRELATION CAN BE MADE BETWEEN STUDENT ACHIEVEMENT AND SCHOOL LIBRARY PROGRAMS LED BY LIBRARY MEDIA SPECIALISTS WHOSE DUAL TEACHING CERTIFICATION UNIQUELY QUALIFIES THEM TO...

Summary:

The role of the library media specialist is diverse. He or she is at once a teacher, an instructional partner, an information specialist, and a program administrator. Library media specialists play an essential role in the learning community by ensuring that students and staff are efficient and effective users of ideas and information. They collaborate with teachers, administrators, and others to prepare students for future successes.

- Teach information skills

- Promote reading advocacy by matching students and books

- Manage information

- Organize and maintain a collection of valuable resources

- Collaborate with teachers to meet the information needs of students

- Assist teachers and students to search out their information needs, critically evaluate the materials they locate, and use technological means to synthesize their findings into new knowledge

- Facilitate booktalking

- Provide resources and activities to promote student achievement

- Collaborate with teachers to provide resources and activities for course, unit, and lesson outcomes

- Provide resources and activities for students that are meaningful now and in the future

- Provide intellectual and physical access to information in print and media resources

- Provide intellectual and physical access to information technologies, either local or Web-based

- Maintain a supportive and nurturing environment in the library and network environment, to increase student satisfaction and achievement

- Provide leadership in the school for achieving school Mission, Objectives and Strategies

Woolls, Blanche. (2004). The School Library Media Manager, 3rd Edition. Westport, CT: Libraries Unlimited. (in publication)

School Libraries Are Important.

A school library and a classroom collection of reading materials are both necessary components of an elementary school program. Each supports the reading and literacy initiatives of the school. One cannot substitute for the other. One—the school library—is a collection of resources that are organized according to a known and accepted system with materials cataloged and classified for universal accessibility. The other—the classroom collection of reading materials—may be organized in a particular manner to service individual classrooms. School libraries staffed by library media specialists ensure that students are effective users of the ideas and information contained in these resources.

AN EFFECTIVE SCHOOL LIBRARY...

+ Is accessible to the total school community, on site or remotely

+ Is cost effective because one book is used by many

+ Provides flexible scheduling and timely access to the collection by all students

+ Offers a broad range of materials—reference, fiction, and non-fiction

+ Addresses a broad range of reading levels

+ Minimizes loss through cost-effective tracking systems

+ Supports learning to read and reading to learn with informational and imaginative text and literature

+ Adds new resources throughout the school year to keep collections dynamic

+ Creates a sense of ownership that is shared by the entire school community

"Results show a scarcity of informational texts in these classroom print environments and activities—there were relatively few informational texts included in classroom libraries, little informational text on classroom walls and other surfaces, and a mean of only 3.6 minutes per day spent with informational texts during classroom written language activities."

—Duke, Nell K. (2000). "3.6 Minutes per Day: The Scarcity of Informational Texts in First Grade." Reading Research Quarterly 35 (2): 202-224.

Roscello, Frances and Patricia Webster (2002). Characteristics of School Library Media Programs and Classroom Collections: Talking Points. Albany, NY: Office of Elementary, Middle, Secondary, and Continuing Education, New York State Education Department.

14 States Can't Be Wrong.*

State Studies Demonstrate the Benefits of School Libraries and Library Media Specialists on Student Academic Achievement.

Summary:

A substantial body of research since 1990 shows a positive relationship between school libraries and student achievement. The research studies show that school libraries can have a positive impact on student achievement—whether such achievement is measured in terms of reading scores, literacy, or learning more generally. A school library program that is adequately staffed, resourced, and funded can lead to higher student achievement regardless of the socio-economic or educational levels of the community.

ALASKA (LANCE, 1999)

- Students in Alaska's secondary schools with full-time teacher-librarians were almost twice as likely as those without teacher-librarians to score average or above-average on California Achievement Tests (CAT5).

- The more often students receive library/information literacy instruction from library media specialists, the higher the test scores.

COLORADO (LANCE, 1993; LANCE, 2000)

- The size of the school library staff and collection explained 21% of variation in 7th grade Iowa Tests of Basic Skills (ITBS) reading scores, while controlling for socio-economic conditions (1993).

- Elementary school students with the most collaborative teacher-librarians scored 21% higher on Colorado Student Assessment Program (CSAP) reading than students with the least collaborative teacher librarians (2000).

FLORIDA (BAUMBACH, 2002)

- In elementary schools where library programs are staffed 60 hours per week or more, there is a 9% improvement in test scores over those staffed less than 60 hours.

- In middle schools where library programs are staffed 60 hours per week or more, there is a 3.3% improvement in test scores over those staffed less than 60 hours.

- In high schools where library media programs are staffed 60 hours per week or more, there is a 22.2% improvement in test scores over those staffed less than 60 hours.

*For full citations of the state studies summarized in this section, see pages 16–17.

IOWA (LANCE, 2002)

* Comparing Iowa elementary schools with the highest and lowest ITBS reading scores, the highest scoring students use more than 2 1/2 times as many books and other materials during library visits.

* Iowa reading test scores rise with the development of school library programs. The relationship between library program development and test scores is not explained away by other school or community conditions at the elementary level.

MASSACHUSETTS (BAUGHMAN, 2002)

* At each grade level, schools with library programs have higher Massachusetts Comprehensive Assessment System (MCAS) scores.

* At the elementary and middle/junior high school levels, students score higher on the MCAS test when there is a school library program.

MICHIGAN (RODNEY, LANCE, AND HAMILTON-PENNELL, 2003)

* At elementary schools with the highest Michigan Educational Assessment Program (MEAP) reading scores, teachers and students are 4 times as likely to be able to visit the library on a flexibly scheduled basis, compared to their counterparts at the lowest scoring schools.

* MEAP reading test scores rise with the extent to which the state's school library programs are headed by certified library media specialists.

(continued)

MINNESOTA (BAXTER AND SMALLEY, 2003)

* In Minnesota schools with above-average student scores on the grade 3, 5, and 8 reading tests, 66.8% were schools where the library media specialist worked full-time.

* Student reading achievement in elementary and secondary schools is related to increases in school library program spending.

* Twice as many schools with above-average scores had full-time library media specialists.

MISSOURI (QUANTITATIVE RESOURCES, LLC, 2003)

* School library services exert a 10.6% statistically significant impact on student achievement.

* The weighted average index scores from the Missouri Assessment Program (MAP) rose with the availability of school library program services.

* The relationship between school library program services and student achievement was not negated by other school or community demographics.

NEW MEXICO (LANCE, 2002)

* New Mexico middle schools with the highest New Mexico Achievement Assessment Program (NMAAP) language arts scores are twice as likely as the lowest scoring schools to provide access to licensed databases via a school library network.

* New Mexico achievement test scores rise with the development of school library programs.

"The extent to which books are borrowed from school libraries shows a strong relationship with reading achievement."

—*"Impact of School Libraries on Student Achievement."* Research Developments: Newsletter of the Australian Council for Educational Research. *No.10 (2003): 4.*

NORTH CAROLINA (BURGIN AND BRACY, 2003)

- School library programs in North Carolina elementary, middle, and high schools have a significant impact on student achievement—as measured by scores on standardized reading and English tests.

- Scores on standardized reading and English tests in the schools included in this study tended to increase when libraries in the schools had newer books, and were open and staffed more hours during the school week.

OHIO (TODD, KUHLTHAU, AND OELMA, 2004)

- *Student Learning through Ohio School Libraries* reveals that 99.4% of students in grades 3 to 12 believe school libraries and their services help them become better learners.

- The study shows that an effective school library, led by a credentialed library media specialist who has a clearly defined role in information-oriented pedagogy, plays a critical role in facilitating student learning for building knowledge.

OREGON (LANCE, RODNEY, AND HAMILTON-PENNELL, 2001)

- Teacher-librarians from high schools with the best Oregon Statewide Assessment reading/language scores are twice as likely as their colleagues from the lowest scoring schools to plan collaboratively with classroom teachers, and their students are more than three times as likely to visit the library as part of a class or other group.

- The relationship between school library program development and test scores is not explained away by other school or community conditions at the elementary or middle school levels or by other school conditions at the high school level.

- Whatever the current level of development of a school's library program, these findings indicate that incremental improvements in its staffing, collections, and budget will yield incremental increases in reading scores.

(continued)

PENNSYLVANIA (LANCE, RODNEY, AND HAMILTON-PENNELL, 2000)

- ◆ The success of any school library program in promoting high academic achievement depends fundamentally on the presence of adequate staffing—specifically each library should have at least one full-time certified school librarian with at least one full-time aide or support staff member. For all three tested grades, the relationship between such staffing and Pennsylvania System of School Assessment (PSSA) reading scores is both positive and statistically significant.

  In 1998-99, three out of five Pennsylvania elementary schools with adequate school library staffing (61%) reported average or above-average reading scores, while the same proportion of such schools with inadequate library staffing reported below-average scores.

- ◆ Pennsylvania middle schools with the best PSSA reading scores spend twice as much on their school libraries as the lowest scoring schools.

- ◆ The mere presence of a large collection of books, magazines, and newpapers in the school library is not enough to generate high levels of academic achievement by students. Such collections only make a positive difference when they are part of school-wide initiatives to integrate information literacy into the school's approach to standards and curricula.

TEXAS (SMITH, 2001)

- ◆ Over 10% more students in schools with librarians than in schools without librarians met minimum Texas Assessment of Academic Skills (TAAS) expectations in reading.

- ◆ This study indicates that library staffing levels, collection sizes, librarian interaction with teachers and students, and library technology levels have a positive association with TAAS performance at the elementary, middle/junior high, and high school levels.

"Every classroom should have a library of materials that is large and diverse enough to provide daily opportunities for students to read self-selected materials. In addition, every school should have a fully funded library that meets the highest of state and/or national standards and a licensed, full-time library media specialist."

—Report of the NEA Task Force on Reading, 2000. p. 7.

The Ohio Study

Selected results from the most recent study...

(TODD, KUHLTHAU, AND OELMA, 2004)

Summary:

The Ohio study sought to understand how students benefit from school libraries and to quantify the school library's relationship to student learning. Nearly 100% of the students who took part in the research study indicated that the school library, its services, and library media specialists have helped them with their learning. The data shows that an effective school library program led by a credentialed library media specialist plays a critical role in facilitating learning, in general, and information literacy, in particular. The data also highlights the impact school library media specialists have when working both as an information-learning specialist and as an educational partner-leader to implement a whole-school library program which articulates library literacy standards and provides learning-oriented development that aligns with achievement goals for the entire school.

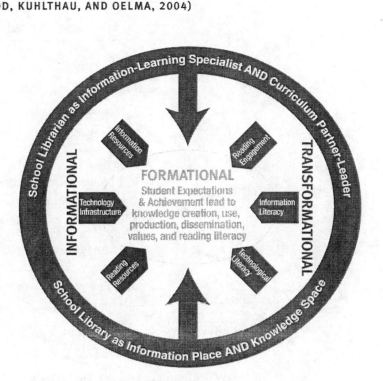

MODEL OF THE SCHOOL LIBRARY AS A DYNAMIC AGENT OF LEARNING

Todd, Ross J., Carol C. Kuhlthau, and OELMA. (2004). Student Learning through Ohio School Libraries. Columbus, OH: Ohio Educational Library Media Association. http://www.oelma.org/studentlearning/default.asp

"The [Ohio] study shows that an effective school library, led by a credentialed library media specialist who has a clearly defined role in information-centered pedagogy, plays a critical role in facilitating student learning for building knowledge."

—*Ross J. Todd, Carol C. Kuhlthau, and OELMA.* Student Learning through Ohio School Libraries, 2004. *http://www.oelma.org/studentlearning/default.asp*

Model posits that as a dynamic agent of learning, a school library's intellectual and physical infrastructure centers on three essential interactive and iterative components:

1. **INFORMATIONAL— The information resource and information technology infrastructure**

   — **Information resources:** Current, multi-perspective, multi-format resources with readability levels aligned with the local curriculum, that support state academic content standards

   — **Technology infrastructure:** State-of-the art technology to acquire, organize, create, and disseminate information and function as a gateway to information

   — **Reading resources:** Reading materials targeted beyond informational curriculum needs, personal pursuits, and pleasure reading, for the development of thinking and informed citizens of their country and world

2. **TRANSFORMATIONAL—Instructional Interventions**

   — **Information literacy:** Development of information literacy for engagement with information in all its forms in the context of curriculum needs, content standards, and subject knowledge creation processes for effective engagement and utilization of information

   — **Technological literacies:** Development of media and technological skills, which include critical thinking and communication competencies, as well as the appropriate and ethical use of technology for information access, retrieval, production, and dissemination

   — **Reading engagement:** Development of approaches to promote and encourage reading for academic achievement and life-long learning through participation in reading initiatives, promotion of literature, reinforcement of reading skills, and fostering a sustained love of reading

(continued)

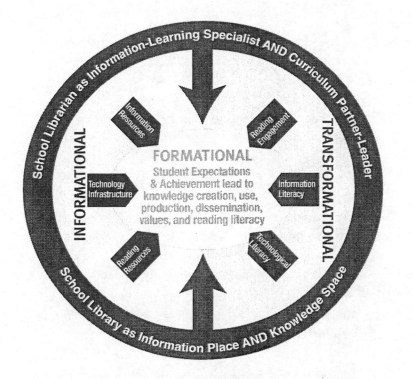

Todd, Ross J., Carol C. Kuhlthau, and OELMA. (2004). Student Learning through Ohio School Libraries. Columbus, OH: Ohio Educational Library Media Association. http://www.oelma.org/studentlearning/default.asp

> "When effective school libraries are in place, students do learn. 13,000 students can't be wrong."

—Ross J. Todd, Carol C. Kuhlthau, and OELMA. Student Learning through Ohio School Libraries, 2004. http://www.oelma.org/studentlearning/default.asp

3. FORMATIONAL — Student outcomes

— **Knowledge creation:** Students achieve through being able to define problems, frame questions, explore ideas, formulate focus, investigate, analyze, and synthesize ideas to create their own views, evaluate solutions, and reflect on understandings.

— **Knowledge use:** Students develop transferable skills for sustaining knowledge beyond the classroom.

— **Knowledge production:** Students can use technology and information tools to produce new knowledge and demonstrate achievement.

— **Knowledge dissemination:** Students can communicate ideas using oral, written, visual, and technological modes of expression.

— **Knowledge values:** Students are ethical, responsible users of information.

— **Reading literacy:** Students have high levels of reading literacy. They become independent, life-long sustained readers.

Todd, Ross J., Carol C. Kuhlthau, and OELMA. (2004). Student Learning through Ohio School Libraries. Columbus, OH: Ohio Educational Library Media Association. http://www.oelma.org/studentlearning/default.asp

As a result of the Ohio research study, it is recommended that:

- All school library programs provide instructional intervention, through a credentialed library media specialist, which centers on the development of information literacy skills for inquiry learning.

- All school libraries, including elementary schools, be staffed with credentialed library media specialists who have educational certification and who engage in collaborative instructional initiatives to help students learn and achieve.

- All library media specialists have a clearly defined role as information-learning specialist.

- All school libraries provide a learning-centered space supported by a strong technology infrastructure.

- All stakeholders engage in sustained and action-oriented discussions in the context of continuous improvement of the necessary resources, technology, and staffing requirements needed to maximize the learning opportunities through school libraries.

Todd, Ross J., Carol C. Kuhlthau, and OELMA. (2004). Student Learning through Ohio School Libraries. *Columbus, OH: Ohio Educational Library Media Association.*
http://www.oelma.org/studentlearning/default.asp

"Simply providing teachers with a generous supply of children's books had little effect on the educational outcomes of students."

—McGill-Franzon, Anne et al. (1999). "Putting Books in the Classroom Seems Necessary But Not Sufficient." The Journal of Educational Research 93 (2): 67-74.

School Libraries DO Work.

"TO BECOME LIFE-LONG READERS, STUDENTS MUST HAVE...

- Access to current, quality, high-interest, and extensive collections of books and other print materials in their school libraries, classrooms, and public libraries;

- Contact with adults who read regularly and widely and who serve as positive reading role models;

- Certified library media specialists and classroom teachers who demonstrate their enthusiasm for reading by reading aloud and booktalking;

- Time during the school day dedicated to reading for pleasure, information, and exploration..."

—*"The Value of Independent Reading in the School Library Media Program."* A Position Statement of the American Association of School Librarians. *Revised July 1999.*

Resolution:
"Credentialed school library media professionals promote, inspire, and guide students toward a love of reading, a quest for knowledge, and a thirst for lifelong learning."

—*"In Support of Credentialed Library Media Professionals in School Library Media Centers."* A Summary of a Board Resolution of the International Reading Association. *May 2000.* http://www.reading.org/positions/cre_libra.html

"Reading development is a process for attaining literacy by integrating oral and written language experiences into the literature and content areas. Spoken language, reading, and writing are learned simultaneously. As students read "real books" and write to communicate, learning becomes relevant, interesting, and motivational and prepares students for life-long learning. Acquisition, organization, and dissemination of resources to support the reading program through the library media center is cost-effective for the entire school district."

—*"Resource Based Instruction: Role of the School Library Media Specialist in Reading Development."* A Position Statement of the American Association of School Librarians.

Resources:

Impact of School Libraries and Library Media Specialists on Student Academic Achievement

ALASKA

http://www.library.state.ak.us/dev/infoemxs.pdf

Lance, Keith Curry, et. al. (1999). Information Empowered: The School Librarian as an Agent of Academic Achievement in Alaska Schools. *Anchorage: AK: Alaska State Library.*

COLORADO

http://www.ala.org/aasl/SLMR/slmr_resources/
select_lance.html

Lance, Keith Curry, Lynda Wellborn, and Christine Hamilton-Pennell. (1993). The Impact of School Library Media Centers on Academic Achievement. *Spring, TX: Hi Willow Research and Publishing.*

http://www.lrs.org/documents/lmcstudies/CO/
execsumm.pdf

Lance, Keith Curry, Marcia J. Rodney, and Christine Hamilton-Pennell. (2000). How School Librarians Help Kids Achieve Standards: The Second Colorado Study. *Spring, TX: Hi Willow Research and Publishing.*

FLORIDA

http://www.sunlink.ucf.edu/makingthegrade/

Baumbach, Donna. (2002). Making the Grade: The Status of School Library Media Centers in the Sunshine State and How They Contribute to Student Achievement. *Spring, TX: Hi Willow Research and Publishing.*

IOWA

http://www.aea9.k12.ia.us/04/
statewidelibrarystudy.php

Rodney, Marcia J., Keith Curry Lance, and Christine Hamilton-Pennell. (2002). Make the Connection: Quality School Library Media Programs Impact Academic Achievement in Iowa. *Bettendorf, IA: Mississippi Bend Area Education Agency.*

MASSACHUSETTS

http://web.simmons.edu/~baughman/
mcas-school-libraries/Baughman%20Paper.pdf

*Baughman, James. (2002). School Libraries and MCAS Scores,
(Preliminary Edition). A Paper Presented at a Symposium
Sponsored by the Graduate School of Library and Information
Science, Simmons College. Boston, MA.*

MICHIGAN

http://www.michigan.gov/documents/
hal_lm_schllibstudy03_76626_7.pdf

*Rodney, Marcia J., Keith Curry Lance, and Christine Hamilton-
Pennell. (2003). The Impact of Michigan School Librarians on
Academic Achievement: Kids Who Have Libraries Succeed.
Lansing, MI: Library of Michigan.*

MINNESOTA

http://metronet.lib.mn.us/survey/index.cfm

*Baxter, Susan J. and Ann Walker Smalley. (2003). Check It Out!
The Results of the School Library Media Program Census,
Final Report. St. Paul, MN: Metronet.*

MISSOURI

http://www.dese.state.mo.us/divimprove/curriculum/
librarystudy/showmeconnection.pdf

*Quantitative Resources, LLC. (2003). Show-Me Connection:
How School Library Media Center Services Impact Student
Achievement, 2002–2003. Jefferson City, MO: Missouri State
Library.*

NEW MEXICO

http://www.stlib.state.nm.us/files/
NMStudyforDistribution.pdf

*Lance, Keith Curry, Marcia J. Rodney, and Christine Hamilton-
Pennell. (2002). How School Librarians Improve Outcomes for
Children: The New Mexico Study. Sante Fe, NM: New Mexico
State Library.*

NORTH CAROLINA

http://www.rburgin.com/NCschools2003/

Burgin, Robert and Pauletta Brown Bracy. (2003). An Essential
Connection: How Quality School Library Media Programs
Improve Student Achievement in North Carolina. *Spring, TX: Hi
Willow Research and Publishing.*

OHIO

http://www.oelma.org/studentlearning/default.asp

Todd, Ross J., Carolyn Kuhlthau, and OELMA. (2004). Student
Learning through Ohio School Libraries: The Ohio Research
Study. *Columbus, OH: Ohio Educational Library Media
Association.*

OREGON

http://www.oema.net/Oregon_Study/OR_Study.htm

*Lance, Keith Curry, Marcia J. Rodney, and Christine Hamilton-
Pennell. (2001).* Good Schools Have School Librarians:
Oregon School Librarians Collaborate to Improve Academic
Achievement. *Terrebonne, OR: Oregon Educational Media
Association.*

PENNSYLVANIA

http://www.statelibrary.state.pa.us/libraries/lib/
libraries/measuringup.pdf

*Lance, Keith Curry, Marcia J. Rodney, and Christine Hamilton-
Pennell. (2000).* Measuring Up to Standards: The Impact of
School Library Programs & Information Literacy in Pennsylvania
Schools. *Greensburg, PA: Pennsylvania Citizens for Better
Libraries.*

TEXAS

http://www.tsl.state.tx.us/ld/pubs/schlibsurvey/
index.html

Smith, Ester G. (2001). Texas School Libraries: Standards,
Resources, Services, and Students' Performance. *Austin, TX:
Texas State Library and Archives Commission.*

Web links verified as of June 2004.

Research Foundation
Paper

Scholastic
Research &
Results

SCHOLASTIC

Scholastic Library Publishing
Grolier • Children's Press • Franklin Watts • Grolier Online
800-621-1115 • fax 866-783-4361
www.scholastic.com/librarypublishing